CROWOOD COLLECTORS' SERIES

Corkscrews

FRANK AND BARBARA ELLIS

THE CROWOOD PRESS

First published in 2009 by
The Crowood Press Ltd
Ramsbury, Marlborough
Wiltshire SN8 2HR

www.crowood.com

British Library Cataloguing-in-Publication Data
A catalogue record for this book is available from the British Library.

ISBN 978 1 84797 113 5

Dedication
This book is dedicated to the memory of Frank Ellis who sadly died before he could complete it. He still had so much more to give to us all.

Typeset by Jean Cussons Typesetting, Diss, Norfolk
Printed and bound in Singapore by Craft Print International Ltd

ACKNOWLEDGEMENTS

Very sincere thanks are due to Joe Paradi, Wayne Meadows and Reinhold Berndt, who all contributed to chapters that were missing from Frank's manuscript. Thanks must go to all those dealers who have given us the opportunities to acquire rare and unusual items. Frank offered his gratitude to Chris Barge, Peter Carr, Dennis Cox (formerly of Christie's), Andrew Crawforth, Ilya Emerson, Sue Emerson, Patricia Harbottle, 'Mac' Jordan, Kevin Shepard, Christopher Sykes Antiques, Gregory Taylor, Philip Trent, Andrew Veitch and Fletcher Wallis. Thanks also to Fred Kincaid, Fred O'Leary and Joe Paradi, who spent endless hours with Frank developing a systematic way of cataloguing corkscrews which became SCReWBase©, and is the basis for this book. Thanks too to the authors whose books were used as reference sources – in particular Gérard Bidault, Bert Giulian, Fred O'Leary, Ferd Peters and Fletcher Wallis. Finally, many thanks to family and friends who encouraged Barbara to continue and complete the book.

PREFACE

As many fellow collectors know, Frank Ellis, the main author of this book, died in May 2008 after a sudden short illness. Barbara Ellis took on the role of organizing the completion of this book, of which about two-thirds was written when he died. Frank's passionate enthusiasm for corkscrews and collecting was well known, as was as his quest for further information and his determination to figure out how each corkscrew worked, and what mechanism was involved. The following piece was written by Frank in September 2007 and will provide an insight into his addiction to corkscrews.

How I started collecting, by Frank Ellis

About twenty years ago, a very good friend Tony was about to have his fortieth birthday. He was impossible to buy presents for because he had no hobbies and no strong interests. He did however like wine and was getting interested in antiques. So what could be better – a wine antique. My wife Barbara and I went off to visit Christopher Sykes' shop in the nearby village of Woburn and were amazed to see the walls covered in corkscrews. It was obvious what present he should have and we bought a simple but elegant straight pull. That evening, whilst watching the television, I was holding the corkscrew and it felt wonderful in my hand. Our friend never got that corkscrew, but we did go back to the shop the next Saturday and bought him another one – and six more for me!

That is how it all started – and it changed my life. From that point on we went out to antique fairs and shops searching for corkscrews. Barbara had a small collection of ceramic and metal decorative owls and decided that if I were going to spend time and money on corkscrews, she would collect antique owls.

About a year later two significant events happened. The first was the sale of the corkscrew collection of Evan Perry, known for his Shire book on corkscrews. It was our first auction. Most of the UK collectors were there and they were very friendly to us newcomers and gave us advice. I got a couple of really nice Henshall types and my first silver sheathed pocket corkscrew. Also, to start my international corkscrew collection, I went home with a German Columbus, and my first French corkscrews: a Zig-Zag and a

My first corkscrew.

Perfect – little knowing how many more I would meet in the future.

After the excitement of my first auction I discovered there was another corkscrew auction at Sotheby's the next day. As I was in London on business that day, I went along. Wow, there was some fantastic stuff and I was successful in buying another silver sheathed corkscrew. The only problem was how to pay? I needed to take it home with me but they would not let me do that if I paid with a cheque – I never thought to take cash in those naive days. A really nice guy in the payment queue realized my plight and offered to lend me some cash as I 'looked like an honest person'. That was Fletcher Wallis (Wally). He told me that the whole antique business depended on trust and that I could give him the money back next Saturday at Portobello Road. So started a long-term friendship with one of the top – if not *the* top – corkscrew dealers in England, and thereafter there were many fruitful visits to Portobello Road.

My collection grew and grew, as did Barbara's flock of owls. I met other corkscrew collectors and found out about the Canadian Corkscrew Collectors' Club (CCCC) from Mike Meakin, whom I met at Christie's. I joined the Club in 1990 and suddenly realized how many corkscrew collectors there were. Within a couple of months, one of the Californian members sent me a list of corkscrews for sale. It was my first real introduction to American corkscrews and I bought all sorts of things including a Negbaur parrot, an Old Snifter and some little medicine bands. I mentioned to him that Barbara collected owls and wondered if he knew where I could get a Hootch-Owl. He replied that

Researching at the National Archives.

A unique Jones.

he had one and we bought it for a very reasonable price.

With the CCCC members' list to hand, I subsequently organized a meeting for a small group of English collectors, which turned into the loosely knit ABCDE Club, or Association of British Corkscrew Devotees and Enthusiasts. A couple of years later we had an informal meeting at our house and Wally suggested the theme of 'registered design corkscrews'. He added that someone should write a book on them to complement his forthcoming book on British patents.

That sowed a seed, which took ten years to come to fruition. Barbara and I launched our new book *Corkscrews: British Registered Designs* in August. The research took years – a multitude of Saturdays. We used to go to Portobello Road for 7 o'clock and then on to the National Archives in Kew, West London, to search systematically through a thousand dirty old books. At times it was frustrating. At other times it was very satisfying when we discovered the original

drawing of an old friend – a corkscrew we had known for years.

My background is as an industrial chemist in the pharmaceutical industry. I am fascinated by different materials and how their development led to different corkscrew designs. For example, you could not make a friction-free worm as used in the Screwpull® until Teflon® had been invented. My analytical mind also likes order, and so it was an absolute delight to work with Fred O'Leary, Fred Kincaid and Joe Paradi on developing SCReW© (Standard Corkscrew Reference Work). I got my love of all things mechanical from my father who repaired bombers in the war and then worked in a small engineering works. What is better than a mechanical corkscrew?

My corkscrew collection is very broad – from mechanicals to brass figurals. Barbara says I will buy anything! But that is not quite true. I once said that I would never collect British brass figurals – then I discovered that many of them were registered designs and so I am now fascinated by them. To limit my

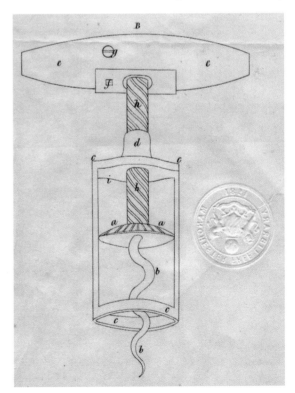

Samuel Henshall's 1795 Patent, Drawing B.

collection, I said I would never collect champagne taps. But Barbara ruined that pledge by buying some for my Christmas presents. I now have a rather good collection of taps!

The core of my collection is English patents and registered designs. People ask, 'What is your best corkscrew?' How do you decide? One of my best English corkscrews has two spikes on a freely rotating collar and a clever cam action that pulls the spikes in towards the centre of the cork when you pull the handle upwards. I believe it is a unique mechanism. It is also marked with the maker's name, Jones.

Another is from Samuel Henshall's 1795 patent – the mechanical corkscrew that most people forget is in that historic document. Who needs an explanation when you can look at a picture? It was originally bought in England and then spent about ten years in France. Beware of fake copies!

Not only have I collected some wonderful corkscrews over the past twenty years, but I have also collected some fantastic friends from the UK, Europe, North America and Australia. We have visited many collections and always experienced great hospitality. We were so impressed and met so many great people at our first CCCC meeting in Vancouver in 1995 that we decided to offer to take the Club out of North America for the first time. The Club has been truly international ever since the London AGM in 1997.

Barbara and I have really enjoyed being part of the CCCC – it is a club that thrives on corkscrews. Corkscrews have taken us to places that we would never have gone – and we thoroughly enjoyed them.

(Article written for the CCCC *Quarterly Worme*, September 2007.)

A rare example of the compound form of Samuel Henshall's 1795 Patent.

INTRODUCTION

Barbara Ellis

The fun of collecting

Most people have a corkscrew in their kitchen as an important functional tool. But not many people are aware of the many different types and designs of corkscrews that have been invented and developed over the last 300 years. Corks began to be used to seal bottles of wine, beer, champagne, perfumes and medicines in the eighteenth century. Since then, inventors have tried to devise easy methods of getting the cork out of the bottle. This challenge has led to numerous innovative, often complex mechanisms, using the laws of physics, the skills of mechanical engineering, the science of new materials and the artistic aspects of design. Until you see a collection or pictures of antique corkscrews, you cannot appreciate the amazing range of products that has been created over the years. It is hoped that this book will spur you into starting to collect these very interesting and useful items.

As a collector myself, I can confirm that there is nothing more exciting than spotting a new find whilst wandering round an antique market, a boot fair or browsing eBay. When you begin, there are obviously many gaps in your collection and plenty of opportunities to fill them. The beauty of corkscrews is that many are very cheap, just a few pounds or dollars, so everyone can afford to start collecting. As your collection grows, it obviously becomes harder. You aspire to better and rarer pieces, which are more expensive, and your available budget starts to become important. You may need to limit your collection by focusing on particular types, such as brass figurals, pocket knives, advertising corkscrews, French patents, or British registered designs. But if your budget is unlimited, you can go on acquiring, as Frank did, tracking

down really rare pieces as well as still picking up unusual cheap and cheerful items. I have often thought 'he must have them all by now' – only to be proved wrong again!

Corkscrews are objects that everyone understands, so tell your partner, children, friends, relatives and work colleagues of your interest, and you will be amazed at what they will come up with. Instead of the boring toiletries and socks for Christmas and birthdays, you may well receive interesting corkscrews to add to the collection. People may come to you saying,

Canadian Corkscrew Collectors Club

11th A.G.M.
Avon, Connecticut 1992

BELOW: CCCC meeting in Amsterdam.

'I found this weird thing in my granny's cupboard' or they may come back from a holiday with 'a strange piece I picked up in a market in Hong Kong'. Old antique corkscrews are obviously the most sought after but modern ones are equally interesting, sometimes copying the old designs, sometimes with entirely new ideas and mechanisms, particularly using modern plastics.

Corkscrews can be found everywhere – antique shops and markets, antique and collectors' fairs, flea markets, junk shops, charity shops, car boot sales, house clearance sales and auctions. You can target these as a day out or en route to a social visit or business meeting. You can also find them via your computer, with many corkscrew dealers on the Internet and of course eBay, which offers a huge number of corkscrews. Get to know your local area and cultivate any possible suppliers who will then keep a lookout for items for you.

Get your partner and family interested in collecting, so you can all go out hunting together, as Frank and I did. Get in touch with other collectors to have the opportunity to see their collections and the chance of buying their duplicates or exchanging corkscrews without any cash involvement.

There are several collectors' clubs you can join, and I can confirm that the ones we belonged to were excellent for buying and selling corkscrews, for meeting fellow collectors and for discussing the finer points of a corkscrew over a bottle of wine or beer. They are also fun for non-corkscrew oriented partners with good food and drink, new places to visit, and an excellent social atmosphere. Beginners are made to feel welcome and join the corkscrew community. They will be amazed at the range of corkscrews displayed for purchase at these meetings, and they will find it difficult not to come away with at least one new piece in their pocket.

There are many books on corkscrews that will provide you with a wealth of information on different types, how they work, patents, registered designs and manufacturers. A comprehensive list is given in the Bibliography.

A very useful comprehensive catalogue is available on SCReWBase©, an extensive CD database of over

---

COLLECTORS' CLUBS

- CCCC, the Canadian Corkscrew Collectors Club (international). Annual meeting in North America or Europe, *Quarterly Worme* magazine.
- ABCDE, the Association of British Corkscrew Devotees and Enthusiasts (UK). One or two meetings per year.
- CFTB, Club Français du Tire-Bouchon (French). Two meetings per year, *L'Extracteur* magazine.
- VK, Verein Korkenzieherfreunde (German). One meeting per year.
- Helix Scandinavica (Scandinavian).
- AICC, Associazione Italiana Collezionisti Cavatappi (Italian).
- GGCC, the Golden Gate Corkscrew Collectors (California, USA).
- ICCA, International Correspondence of Corkscrew Addicts (membership by invitation).

6,000 corkscrews. These are shown with pictures, descriptions, information on patent and registered design numbers and manufacturers, and bibliographic references. The database is searchable by type, manufacturer and patent or design number, so you can readily identify your new acquisition, or compare it to the numerous variations shown.

Displaying and cataloguing corkscrews

Corkscrews are objects of great beauty to the collector. However, their family members may not agree and may not appreciate the attractions of a rusty lump of metal adorning their rooms. Frank and I reached a compromise where we allowed each other space to display our separate collections. However, I know of one British collector who is not allowed to display any

Frank with some of his corkscrews.

corkscrews at all, has to keep them hidden in boxes, and can only reveal them when fellow enthusiasts visit. The luckiest collectors are those in North America who all seem to have huge basements that they can convert to corkscrew dens, often with a working bar attached.

There are many ways to display corkscrews. They can be hung on boards, on hooks or on racks – some even have handy hanging rings. Some can stand on shelves, unaided or inserted into large corks, or sometimes on an old plastic lid with a hole drilled in the top to allow the worm to drop through. Display racks can be created from tiered rows of boards with holes drilled into them. Special Perspex or Lucite stands with tubes can be bought that will accommodate the worm. Other corkscrews can be stored in drawers – the old Victorian collectors' chests of drawers used for displaying butterflies and eggs are excellent if you can find them and have room, but old office stationery cabinets used for envelopes are also very useful.

A question often debated by collectors is how much should you clean up and restore an old, rusty or damaged specimen. This is really up to each individual.

There are purists, who would do nothing, through to those who virtually reconstruct the corkscrew beyond recognition. Any loose rust can be brushed away gently and dirty handles cleaned. Some people will replace broken handles or worms, but this must be done carefully without damaging the patina of the shaft, and with appropriate similar replacements. Brass and bronze barrels and frames should not be cleaned as this will destroy the natural patina that has been acquired over the years. The value of such corkscrews can be significantly reduced if they have been acid dipped to the bright metal level. Some old patinated steel examples have also been ruined by acid dipping. Silver can be cleaned, but not too often, as you may polish away important hallmarks.

Buyers should look out for clear signs of patina change and grip marks near the handle, indicating that something has been done to the corkscrew. The collector will gradually build up experience and a gut feeling that the corkscrew looks 'wrong', because of the handle or worm. Contact with other collectors is most useful as a means of joining in discussions of 'does this look right to you?', as well as giving alerts to fakes in the market and on eBay. Some specific points to look out for are highlighted in various sections of this book.

As your collection grows, you will need to start cataloguing as, unless you have a superhuman brain, you will forget what you have and will not recall particular markings or variations in design. You can invent your own cataloguing system, or use basic simple types for grouping – for example, bows, frames, levers and so on. However, as the collection increases and you acquire more sophisticated examples, you may need the ultimate SCReW© Code system.

This was devised over a number of years by the 'gang of four' – Frank, Fred Kincaid, Fred O'Leary and Joe Paradi. Many hours of e-mail, phone and face-to-face discussions took place to create this epic piece of work. A guide is given in Appendix 3, showing the classes, the codes and the decision tree to select the right class. The code has many loyal followers, who might refer to an example as an 'MRf' or an 'LSc'. As a non-user who just wanted to check if Frank had a particular corkscrew, I found it rather complex to identify which coded drawer to look in, but the thumbnail pictures are very helpful in identifying the class.

It is useful to set up a simple computer spreadsheet to catalogue your collection and record where you bought each item, how much it cost and what its current value is. This is useful for insurance purposes and for you to see if the collection is gaining value as an investment. Some pieces have increased in value significantly due to rarity and demand from keen collectors. Some collectors keep a portfolio of photos in hard copy, or on their laptop or other portable electronic device. SCreWBase© can be bought with Corkscrew Collector – a spreadsheet already set up for you to enter and record key details of your corkscrew and to add images.

Markings on corkscrews – patents and registered designs

Corkscrews with markings are usually most desirable. The markings may be advertisements and this is a whole sector in which to specialize. They may show the name or trademark of the manufacturer or designer, which can be important, or the retailer, which is interesting, but less important. Frank had a particular love of corkscrews made by Robert Jones of Birmingham, variously marked showing the different stages of the family business that made high-quality corkscrews. Collectors in different countries have their own favourite manufacturers to collect, for example Pérille in France, and Williamson in the USA. Items by the famous designer Hagenauer are very keenly collected. You can even try to collect corkscrews marked with your own name – we have a modest corkscrew marked 'Ellis', advertising a wine dealer. Other markings give the trade name of the corkscrew, such as Nifty, Hercules, Rapide, Surprise, and many other evocative names. These are more highly prized than un-named versions.

Patent and registered design markings are very important and can add significant value to a corkscrew. They can show the inventor of the patent or the design, and indicate the date when the patent was filed or the design was registered. Many examples are shown later in this book. Several of the books listed in the Bibliography cover patents and registered designs from different countries. Sometimes a corkscrew appears to be marked as a patent, but no patent can be identified. This could be because the patent was never granted, or the inventor failed to pay the patent fees, or simply because the unscrupulous manufacturer wanted the customer to think the item was unique and hence more expensive. Several examples of this 'fraud' can be found in this book.

A patent is granted for an invention that is 'new' or 'novel' in terms of mechanism, construction or function. Patented corkscrews are very collectable as each has a unique mechanism or feature for removing the cork. A registered design is not the same as a patent. It is the actual design and what it looks like that is important. Registered design corkscrews are also very collectable as each has a unique shape or appearance, so has aesthetic appeal. Sometimes, the patented mechanism or registered design does not work properly or breaks easily, and such corkscrews are therefore difficult to find as manufacture would have been stopped and broken examples thrown away. These rarities are keenly sought by collectors and can fetch very high prices due to their scarcity. They need to be handled carefully and the collector should avoid trying to see if they work – several rare pieces have, tragically, been broken in this way. One problem today is that modern corks are often made from cork composites, which are more compacted, or they are made from synthetic plastic and rubber materials, which are much harder than the old traditional corks. The delicate mechanisms designed for the old softer corks may be damaged if they are used on today's corks, so be very careful!

British patents are marked 'Patent', 'Pat', 'Pat^{d}', or sometimes just 'P'. The first British corkscrew patent was granted in 1795 to Samuel Henshall.

British registered designs are shown in several different ways. The first British registered design was granted in 1840 to Robert Jones and Son, and examples are marked with the name, number and date. In the period 1842–83 a diamond registration mark, sometimes called a lozenge, was used. This indicated the exact date of the registration, the class of material used (e.g. metal, wood) and the bundle, which was the number of items registered on that day. To complicate matters, there was one arrangement of codes for the period 1842–67, and another for 1868–83, as shown below, but it is easy to tell one from the other. The day and bundle were always numbers whereas month and year are coded as letters. So from the position of the numbers (day and bundle) it is easy to see which series the diamond belongs to. If the numbers are at the bottom and right hand side of the diamond, it covers 1842–67. If they are at the top and left hand

Robert Jones II, 7 October 1842.

side, it covers 1868–83. Examples are shown below and a list of codes is shown in Appendix 2. The diamond mark is a beautiful feature on an old corkscrew, indicating its age, and is a statement of quality.

From 1884, the diamond mark was no longer used and a simple numbering system was introduced starting at number 1. Items are marked 'Registered', 'Reg.', 'Reg. No.', 'R^{d}', or 'R^{d} N^{o}' together with the number. The numbers identify the year of registration, as shown in the table in Appendix 2.

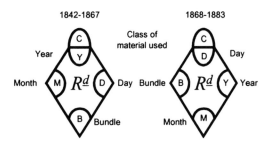

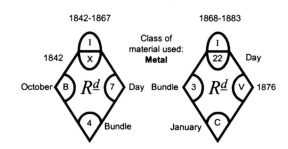

Examples of diamond marks.

USA patents are usually marked PATENT or PAT'D with the date of patent issue. The first utility patents for corkscrews were granted in 1860 on the same day to M.L. Byrn and to Philos Blake – there is controversy over which patent should be regarded as the first.

USA design patents apply to appearance rather than what the item does, and are equivalent to registered designs. Utility patents and design patents are on a different numbering system, and design patent numbers are lower since fewer were issued. This can be rather confusing, particularly if the 'Des.' or 'D.' designation is not shown alongside the 'Patent' marking.

French patents or *brevets* are marked 'Breveté' or 'B^te' and 'SGDG', which is *Sans Garantie du Gouvernement* ('without government guarantee'). The first French patent was filed in 1828 by François Rever. Patent numbers are rarely shown.

French registered designs are marked 'Déposé' or 'Modèle Déposé'.

German patents are marked 'DRP' for *Deutsches Reichspatent* ('patent of the German Empire'). Some are marked 'Ges.', 'Gesch.', or 'Ges. Geschützt' (abbreviations of *gesetzlich geschützt*, meaning 'protected by law'). More recent patents after 1948 are marked 'DBP' for Deutsches Bundes Patent ('patent of the Federal Republic of Germany'). The first German patent was granted in 1878 to Benjamin Lew. Before 1877 some patents were granted in individual German states.

German registered designs are marked 'DRGM' until 1945, for *Deutsches Reichs Gebrauchmuster* ('registered design of the German Empire'). After 1945 they are marked 'DBGM', for *Deutsches Bundes Gebrauchmuster* ('registered design of the Federal Republic of Germany').

Italian patents are marked 'Brevetto' or 'Brevettato' ('patent' or 'patented').

Patents and registered designs were often filed in several different countries to give better protection to the inventor, so each corkscrew may have several different patent or design numbers assigned to it. The specialist books and SCReWBase© provide this information.

Some items are marked 'Pat. Pend.', or 'Pending',

Edwin Wolverson's Holborn Signet, 22 January 1876.

or 'Patent (or Registration) Applied For' – this may be true and it may be an early version of the corkscrew before the patent or registered design has been filed and granted. In many cases, however, no patent or registration can be found, meaning that either it was not granted, or the inventor did not pay the fees, or they were trying to imply that the item was a unique invention, misleading the customer.

Sometimes the markings do not match the original patent or design registration documents. As always, mistakes are made in production, with workers picking up the wrong stamp or mould, particularly if they are working on several products for different customers. These errors do not usually detract from the value of the corkscrew, and wrong markings are sometimes specially cherished by collectors.

Patent and design registrations numbers are usually

up to seven digits long, with early examples being shorter. It is sometimes confusing to see just a three- or four-digit number on a corkscrew – this is usually the manufacturer's design pattern, mould number or catalogue number.

Unmarked versions of patents and registered designs are usually later versions made after the patents or registrations have expired, often by other manufacturers as well as the original inventor. Many collectors start with unmarked versions, which are cheaper, and upgrade to marked examples when they can. However, some patents and registered designs were never marked, including some very rare examples.

Other markings may refer to the materials used, and are covered in the next section.

Materials

A wide variety of materials have been used over the years to make corkscrews, with new materials allowing new innovations. The earliest corkscrews were made of wrought iron or steel. Early sheaths and frames were made of flat pieces of steel which were heated and bent to form a tube and then welded using brass, giving a brazed seam. This is described in more detail in the section on pocket and protected corkscrews.

Early pieces were also made with silver handles and sheaths. Some of the silver pieces will be hallmarked to indicate the place of manufacture. Most European countries have their own hallmarking system indicating the town in which the item was made and the date period. British hallmarks are very specific, with up to three symbols indicating the town where the item was made, the precise year of manufacture and the king or queen on the throne at that time. These can be deciphered using readily available silver hallmark books or specialist sites on the Internet. Small silver pieces were not always hallmarked or the hallmarks may have been rubbed away through too much cleaning; this can make dating the item difficult. The style and weight of the item will provide a guide, with

more modern pieces being heavier, as discussed later in the section on pocket and protected corkscrews (Chapter 4). More modern silver items from most countries are now marked 'sterling', sometimes with a number indicating the grade of silver. The British hallmarking system still continues today, although there are moves from the EU to abolish it.

Gold was of course used for very special pieces. Old items can be hallmarked, but these are often difficult to identify, and many pieces are not marked. The collector should take care since recently made items are being sold as antique corkscrews at highly inflated prices. The style and the worm will provide clues as to the authenticity of the item.

Brass is an alloy of copper and zinc and began to be made in commercial quantities in the mid eighteenth century. It was used to make corkscrew barrels and frames, particularly in England, which was the centre of the Industrial Revolution, and more particularly in Birmingham, which was for a long time one of the centres of corkscrew manufacture. Many brass figural corkscrews were made from the early twentieth century, a peculiarly British genre.

Bronze is an alloy of copper and tin and was also used to make corkscrew barrels and frames at a similar time to brass. It has a much darker patina than brass, looks classier, and was used for the more high quality pieces. As mentioned before, brass and bronze should not be cleaned too vigorously and should never be acid dipped, as this removes the patina achieved slowly over the years and significantly reduces the value of the item.

Pewter is an alloy of tin and lead and is a relatively soft metal. Although it has been known and worked with for hundreds of years, it is somewhat surprising that its use for corkscrew handles did not really become popular until the mid twentieth century, when it was particularly made use of in Scandinavia for distinctive ornamental features.

Aluminium did not become commercially available until 1886. It is a very light metal and not many corkscrews were made from it.

Most steel corkscrews were chrome or nickel or brass plated in the twentieth century. In the mid to late nineteenth century a bronze wash finish was applied, giving a characteristic orange-red colour to many British corkscrews of this period. This bronzing did not wear very well, so do not be surprised if you only see remnants of it on the frame. In the twentieth century aluminium was sometimes anodized giving a range of metallic colours as used in the Valezina corkscrew.

It is useful to check the components of a corkscrew with a magnet to help identify the metal they are made from (for example, to differentiate between

WORMS

There are several different types of worm and it is useful for the collector to learn the correct terms for describing them, as shown below.

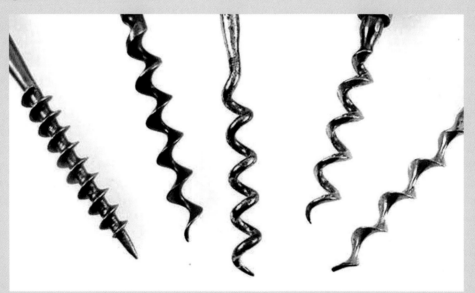

From left to right:

Archimedean – This is named after the Archimedes water screw. It can be seen on some very early corkscrews, where the spiral is brazed on to the shaft. It is also seen on many Italian corkscrews and on very modern corkscrews. It is not very practical as it drills a hole through the cork.

Bladed worm – This is either cut or forged and is one of the most common worms. It has a solid centre core, which increases resistance to breakage but tends to weaken the cork. Some bladed worms have a centre point at the end, similar to the Archimedean point.

Wire helix – This is formed from a round wire shaped around a mandrel and is very common as it was very easy to make. It has an open centre. It may be grooved along its outside surface to allow easier cork penetration, and is then known as a fluted worm. There are also double helix wire worms, which are a clearly defined group.

Bladed helix – This looks like a cross between a bladed worm and a wire helix. It has an open centre and a non-round (triangular, oval, rectangular, etc.) wire cross-section.

Speedworm – This is designed for faster cork penetration. It looks like a bladed worm with steeper pitch. There are many variations and most have a solid centre. It is often found on bar screws.

brass and brass-plated steel). Iron and steel are magnetic, but some modern stainless steels are not magnetic, so this is not a foolproof method.

Corkscrew handles and frames can be made from a huge variety of natural materials. The simplest corkscrews often have wooden handles, which may be polished, varnished or painted. Boxwood was popular in France, used for very distinctive handles and frames. Antlers are outgrowths of bone carried by deer and provide a tough material for handles. Horn is modified skin tissue, obtained from cows, goats and sheep, and is quite soft and flexible. It is best worked by heating with steam and applying pressure – under these conditions it becomes 'plastic'. Most corkscrew handles made of horn seem to date from around the turn of the twentieth century.

Bone and ivory were very commonly used for early corkscrew handles. These are warm to the touch and easily carved. Bone is rather grainy and coarse and residual blood vessel channels can be seen running through it. There is a limit to what can be done with bone, due to its hollow centre. Many early British corkscrews have turned bone handles, usually with end caps to cover the hollow hole. Ivory from elephant or walrus tusks is technically a tooth and is solid with no hole up the middle. Ivory was mainly used for small solid handles or small sheaths, particularly for perfume or medicine corkscrews, or for more ostentatious carved decorative handles for corkscrews. There are restrictions on trade in ivory, and collectors need to be aware of these.

Synthetic materials such as rubber and plastic began to be used in the early twentieth century. Celluloid (cellulose nitrate) was used for making decorative moulded figural corkscrews. Bakelite (phenol formaldehyde), which was rather brittle, was sometimes used for handles. More modern acrylic plastics such as perspex or Lucite are tough and can be cast into transparent blocks to produce artistic effects. The more common polyethylene, polypropylene and ABS (acrylonitrile butadiene styrene) are used to good effect in modern corkscrews, particularly for figural representations. Other innovations include Teflon® coating of the worm, which reduces friction and helps cork removal.

It is useful to carry a magnifying glass with you to inspect the corkscrew more closely, to check the fixture of the worm to see if it has been interfered with, to check the material and patina of the handle and frame, and to check to see if there are any markings that can identify the corkscrew, sometimes hidden below rust or dirt. And of course you need a full wallet and a large bag to carry your new treasures back home.

Worms come in different lengths, but should usually have four turns and a sharp tip. Sometimes the tip is broken, or there are fewer turns. The collector has to decide if this is acceptable or not.

Most corkscrews are right-handed, but there are left-handed ones as well, sometimes made as a joke in the past, as they are impossible for right-handed people to use. It is important to know the difference between right and left, as different handed threads were used on many mechanical corkscrews and are an important part of their description. A right-handed thread runs from top right to bottom left, and a left-handed thread runs from top left to bottom right.

How to use this book

This book is aimed at beginners and people who have started a small collection and want to know more. It is divided into sections by type of corkscrew, starting with the simplest, the straight pull corkscrew. The early sections cover basic design features, giving descriptions of worm types and fixings in more detail, and the later sections then pass on to the more complex type of corkscrews. The sections are broadly based on the SCRewBase© cataloguing system (Appendix 3), but they do not follow it exactly. The order of the sections is deliberately different to make it easier for the beginner to move slowly and more logically through the range of corkscrew types, and not be led by the alphabetic constraints of the SCReW© Code. Simplifications have been made as deemed appropriate by the co-author, as a 'relative' beginner. Apologies are made to the ardent followers of the Code who may be upset by this deviation.

STRAIGHT PULLS

When it comes to opening a bottle of wine, straight pull corkscrews are the ones that come to most people's minds. There is nothing complex about them mechanically – you just screw them in and pull hard. The removal of the cork is down to brute force, with one exception, where they have been adapted for use with a lever. Many corkscrews in this class look like the letter T and are often called 'Tees' or 'T-screws'. Their collectibility lies in the shape of the handle, the material that it is made from, the design of the shank and the presence of advertising. Some straight pulls have one or more holes in the handle to put in one, two, three or even four fingers to get a good grip. There are also eyebrow shaped handles for two fingers. A small set of straight pulls have a vertical handle. These are not T-shaped and the user has to grip them with their palm and fingers to get a good grip. As they are mostly designed for opening small medicine and perfume bottles that had small corks, there is no requirement for too much brute force.

Simple T-shaped straight pulls

There is huge variety of corkscrews with handles made of different materials and with different designs, and only a selection can be covered here. Many are relatively inexpensive but some, due to age or decorative style, can be highly priced. This type has the advantage of a simple construction and gives the user a good solid grip while holding the bottle with the other hand.

The images below show different examples of how the corkscrew is put together, which the collector

should try to recognize. The main problem in construction is how to fix the shank, the metal part carrying the worm, to the handle, especially if it is made of wood or bone. The common solutions are for the shank to be passed through a hole in the handle and either the end is threaded and a small nut is then screwed down on to it to grip the handle, or a small washer is passed over the end of the shank which is then hammered down, as if it were a rivet, on to the washer. The former method allows the handle or worm to be changed relatively easily in case of damage. The second method makes it very difficult to take the corkscrew apart. Another method of fixing the handle to the shank is to hammer a nail through either the end or the side of the handle through a pre-drilled hole in the shank. With metal handles such as eyebrows, the shank is often screwed into the base of the handle. A simple solution for wire shanks was to make a twisted wire handle or simply to wrap the wire round a wooden handle.

Many antique wood- or bone-handled corkscrews have a brush fitted at one end. Visitors who see your collection will normally ask, 'What is the shaving brush for?' One can either proffer a whimsical notion that it was used by butlers in the wine cellars of grand houses to spruce themselves up before important dinner parties, or, more prosaically, that it was to clean dust and perhaps wax debris from the bottle before and after opening. In the case of bone handles, which are hollow and need the ends of the handle to be covered to give a neat finish, it may have been cheaper to insert a bristle brush rather than adding a lathe-turned end cap.

Straight pulls with wooden handles. *Clockwise from bottom left:* Painted 'marble texture' handle fixed to the plain shank by a nail through the end (mid twentieth century); plain handle with a hammered fixing to a flat steel shank (marked 'B & Co.', early twentieth century); simple turned handle with a brush fixed by a top nut to a slightly balustered shank and plain worm (mid nineteenth century); simple turned handle and shank fixed with a top nut, with a fine Archimedean worm (mid nineteenth century); complex turned handle with a brush and equally complex shank with a fluted worm (mid nineteenth century); turned fruitwood handle with a hammered fixing to a square shank (marked 'I. Sorby', a Sheffield maker, mid twentieth century); simple black painted handle fixed to a candy twist shank by a nail through the front (early twentieth century).

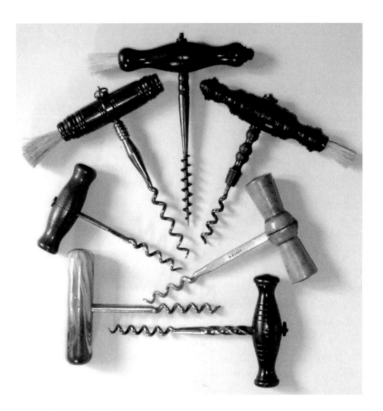

Straight pulls with handles made from animal materials – antler, horn and bone. *Clockwise from bottom left:* Antler handle with a hammered fixing to a fancy steel shank (late nineteenth century); antler handle with nickel-plated brass end caps with a hammered fixing to a fancy steel shank (late nineteenth century); cow horn handle fixed by a top nut to a fancy shank (late nineteenth century); antler handle with a hammered fixing to a square steel shank with a fluted worm (late nineteenth century); horn handle with nickel-plated brass end caps, fixed by a top nut to a steel shank (late nineteenth century); turned bone handle with bone end caps, fixed by a top nut to a steel shank (early nineteenth century); medium-sized French corkscrew with a cow horn handle fixed by a pin through it to a slightly balustered steel shank (late nineteenth century).

Straight pulls with handles made from metals and synthetic materials. *Clockwise from bottom left:* Brass handle with a hammered fixing (mid nineteenth century); plated steel handle with the shank screwed into it (marked with a War Department arrow and 'W & C' (Willetts & Coney), mid twentieth century); nickel-plated hollow brass handle advertising Thorne's Whiskies with a flat steel shank (early twentieth century); moulded vulcanized rubber handle fixed by a top nut to a fancy steel shank (late nineteenth century); glass handle fixed to a plain shank by a band around the centre (made by Lindshammar Glass, Sweden, mid twentieth century), silver-handled corkscrew (hallmarked for Birmingham, 1938); amber-coloured phenolic resin handle (mid twentieth century).

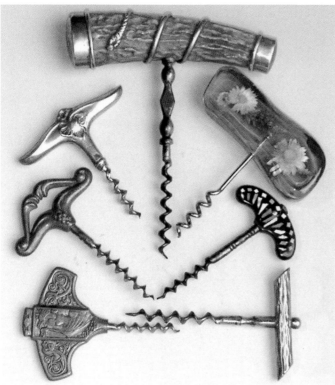

Straight pulls with decorative handles

Straight pulls with decorative handles. *Clockwise from bottom left:* Three Scandinavian straight pulls with pewter handles with one showing a Viking ship and marked 'Norway' (mid to late twentieth century); antler handle with silver end caps and a silver snake coiled around it (probably American, early twentieth century); gaudy acrylic plastic handle with embedded flowers (mid twentieth century); horn handle with mother-of-pearl inserts (French, late nineteenth century); silver-plated brass handle with a tree bark effect (late nineteenth century).

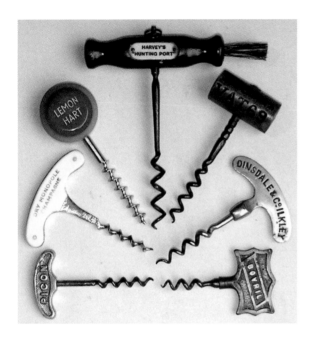

Straight pulls with advertising handles

Corkscrews with advertising are an interesting specialist sector for collectors. *Clockwise from bottom left:* Plated steel handle advertising Picon, a French aperitif (early twentieth century); steel core handle with plastic covers marked 'Dry Monopole Champagne' on one side and 'Hennessy Brandy' on the other (mid twentieth century); novelty left-handed worm and two-colour phenolic plastic handle advertising Lemon Hart with 'try it always' on the other side (mid twentieth century); wooden handle with celluloid inserts promoting Harvey's 'hunting port' and John Harvey & Sons Ltd Wine Merchants, Bristol, England (early twentieth century); drum-shaped wooden handle (mid twentieth century) with whisky advertising for Sanderson's Vat 69 on both sides (other advertising is known); flat steel handle (early twentieth century) stamped 'Dinsdale & Co. Ilkley' on one side and 'Wine Merchants' on the other (other advertising is known); steel handle with a copper wash advertising the beef drink Bovril and stamped 'R^d N° 129857' – derived from the 1889 British registered design from T. Wilkinson & Sons, Birmingham.

French straight pulls

French straight pulls have a classic elegant style – most have bladed worms. *Clockwise from bottom left:* Three steel-handled straight pulls stamped 'J-P' on the handle or shank, for the maker Jacques Pérille (late nineteenth century); high-quality corkscrew with an ivory handle, faceted shank and delicate Archimedean worm (late nineteenth century); ribbed wooden handle with a central brass band stamped 'LB Paris Déposé' (made by Leboullanger, late nineteenth century); horn and bone sandwich handle (late nineteenth century); brass handle with a horn insert and stamped 'Bauer' (late nineteenth century).

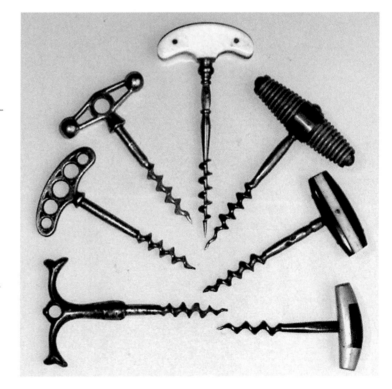

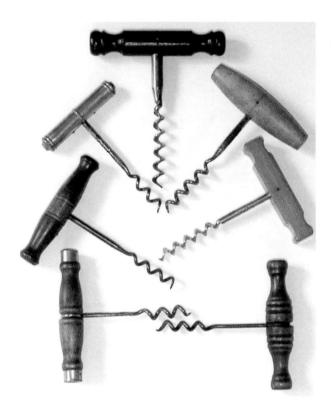

American straight pulls

American straight pulls have a style of their own, often with simple wire worms. *Clockwise from bottom left:* Simple wooden handle with nickel-plated end caps with the wire of the shank wrapped round it (early twentieth century); wooden handle with a central brass band stamped 'Patented Apl. 4th '85' and 'May 5th '85' for the two piece handle construction and the two pins underneath that hold it together, as shown in Edward Haff's patent of 1885; unmarked Haff with a wooden handle covered by a nickel-plated brass sleeve and fixed with two pins underneath; two wooden-handled straight pulls stamped 'Williamson's' on the shank (mid twentieth century); phenolic plastic handle stamped 'Wiliamson's' on the shank (mid twentieth century); simple wooden handle with the wire of the shank wrapped round it (early twentieth century).

Twisted wire straight pulls

It is amazing what can be fashioned from twisted wire. *Clockwise from bottom left:* Simple wooden dowel handle with one loop of wire round it and a twisted wire shank (late nineteenth century); uncommon British example stamped on the wooden handle 'Rᵈ Nº 21189' for Berkeley's registered design of 1885, in which the ends of the two wires are hammered over on to washers; more common Berkeley registered design from 1885, stamped on the wooden handle 'The National Rᵈ Nº 28303' (also known without the hanging loop); one of the two loops of wire that go round the handle of this American piece is stamped 'Williamson's' (late nineteenth century); the twisted wire on the handle surrounds a steel central rod (British, late nineteenth century); one of the loops at the end of the handle is stamped 'Rᵈ Nº 50027' in tiny writing for the 1886 registered design of W.T. Taylor & Co., wire drawers of Birmingham, England; much more common unmarked version with the end loops bent upwards (late nineteenth century).

Miniature straight pulls

These delightful miniature straight pulls were used for opening perfume or medicine bottles. They are usually less than 3in (8cm) long. *Clockwise from bottom:* Ebony handle and octagonal scalloped shank (early twentieth century); ivory handle with a phoenix crest (late nineteenth century); plated steel handle with bladed worm, probably German (early twentieth century); bone handle, brush and bladed worm, probably German (early twentieth century); silver handle (hallmarked for Birmingham 1898); finely turned wooden handle and fancy shank (late nineteenth century); ribbed wooden handle with a central brass band in the Leboullanger style, probably French (late nineteenth century); Clough's Patent Medicine Dial, which is left in the medicine bottle to remind you what time to take the next dose and then thrown away with the bottle (around 1900); delicate mother-of-pearl handle with slender bladed worm (late nineteenth century); plated steel handle with bladed worm (early twentieth century).

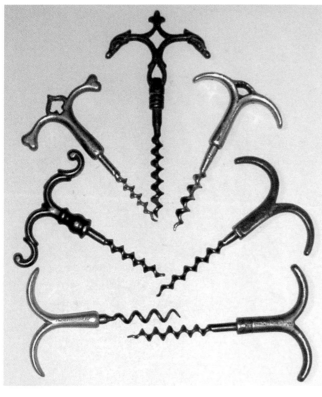

Straight pulls with eyebrow handles

These have characteristic handles known as eyebrows. *Clockwise from bottom left:* Aluminium handle stamped 'Commercial G.F. Hipkins & Son' (around 1900); fancy curved steel handle, probably French (mid nineteenth century); plated steel handle with a hole in the shape of a playing card 'spade' – the other three suits also exist – probably French (late nineteenth century); decorative steel handle with serpent heads at either side, possibly German (mid nineteenth century); plated steel handle stamped on the shank 'J-P' for Jacques Pérille, French (late nineteenth century); steel handle stamped 'R. Jones & Son' (late nineteenth century); simple steel handle stamped 'Willetts & Coneys Ltd' and 'N° 51221' (a catalogue number) (early to mid twentieth century). Other markings are known: 'W&C L^td', 'C.T. Willetts L^d', and 'Berkeley & C° L^td'.

Straight pulls with finger holes

These straight pulls have finger holes to make it easier to pull the cork. *Clockwise from bottom left:* Commonly known as a 'cellarman's corkscrew', this has a thick steel loop handle and a short shank – this one is stamped 'Farrow & Jackson Ltd London' (late nineteenth century); wooden handle and stamped under the finger hole 'Holborn Signet' and a registration diamond indicating the 1876 British registered design of Edwin Wolverson; two unmarked variations of Wolverson's registered design, one is bronze washed steel and the other brass; simple thick wire corkscrew stamped 'J-P' for Jacques Pérille, French (late nineteenth century); unusual three-finger pull made from plated steel (early twentieth century); heavy gauge wire corkscrew with two twists round the shank and stamped on the handle 'Tony Dussieux 5' (French, early twentieth century).

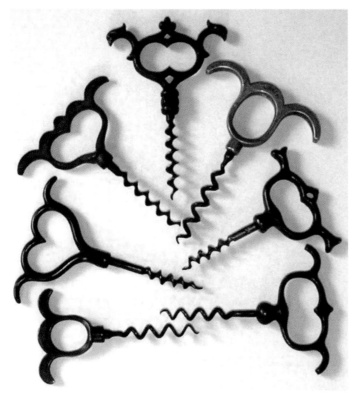

Three- and four-finger pull corkscrews with finger holes. *Clockwise from bottom left:* Three-finger pull corkscrew stamped 'The Signet' with a registration diamond for the 1876 registered design of Edwin Wolverson; heart-shaped four-finger pull (late nineteenth century); uncommon steel corkscrew with a bronze wash named 'The Union / H.A. Knox & Co.' with a registration diamond for the 1876 registered design of Joseph Page; very decorative four-finger pull with serpent heads, possibly German (late nineteenth century); aluminium three-finger pull handle stamped 'Signet' and 'G.F. Hipkins & Son', with a triangular section worm (around 1900); four-finger pull stamped 'J-P' on the shank for Jacques Pérille, French (late nineteenth century); relatively common steel four-finger pull (late nineteenth century).

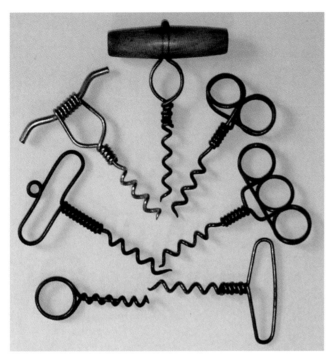

Straight pull wire corkscrews with finger holes. These are all probably English from the late nineteenth century, manufactured by Berkeley and Co. or D.F. Taylor & Co. *Clockwise from bottom left:* Single piece of wire with end wrapped by the worm; wide loop handle with hanging ring; 'bull's horns' shape with a heavier piece of wire across the top; wooden-handled example very similar to the National shown earlier; complex two- and three-finger hole corkscrews, both made from a single piece of wire; simple loop handle.

Straight pulls with lever holes

These straight pulls have holes for use with levers, particularly Lund-style levers, described in Chapter 6. *Clockwise from bottom left:* Bronzed steel example marked 'Lund Patentee & Maker / 57 Cornhill & 24 Fleet St London', referring to the 1855 patent; two examples with wooden and ivory handles, both marked round the lift hole 'Lund Maker 57 Cornhill'; wooden handle with the shank marked 'Lund Patent London'; bronzed steel marked 'Holborn Lever' on both sides for use with the corresponding lever; unmarked bronzed steel examples. The Lund-style worms are found with a variety of markings including 'Day & Sons Crewe', 'Farrow & Jackson / London', 'Improved / Corkscrew', 'London / Lever', 'London / Patent', 'Lund / London', 'Lund's Patent / London', 'Lund Patentee & Maker / Trade Mark' with a picture of a milestone, described later in Chapter 6; 'Patent / Lever'.

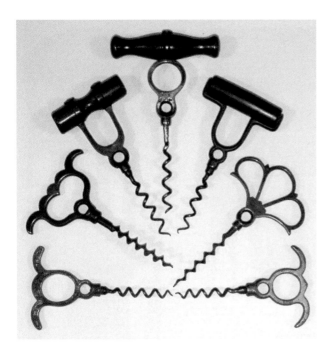

Straight pulls with lever holes and finger holes. *Clockwise from bottom left:* Three-finger pull marked 'The Lever Signet' with a diamond registration mark for the 1876 registered design of Edwin Wolverson (many examples have an unmarked pseudo-diamond); fairly common four-finger pull with lever hole (mid nineteenth century); wooden handle single-finger pull marked above the lever hole with a diamond registration mark for the 1879 registered design of James Henry Stone; signet pull named 'The Twin' with a diamond registration mark on the other side for the 1877 registered design of James Henry Stone, made in both steel and brass; often referred to as having a 'roller handle', this corkscrew is derived from Wolverson's 1878 registered design (this example is marked with a diamond registration mark, but they are usually unmarked); attractive three-finger pull named 'The Plume' with a diamond registration mark on the other side for the 1877 registered design of Benjamin Law, made in both brass and plated steel; unmarked bronzed wash example in the lever signet style (mid nineteenth century).

Straight pulls with vertical handles

Straight pulls with vertical handles are not very practical for use with wine bottles. Most are quite small and were used for perfume or medicine bottles. *Left:* Modern acrylic handle with an embedded cockerel for Portugal. *Right:* Perfume or medicine screws from dressing case sets, mid to late nineteenth century *(from left):* two mother-of-pearl handles; wooden handle; two bone handles; decorative silver handle hallmarked for Birmingham 1893; silver handle hallmarked for London 1939.

Dressing case sets

People used to travel in style with large leather or wooden dressing cases containing combs, hairbrushes, boot hooks, a variety of jars and bottles for perfumes, lotions and powders, and smaller leather inserts with manicure, shaving or needlework utensils. These inserts can often be found separate from the whole case and usually include button hooks, tweezers, nail files and, of course, the all-important corkscrew. However, they often have missing items, so it is important to check that the style, colour and markings of the items are all the same. Some dressing cases have folding bow, picnic or roundlet corkscrews rather than straight pulls.

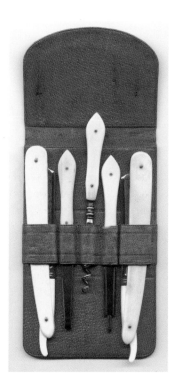

Left: Dressing case set with monograms on the ivory handles, with the scissors marked 'Lund 57 Cornhill' (mid nineteenth century). *Right:* Gentleman's dressing case set with two razors.

Straight pulls belonging to tool sets

These are typified by the Bonsa tool set in a leather case. The tools are marked 'Bonsa' or 'D.R.G.M.146827 Registered' for the German registered design of 1900 from Böntgen and Sabin (from which the trade name Bonsa is derived). The tools snap into the handle and are held in place by a spring-loaded lever. Other similar sets are known, named Sabina, Blosta, and Electron.

FIGURALS

Corkscrews are called figurals when the whole item, or a significant part of it, represents a tangible object. There is a multitude of designs, prices are normally modest, and because there is a reasonable supply, it is a fun and exciting class to collect. They were mostly designed as souvenirs or as novelty items and are therefore perfect gifts. Even your non-specialist friends will like these corkscrews and be able to seek them out and give them to you as presents.

Due to the inventiveness of designers, the diversity of corkscrews with figural aspects can cover the whole spectrum of a collection. Most of the figural corkscrews covered in this chapter have no mechanical features to them – they are simple straight pulls. There are certainly plenty of mechanical corkscrews that do have figural features, such as the 'Hootch-owl' and 'Anna G' in the Levers class, but they are referred to in the relevant chapter to avoid duplication, cross-referencing and complication. This chapter also does not cover the popular 'Lady's Legs' in which the legs cover the worm, as these will be found in Chapter 4.

One exception has been made for Syroco figures, which usually have a partial puller bell, but are included here.

There are two ways of considering figural corkscrews as a basis for discussion. We could look at a page of cats, a shoal of fish, a fleet of ships and a collage of people's heads and so on. This is the way the SCReW© Code classifies them and the way they are presented in Don Bull's *The Ultimate Corkscrew Book*. However, I feel it is best to consider the different styles of figurals and illustrate them with a diversity of examples, but still grouping subjects where possible.

British brass figurals

This is a specific and niche area for the collector, who can add an educational element to the hobby by researching the historic background to the subject.

In the early part of the twentieth century, rail travel

STYLES OF FIGURAL CORKSCREWS

- British brass flat backs or hollow backs – a very specific genre and distinctive design with a cast brass handle.
- Combinations – in which separate parts fit together to form a whole figure.
- Free-standing figurals – the corkscrew is designed to stand up on its own as an ornament rather than lie in a drawer.
- Hinged worm – usually to add extra novelty and interest to an item.

- Plain sheaths – in which the worm of the corkscrew has a non-figural cover and adds nothing to the design.
- Sheathed figurals – the opposite of the one above: it is the sheath or body that is important and the plain corkscrew just fits into it.
- Straight pull figurals – the simplest of them all with a figural handle and a plain non-hinged worm.

Above and left: Examples of markings: 'Reg 682891' and 'R^d 767310 C & A'.

Various handle styles. *Left to right:* With an eyebrow above the handle, the face on this corkscrew is from a pillar capital found in Wells Cathedral in Somerset and has been referred to as 'toothache man' (although unmarked, it is derived from the registered design number 716770 from 1925). With an eyebrow below the figure, the next corkscrew is named 'Jenny Jones' and shows the Welsh girl on her way to London to buy a Bible and inspiring the foundation of the Bible Society (Reg. No. 706696 from 1924). With a pseudo-eyebrow below the figure, the central corkscrew is named 'Fox Hound' and is from a series of six registered designs for dogs (Reg. No. 692111 from 1922) – the other dogs are 'English Setter', 'Greyhound', 'Wire-haired Terrier', 'Cocker Spaniel' and 'Bulldog'. Next, with a finger and hanging ring above the figure, the 'Bear and Ragged Staff' is the symbol of the county of Warwickshire (Reg. No. 535916 from 1909). Finally, the corkscrew with no eyebrow or finger ring but just a hanging hole is named 'Dartmoor Pisky' (Reg. No. 809103 from 1936).

Left to right: Smiling cat (catalogue number 18834, Reg. No. 588482 from 1911); thistle, the emblem of Scotland (Reg. No. 779768 from 1933); 'Whitby Abbey' (Reg. No. 803165 from 1935), depicting the Abbey of the picturesque harbour town on the North Yorkshire coast; 'English Setter' (Reg. No. 692076 from 1922).

became more popular and accessible to the working population. Workers were also getting an entitlement to holidays. They went on day trips and they took souvenirs back home. Various brass novelty items were produced to satisfy this new market, with corkscrews being just one of the many items, which included ashtrays, door knockers, toasting forks, cap lifters, shoe horns, button hooks and table bells. Some, but not all, of the cast brass handles of these items were registered designs and were covered by copyright. If you have a look on the back of the brass handle you might see a registration number starting 'Reg' or 'RD'. The number will identify the designer and the date of registration. The number was included at the casting stage and it is often rather unclear and difficult to read. An in-depth study of British registered designs for corkscrews can be found in Ellis and Ellis.

There are a number of basic handle designs. Some were designed for the job of removing corks from bottles, but others are not very practical and are extremely uncomfortable to use.

Collectors should be aware that the market for figural brass corkscrews has been so buoyant that handles have been removed from toasting forks and other similar items, and a new shank and worm screwed into them. It is usually quite obvious to the corkscrew collector when this has been done, but not always. There are no rules for telling an authentic brass figural from a marriage, but there are some generalizations which should be borne in mind. The presence of an eyebrow handle, either above or below the figure, is a good sign that it was made as a corkscrew. Bright marks from grippers on an otherwise unmarked shank are a sign of a marriage. Most toasting forks have a

MANUFACTURERS OF BRASS FIGURALS

Brass figural corkscrew handles were made by a small number of manufacturers as listed below:

Crofts and Assinder – corkscrews stamped 'C & A'.

Lloyd Pascal & Co. – corkscrews stamped 'ELPEC' (from El P *et* Co.).

John Jewsbury and Company Limited.

Pearson-Page Company Limited, which was taken over by Jewsbury and Company Ltd to form Pearson-Page-Jewsbury Co. In the late 1940s, Pearson-Page-Jewsbury Co. Ltd registered the trademark 'Peerage', which is used on later corkscrews.

swollen knop or lump under the handle, whereas corkscrew handles normally do not. Genuine old straight pulls have simple helical wire worms (circular section) or ciphered worms (triangular section). The presence of a bladed or Archimedean worm should raise doubts in a collector's mind unless they are post 1945.

Below, Left to right: 'Victory' (Reg. No. 708751 from 1924), showing Admiral Nelson's flagship in the Battle of Trafalgar, 1805; the 'Fowey Ship', double sided (Reg. No. 782287 from 1933), probably promoting an inn in the harbour town of Fowey in Cornwall; 'Longships Lighthouse Land's End' (Reg. No. 803797 from 1935), showing the lighthouse off the coast of Cornwall; 'The Canterbury Cross' (Reg. No. 701922 from 1923), representing the ancient stone cross in Canterbury Cathedral.

Left to right: 'Southwold Town Crier' (Reg. No. 682891 from 1921), showing the man who walked round the town proclaiming the day's news; 'Black Boy' (Reg. No. 707063 from 1924), with a loose finger pull ring; Pompadour (Reg. No. 767262 from 1931), perhaps produced after the release of the 1927 film *Madame Pompadour*, about Louis XV's famous mistress; cross-legged Dutch boy (Reg. No.767310 from 1931).

There are many pixie designs, most of which refer to places in the southwest of England. *Left to right:* Double-sided pixie leapfrogging over a toadstool (Reg. No. 791362 from 1934); 'Dartmoor Pixies' (Reg. No. 791359 from 1934); 'Dartmoor Pixie' (Reg. No. 711001 from 1925) – this design is also found named 'Devon Pixie', 'Exmoor Pixie', 'Haytor Pixie' and 'Cornish Pixie'; 'Jolly Monks' (Reg. No. 592516 from 1911).

Combination figurals

These are figurals in which separate parts fit together to form a whole figure.

In all of these examples the worm is hidden inside part of the object and therefore many of them have a long tubular section as part of the design. There are a host of keys and anchors waiting for the collector with a modest budget and a keen eye for checking what might be hiding inside.

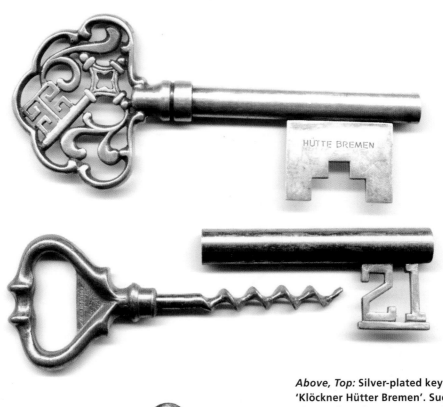

Above, Top: Silver-plated key marked 'Klöckner Hütter Bremen'. Such keys are often referred to as 'Bremen keys'. *Bottom:* Brass key (Reg. No. 871997 from 1953). The 'bit' is formed as the number 21 for a coming of age gift as the 'key to the door' of the home.

Left: Viking longship with a sail marked 'Norway Calling'. By removing the tubular mast the worm is revealed and the upside-down ship makes quite a comfortable straight pull. *Right:* Anchor with the worm housed in the central part.

Top: Ice axe with a cap lifter hook on the shank, the point actually designed to chop ice. It is marked under the blade 'Ges. Geschütz' for the German-registered design. *Bottom:* Brass gun with a screw-on barrel and a hammer that can be used as a cap lifter. *Below:* Ceramic seal made in the UK by Wade in the 1960s with the worm attached to the ball.

In 1958 Paul Gladman registered two designs as 'mantel ornaments' with corkscrews or cap lifters clipped behind them. The sailor with a lifebelt is marked 'Reg. No. 887319' and also '887318'. The second Gladman design was a shield with a heraldic lion, marked on the back 'Reg. No. 891381' – both the Scotsman and the helmet are corkscrews. Gladman probably designed other bar sets as well, such as Andy Capp and Flo behind their bar, marked 'Made in England' on the back. Andy is a cap lifter and Flo a corkscrew – they featured in a cartoon strip by Reginald Smythe, which ran for many years in the Daily Mirror from 1957. The figures and the bar come in a variety of colours. A related Zulu warrior complete with cocktail stick spears behind a shield is also known.

Left: When it is all put together, with the cap lifter hook inside the plastic base section and the cover on the worm, this is a promotional item for Acrow, who made jacks for propping up buildings. An added novelty is the pencil sharpener in the top section of the jack.

Below: Syroco figurals, made by the Syracuse Ornamental Company of Syracuse, New York. They were made by compression moulding of a composition of wood powder and thermoset resin. There are six figures to collect – Indian, man with top hat, waiter, monk, clown, and (the rarest and missing from this set) the knight. The clown has been opened up to show the corkscrew with its characteristic bell which helps to pull the cork. The worms and bells were supplied by the Williamson Company. Figures were either painted or stained with a walnut finish, so there are variations to collect. Other corkscrews with faces or dog heads were also made by Syroco, but without the body part.

Anri Figurals. These wooden figurals were produced in Northern Italy by Antonio Riffeser (An-Ri) and hand carved by local villagers. The heads carry corkscrews or bottle openers. There is a huge variety of jolly monks, barmen, sailors and others. There are also drunks leaning on lamp posts, or sitting on benches with a set of friends bearing bottle openers or bottle corks.

Free-standing figurals

There are numerous examples of free standing figurals designed as ornaments and they vary widely in quality and price, depending on the designer and their artistic appeal. Just a small selection is shown here.

Left to right: Gent in a bowler hat resting on a 'shooting stick' with a hip flask (unmarked); brass motor cycle (marked on the base 'Des. Reg. 873699' for 1954); crawling chimpanzee marked on the body 'RT London'.

Between 1932 and 1936, Pearson-Page-Jewsbury Co. Ltd registered twenty-two designs for a series of cute animals. Just four are shown here. The 'just good friends' dog pair is one of the most common (Reg. No. 779325 from 1933), and the pig (Reg. No. 779326 from 1933) is probably the least common. The dog standing on his hind legs looks like Bonzo, a mischievous cartoon pup who appeared weekly in *The Daily Sketch* in the1920s and was created by George Studdy. The upward curve on the rear feet acts as a cap lifter. The corkscrew is not common (Reg. No. 780441 from 1933). The dachshund with cap lifter front feet is a 1936 model (Reg. No. 811349).

There are a number of very well carved or machined wooden dogs like this poodle with a corkscrew tail. The Red Devil is unmarked, but although it appears to be derived from a US design patent from Gerald Youhanaie of 1985, it is clearly much older than that. The triangular base incorporates a cap lifter.

Two well-made corkscrews both marked 'RЯ' 'Made in Austria'. The mark is believed to be the symbol for Richard Rohac, active in the 1950s. It has in the past been attributed to Rena Rosenthal who distributed Hagenauer items in New York in the 1930s. (Information from Wayne Meadows.)

Other Austrian figurals were designed by Walter Bosse and his partner Herta Baller in the 1950s and '60s. The monkey is marked 'Bosse, Austria'; the cute Bambi and Scottie dog are both marked 'Baller, Austria'. (Information from Wayne Meadows.)

Figurals with hinged worms

A hinged worm can add extra novelty and interest to an item or be used merely to hide the worm and not ruin the figural outline. Once again, there are many examples to collect without stretching the budget too far.

Below: Typically French! (The wooden corkscrews of course, not the subject matter.) Both the *gendarme* and the *matelot* can modify their angle of dangle due to a pin through the loop on the end of the worm. Both have a cap lifter behind them. The Viking is more demure with a hinged 'sword' behind his shield, and the horned helmet designed as a cap lifter.

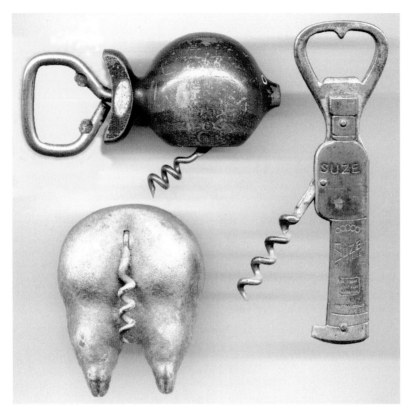

Top: Wooden fish with a cap lifter tail and a folding worm. The silvered label on the tail is too worn to be readable. *Right:* French folding corkscrew in the shape of a bottle with a cap lifter head. The advertising is for 'Suze Gentiane'. *Bottom:* This pig's bottom with folding corkscrew tail has an unusual pink furry finish. It was also made in plain aluminium. The opposite side has a flat steel plate with a cap lifter cut out and is marked 'Colonial Crafts Pat. Pending'. The patent has not been found to date.

Top: Horse's head with the reins acting as a cap lifter hook, and marked under the folding worm 'Made in USA'. *Bottom:* Brass fish with a cap lifter tail and the upper lip fashioned as a can piercer.

This elegant corkscrew is an example of the highly collectable Art Deco designs made by the famous Hagenauer family in the 1930s. It is marked with the 'wHw' logo on the cap lifter hook and 'Made in Vienna, Austria'. Not all Hagenauer corkscrews have folding worms.

Below: American examples. *Left to right:* The parrot has a cap lifter beak and is marked on its feet 'Negbaur USA Pat'd'. There are a number of different finishes for the parrot derived from Manuel Avillar's USA design patent of 1929. The gentleman is marked on the base 'Old Snifter' and under the umbrella 'Negbaur N.Y. Made in USA Pat'd'. Turning the head makes the hinged worm pop out from the back, the essence of John Schuchardt's patent of 1935. This example has the hands and umbrella fashioned as a cap lifter. The gentleman without an umbrella does not have a twisting head, but sometimes has a hat that pulls off to provide a small cup for a nip of spirits. It is marked 'Old Snifter' and 'Demley'. It has often been reported that the image is of Volstead, the man who introduced the Prohibition Bill to the US Congress in 1919. However, Don Bull's research (*Ultimate Corkscrew Book*) led to the conclusion that these figures are derived from a cartoon character created by Rollin Kirby to lampoon the 'dry' prohibitionists.

British examples. *Left to right:* The Scotsman wears a kilt, clutches a bottle of whisky and has a hinged worm as his stick. On the back it is very poorly cast with 'Reg. Nº 852412', for the registered design of George Leslie Tirebuck for 1947. It is very likely that the 'What a day' figural was also designed by George Leslie Tirebuck. The girl has a pigtail worm and carries a hot water bottle on the way to bed. The example is marked 'Regᵈ'. on the back. The golf bag is a rarer design from Tirebuck and is clearly marked 'Regd.' and also has a cap lifter hook on the side. It was registered in 1955.

Three celluloid picnic-style corkscrews with black plastic sheaths that fit over the worm to protect the point and also act as a cross bar for pulling out corks, using the hole in the handles. The bodies are made in two halves which are filled with zinc oxide powder and glued together. Significant areas of rust and corrosion can be seen where the steel shank meets the celluloid.

Plain sheathed figurals

These figural corkscrews have a plain sheath to cover the worm, adding nothing to the representation of the image. There are not many examples to collect unless you like celluloid figures, or you are lucky enough to find a treasure trove of eighteenth-century corkscrews – or if you can afford Dutch silver.

One of the very first plastics that had commercial applications was celluloid, or cellulose nitrate. Celluloid could be easily moulded to make decorative items, such as corkscrew handles. However, it had an inherent problem since moisture in the atmosphere hydrolyzes it very slowly to nitric acid, which will rust steel. Look carefully at the point where the steel shank goes into the celluloid – the corrosion is much worse there than anywhere else. This is a sure sign of age and authenticity.

Left: British brass figurals with a brass sheath are not common but not particularly expensive when you find them. This one depicts Wells Cathedral on both sides. *Right:* The chrome on brass penguin has a plastic sheath, which covers a rather weedy worm. It is marked on the base of the sheath 'Dura' and is derived from a US design patent of 1933 from The Reynolds Spring Company.

Late-eighteenth-century sheathed corkscrews. *Left:* The small dog is delicately carved from ivory and the steel sheath has a brazed seam and covers a wire worm. *Centre:* The salmon is silver plated with an Archimedean worm protected by a dimpled sheath. *Right:* The bent steel leg is very detailed and the sole of the boot was probably intended as a pipe tamper. It has a wire worm and a pricker which inserts into the knee to form a T-handle.

Silver sheathed figurals. The screw-on silver sheaths of these Dutch corkscrews are very decorative. Larger bases sometimes carried a seal and smaller bases may have been intended as pipe tampers. Some bases unscrew to reveal a pricker or piercer as in the carousel horse example shown. Dates range from the mid eighteenth to the late nineteenth century. Early examples may be hallmarked and are quite light; later examples are much heavier.

Figural sheaths

In these corkscrews it is the sheath or body that is figural and the worm, usually with a cap lifter, fits into it. There are relatively few examples, mostly from the USA and usually made of a heavy lead alloy.

The fish is marked 'JB' on its mouth. 'JB' was the trademark of Jennings Brothers Manufacturing Company in the early twentieth century. The coffee pot is marked 'JB 301' on the base. The owl is marked 'JB 3572' on the base. Other JB examples to look for are a horse's head, a seahorse and 'Little Brown Jug'. The silver boot is marked on the base 'Sterling 738' with a trademark 'R B Co' for R. Blackinton.

Straight pull figurals

There are numerous straight pull corkscrews with figural handles for the collector, ranging from early nineteenth-century steel examples to present-day plastic ones.

Left to right: Steel handle in the shape of a hand gripping a bar; brass pistol from about 1880, the square steel shank stamped 'Gagnepain', the French maker; and a detailed cast steel fish with two eels wrapped round it, the shank stamped 'Gau?ret'.

Left: Hugh McBride's British patent of 1888 in the shape of a champagne cork with two slots in the top. The boxwood handle is marked 'Patent No. 7431' on the handle and 'McBride's Patent Dry Monopol' on the shank. (Collectors often wonder why the handle and shank are at an angle. One explanation is that the corkscrew may have been designed as a promotional table place marker or menu holder. When the cork is placed on its base, the point of the worm sits on the table and a name card can be inserted in one of the slots on the top.) *Centre:* A promotional corkscrew from the 1970s advertising Vat 69 whisky (the plastic sides of the handle are pinned to a steel core and the shank is stamped 'Foreign'). *Right:* An uncommon corkscrew derived from C.T. Willetts' British registered design of 1893. The boxwood handle is stamped 'Registered' in an arc.

Left: Plated brass handle comprising a tankard and cap lifter, marked on the back 'Reg. No. 880690' for Walden and Gladman's British design of 1956. *Centre:* Very heavy plated corkscrew with two horse heads, stamped 'Christian Dior Made in England' above the worm (late twentieth century). *Right:* Ceramic handle promoting a drain pipe company with the trademark 'IAI'. The shank is stamped 'Dreko German DR', for an East German corkscrew manufacturer (second half of the twentieth century).

Scandinavian figurals from the early twentieth century. *Left:* Unmarked smiling dolphin made of pewter. *Centre:* Two seahorses made of pewter, marked 'Danmark' and the trademark of Just Andersen. *Right:* Bronze corkscrew depicting Pan and Bacchus fighting over a bunch of grapes, from a 1920s Danish design by Mogens Ballin.

Pearson-Page-Jewsbury Co. registered numerous animal designs in the 1930s, as described earlier. The designs also included the straight pull figurals as exemplified by the crouching dog (Reg. No. 779330 for 1933) and the reclining pixie (Reg. No. 779331, also 1933) shown here. *Centre:* Silver salmon, Reg. No. 254376 for Henry Well's British registered design of 1895, and hallmarked for Birmingham 1899, with the maker's mark, 'HW'.

Left: Running goat marked 'RЯ Made in Austria', by Richard Rohac (as mentioned earlier). *Centre:* An unmarked heavy American eagle with a cap lifter beak and can piercer tail. *Right:* A delicate heron, probably from a dressing table set, marked 'Reg^d 164209' for the 1891 British design registered by Alexander Jones and Co., travelling bag makers.

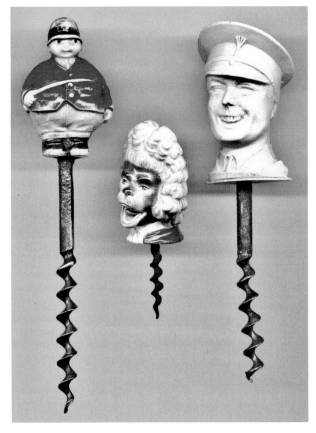

Left and right: Celluloid figurals made without sheaths depicting a fat huntsman and Edward VIII, the British king who abdicated in 1936 because of his love for Mrs Wallis Simpson. *Centre:* Porcelain monkey in a wig, made by Meissen, marked with a crossed sword mark as used in the period 1815–1923.

KNIVES

The folding blade pocket knife has a long history and the excellent book by Peters and Giulian covers them in great detail, from the introduction of the 'back spring' in 1660, which ensures that the blade stays closed in the pocket. It seems to be a manufacturer's mission to incorporate a host of other tools on such pocket knives and many of them have a corkscrew. It is this sort of knife that this section will cover, and there are an endless number of styles and variations to collect. The flat scales or sides of a pocket knife pro-vided the perfect platform for advertising and this provides another fruitful area for collectors. Indeed, there can be brisk competition between the knife collector, the collector of advertising and the corkscrew collector.

The thick part of the blade next to the hinge is called the 'tang' and this often bears the mark of the manufacturer, which helps with identification and dating. The most important centres for manufacturing pocket knives in Europe were Sheffield (England),

Bottle-shaped knives

Top left: **French knives of this type are relatively easy to acquire and because of their shape and what they promote, they are called 'champagne knives'. They have horn scales, sometimes with a metal insert for the advert, and a short curved blade for cutting the wire on champagne corks. The one shown advertises 'Moët & Chandon Epernay' and the main blade is marked on the tang 'Sauzedde Biat'.** *Top right:* **The brass scales of this Italian knife promote 'Trinchieri Torino' on both sides. Just below the 'bottle' top it is marked 'ARI BEM'.** *Bottom left:* **There are a few versions of the Maggi knife and, whilst they are not uncommon, they can command good prices. They can have one or two blades. The example shown is marked 'Maggi für jeden Tisch Maggis Würze'. It has more writing on the other side promoting flavouring for soup and food. Other versions promote Maggi's Aroma sauce.** *Bottom right:* **This French knife is stamped 'Orangina Gazéifiée à la Pulpe d'Orange'. It has a cap lifter slot on the other side.**

Thiers and Laguiole (France), Solingen (Germany) and Eskilstruna (Sweden) and you will probably find one of these names on most of the knives you collect.

Knives can be categorized by shape, by specific tools attached to them (such as a cap lifter or can opener), or by type, such as pocket knives.

Bottle-shaped knives

The general flat shape of a pocket knife renders it ideal for creating figural versions. For the producer of bottled goods – drink, seasoning or anything else – the pocket knife was a prefect promotional aid.

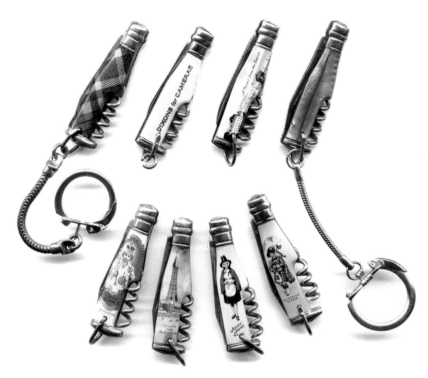

These single-blade small knives (48mm) are in the shape of a bottle and come in a variety of patterns. They were made in the early 1950s by Richards of Sheffield and the tangs are always marked with their name and a lamppost trademark. The scales are celluloid and the light-coloured ones are made to look like mother of pearl. Some have a key ring attached. Examples shown are: tartan, plain (sometimes with advertising such as 'Dixons for Cameras'), 'A Present from the Seaside', mottled grey (and other shades), 'Queen Elizabeth II Coronation 1953', 'A Present from Blackpool', 'Jenny Jones Wales', and 'Scottish Piper'. Others known include 'R.C.M.P. Canada', and 'Rodeo Canada'.

Other figural knives

Top left: With its shape like a leg, this quality American knife promotes 'Brownbilt Tread Straight Shoes' with the tang marked 'Utica Cutlery Co., Utica N.Y.' *Centre left:* The small knife with pale green plastic scales in the shape of a shoe or sabot is probably French from the mid twentieth century. *Bottom left:* The scales of this chunky German shoe knife are horn and the two blades are both marked 'Ges. Geschützt'. *Top centre:* This beautifully made French knife is marked 'Déposé Touriste' and depicts a gentleman in a peaked cap. The larger blade has a trademark of a tent and the word 'Camp'. *Bottom centre:* This picnic knife, marked on the back 'Made in China' is of much poorer quality. It has a fork, spike and can opener, and a very weedy worm that is unlikely to last beyond opening one bottle. *Right:* These two knives in the general shape of a leg are typical of the production of Laguiole, a small town in France. The upper one is newer with black plastic scales and the blade marked 'Veritable Laguiole'. The lower knife is of much higher quality with real horn scales, a blade marked 'Laguiole Besset Jne' and, as with all of the older knives, a decorated back spine with a bee motif.

Knives with cap lifter hooks

The success of the crown cap resulted in knife designers incorporating cap lifter hooks on to the knife blades or the scales of pocket knives. There are many different designs and only a few are shown here.

Examples of cap lifters on the knife blade itself. Richards of Sheffield was very successful in making cheap knives for the masses in the 1950s. The blade is unusual with its cap lifter hook, a concept that was patented in the USA by James Heath in 1909. The patent had expired by the time Richards made these. The scales are celluloid and some of the patterns are the same as the small bottle knives. *From the top:* **Tartan scales; 'An Irish Leprecaun', 'Good Luck'; 'Kruger and De Wet'; 'Queen Elizabeth II, Coronation 1953'; plain and advertising 'Fly by B.O.A.C'; and finally a knife with silver scales hallmarked for Sheffield 1951 and made by Needham, Hill St, Sheffield.**

Here the cap lifter appears on the knife scales. *Top:* **This knife is marked 'D.R.G.M. Made in Germany', but there is no number to identify the registration. It reads 'Drink Clarke's Gold Medal Mineral Waters, Scarborough'.** *Left:* **The tang of this American knife is stamped 'Ideal USA'.** *Centre and right:* **Two versions of this design are shown; one with decorative brass scales and one with plastic scales. The tang of the one on the right is marked 'Fine Quality Foreign'.** *Bottom:* **'Schweppes's Table Waters, Cordials etc.' are promoted on this knife along with a picture of a soda syphon.**

Top left: The cap lifter is marked R^d N° 610074, which denotes Ibberson's 1912 registration. However, the registration document shows a very different design with a double hooked cut-out part way down the edge of one of the scales. *Bottom left:* The knife has a cigar cutter hole, a cap lifter hook and screwdriver at the end. Colman's Mustard is advertised on one side. The design (Reg. No. 750382) was registered by John Clarke & Son Ltd in 1929. Examples are also known without the cigar-cutting hole. *Centre:* This is one of a number of German knives promoting various drinks, in this case 'de KuYper's Square Face'. *Top right:* The knife (Reg. No. 750460) has 'Pull' to the left and 'Lift' to the right of the cap lifter. It is also stamped 'The Two-Way Crown Cork Opener'. The 1929 registration was from George Gill & Sons. *Bottom right:* With its characteristic hooked cap lifter (Reg. No. 709835), this knife was a relatively successful

design and examples exist with polished steel scales and bone scales. The example shown has only one blade but they were made with a variety of blades and tools. The 1924 registration was from Brookes & Crookes Ltd of Sheffield. *Bottom centre:* This knife (Reg. No. 766603 for Herbert Needham's 1931 design) has a screwdriver tab and a cap lifter hook stamped 'Crown Cork Opener'.

Knives with cartridge extractors

Pocket knives with corkscrews were made with shot gun cartridge extractors at the end for the huntsman. *Left:* The knife has antler scales with a square metal insert promoting 'Spratts Patent' (for farm animal feeds). At one end is the cartridge extractor marked 'Sheffield' and 16 on one side and 14 on the other for cartridges of different gauges. The button hook of this example also has a cartridge extractor stamped 12, thus covering all key sizes. The knife was made by Joseph Westby and was also available with nickel-plated steel scales. *Right:* This knife is named 'Thornhill's New Shooting Knife' and 'patent' next to the bell trademark for Brookes & Crookes. The blades are marked 'Thornhill & Co., New Bond Street'. The extractor end is stamped '12' on one side and '16' on the other, but the unusual feature of the knife is the small curved blade, which has a serrated file on one side. It is marked 'Graduating Extractor' on the visible side and has a small lug on the back of the tang, which can grip a non-standard-sized cartridge. This concept was patented in Britain in 1892 by Westby & Levick, electroplate manufacturers in Sheffield. Joseph Westby started his apprenticeship with Brookes & Crookes and set up on his own in 1893. This probably explains why the knife has the bell trademark and suggests that Thornhill was the London retailer.

In the late nineteenth century there were a number of designs for variable cartridge extractors as tools for knives. *Left:* The Y-shaped adjustable extractor is marked 'registered' twice with a diamond mark for 1880 for Stacey & Shaw's Sheffield design. It was made by Mitchell and Company. *Centre:* This knife has a swivelling cartridge extractor. It bears a diamond registration stamp for George Butler & Co.'s design of 1881. Not all examples have the diamond mark. The stem of the cartridge extractor has Butler's trademark 'Art' in a circle and the extractor itself is stamped '12' and '16' for the different cartridge sizes. The tangs of the blades of the knife shown are stamped 'Art Geo Butler & Co, Sheffield'. *Right:* The lazy tongs extractor is not common and the tang marked 'F. Herdera Sn Solingen' shows that this is a German knife, despite having a typical British shape.

Horseman's knives

Horseman's knives have a long tool with a curved end for cleaning horses' hooves. The hoof hook usually locks in place on the back of the knife with a slight spring action. *Left:* The stamping on the tang on one of the blades, 'T. Turner & Co, Sheffield, Cutlers to His Majesty', dates this knife to the early twentieth century. It has nickel-plated steel scales. *Top:* This perfect miniature horseman's knife has mother-of-pearl scales and was probably intended as a charm rather than a tool for very small ponies. *Right:* The antler scales of this utility knife have small slots in the ends to accommodate a pick and a pair of tweezers. It was made by G. Butler & Co. of Sheffield in about 1880.

Pocket knives

These are classic examples of British pocket knives of the Victorian era, carrying a variety of tools. *Top left:* The gentle humped back was made to take a corkscrew and this example has a diamond registration mark for William Singleton's registered design of 1874. This example was made by Mappin & Webb. *Top right:* This small knife is of a similar age and was made by George Butler of Sheffield. It has an asymmetric hump, probably more common than the one on the left. *Bottom left:* The two screw bolts are for repairing the bridles of horses whilst out riding and the long blade (left) is for trimming hooves. The tangs of this well-made knife are marked 'F.A. Barnes, 37 Ship Street, Brighton'. *Bottom right:* Although the scales promote George Goulet Champagne, the knife, with its 'crown cap opener', was made in Sheffield by G. Butler & Co. and has their 'Art' trademark on the tang.

These are pocket knives with scales made from natural materials. *Top left:* This miniature knife has mother-of-pearl scales and a tiny pair of scissors. A nail file folds out from the back of the knife. *Top right:* The dumb-bell-shaped knife is an unusual shape and has bone scales promoting 'Champagne Vve A, Devaux, Epernay'. *Bottom left:* This fine quality miniature knife has tortoiseshell scales and the tangs are marked 'Harrison Bros. & Howson'. *Bottom:* 'Rodgers, Cutlers to Her Majesty' made this knife with ivory scales. Rodgers of Sheffield was famed for its massive stocks of ivory and it is reported that in 1878 Rodgers used 26 tons of ivory, comprising 2,561 tusks averaging over 22 pounds in weight each, for ivory handles for their cutlery.

Pocket knives with decorative scales. *Top:* This German knife celebrates a year's production of 165 million blown-glass bottles at Gerresheimer Glashuttenwerke and shows a man blowing glass. It has a blade for manicuring nails and the tang is marked 'Paul A. Henckels, Solingen'. *Centre left:* This lower-quality knife has pressed aluminium scales with images of Kruger and De Wet with banners on the other side for Transvaal and Oranje Vrijst in South Africa. *Centre right:* There are many French knives with pressed brass scales showing sporting scenes. This one is slightly different: it has the image of an old man on one side and a dancing girl on the other side and is marked 'Déposé'. One of the blades is a can opener and the large blade is marked 'Pradel'. *Bottom left:* The scales show a German girl carrying about eight steins of beer on the front side. The other side shows intertwined vines and the 'twins' trademark of 'J.A. Henckels of Solingen'. It also has their mark on the tangs. *Bottom right:* The silver scales of this miniature knife are engraved with leaves and flowers. It is hallmarked for Birmingham 1892. Surprisingly for a British knife, the tangs are not marked.

Pocket knives with can opener blades

Left: This is the 'official knife' of the 'Canadian Girl Guides' and has a beaver emblem and the motto, 'be prepared'. They were certainly well prepared with this knife for opening cans, beer bottles and wine bottles. The other side is marked 'R^d N° 717020' and 'C. Johnson & Co. Sheffield' on the tang. The design of the wicked looking can opener blade was registered in 1925. *Centre:* The second 'Girl Guides' knife has similar features and was made by W. Mount & Son Sheffield. Although it is marked 'Reg. N° 494338', it is not a registered design but a statement that the trademark 'Girl Guides' was registered in 1928. *Right:* This large knife is from Germany and marked 'Mercator D.R.G.M.' on the spine. One of the scales is marked 'Special' and the tang is for 'Mercator Solingen'. The large blade locks in the open position and is released by the lug on the spine. *Bottom:* This knife is collected by fishing enthusiasts as well as knife and corkscrew collectors. It is marked for the famous maker of fishing tackle, 'Pegley Davies Anglers Knife', and shows a series of hook sizes on the opposite side. It also has a 2½-inch ruler for the minnows that didn't get away.

Watts' patent knives

John Robert Watts was a long-established maker of cutlery and penknives in Sheffield, England. Many knives are marked Watts, but a specific type was marked 'Watts's Patent' (sometimes Watts') on a large spring-loaded arm, which can be locked in the closed position with a sliding catch. The patent refers to the 1892 patent from Watts, which shows a wire cutter with the locking catch but no corkscrew, and his 1901 patent, which shows a corkscrew pivoted to a combination tool with knife, cigar cutter and button hook.

Top left: The jaws are a wire cutter and there are two standard blades. The tangs are marked 'John Watts Sheffield Est^b 1765'. It is also marked 'cigar cutter' round the hole and 'Made in Sheffield, England' on one of the scales. *Centre left:* The promotional knife for Dry Monopol champagne is quite well known and has 'Heidsieck & Co.' on the other side. *Top right:* It is less common to find the adjustable cartridge extractor version of Watts's Patent. This example is marked 'Made in Sheffield, England' and the other side is marked as a 3-inch ruler. *Centre right:* Made for fishermen, this complex tool has a master blade stamped 'John Watts Sheffield', a pair of folding scissors, and a hollow ground sharp-edged blade, which is possibly a fish scaler. The main jaws are for preparing lead shot weights. *Bottom:* Watts also made a specialist knife for cyclists and the jaws in this example are for use with tyre valves. The blunt-edged tool with a rounded end is for removing tyres from wheel rims. Although it is marked 'Watts's Patent' on the lever arm, the tangs show that it was made by W. Thornhill & Co., 114 New Bond St.

Below, Top: Most Watts's patent knives were made with metal scales but this is a tortoiseshell example. The lever arm promotes Château de Condé, Epernay. *Right:* This knife is clearly related to the Watts type in concept but was the subject of a 1904 design registration from Thomas Turner & Co. The lever arm is marked 'R^d N° 435493 Thomas Turner and Co. Cutlers to His Majesty'. The scales bear a host of promotional detail for 'E.J. Churchill, Practical Gun and Rifle Manufacturer'. The registration was for the small locking clip that holds the lever arm closed and can just be seen as a small notch on the right-hand side. There are very few of these knives around and the clip is usually faulty. *Bottom:* The knife that is pictured is identical to the drawing for the 1908 registered design of George Butler & Co. The knife is only marked on the tang with 'J. Beal & Sons Sheffield'. The locking device in this case is a small flip-over catch at the right-hand end.

Knives with extended worms

Although many pocket knives have a corkscrew as one of the tools, a big problem is that with the folding corkscrew hinged close to the middle of the knife, it cannot be much longer than half the length of the knife and thus has little or no shank. This makes it rather difficult to get your fingers under the handle at the point of pulling out the cork. A number of innovative solutions were developed to get round this problem, to enable a full-length worm and shank to be used.

Top left: The 'Charles Heidsieck' knife has bone scales with nickel end sections. It has two normal blades and a short serrated curved blade for cutting champagne cork wires. The worm has a long shank, at the end of which is a small upturned lug. The shank slides along the back of the knife in a channel and through a small revolving ring, so that the end can ultimately pivot in the ring to turn the worm perpendicular. One of the scales is marked 'Registered', which is probably a reference to Müller's 1896 D.R.G.M. registration and British patent. The tangs are marked 'Made in Germany'. *Top right:* Müller's revolving ring must have been quite labour intensive to manufacture and it is believed he simplified the design as in this example, although a registration document or patent has not been identified. The end of the shank is shaped like a 'J' and this type of knife is often referred to as a 'J-hook'. The 'J' can pivot round a fixed pin and the structure is easier to manufacture. The knife has antler scales and the tangs are marked 'L. Herder & Son Germany' and 'L. Herder & Son Phila. PA.', suggesting it was made in Germany and exported to America. *Centre:* In this knife from the mid twentieth century, the details of the shank are hidden inside the plastic scales of the knife, but it is another J-hook. *Centre left:* The double folding worm in this example is hinged on the back of the knife and also has a spring-loaded hinge in the middle of the shank. It has two standard blades, both marked 'Petty & Sons, Sheffield'. *Centre right:* This is a very delicate knife with J-hook worm, probably for ladies' use, as it has standard and manicure blades, marked on the tangs 'Balke & Schaal, Solingen'. *Bottom left:* Müller created another design concept in 1897 with a pin through the end of the shank for rotation and a slot in the scales of the knife for the shank to slide in. The blade tang is stamped 'D.R.G.M. 72,477 Paul Henckels Solingen' and the scales promote 'Champagne Vve A. Devaux Maison Fondée en 1846'. *Bottom right:* A slot in the shank offered yet another solution of storing the worm along the back of the knife. The scales are mother-of-pearl and the main blade is stamped 'Wedekind & Co London, Patent No 25659', which refers to Alfred Williams' 1896 British patent, following Kastor & Co.'s 1896 German registration and 1897 US patent.

Top left, bottom left, bottom right: These are examples of Hammesfahr's 1897 German patent for a very clever solution to the problem of extending the length of the corkscrew. The shank is in two halves connected by a pin. From the closed position *(bottom left)* it is swivelled round through 180° (bottom right) and then the whole corkscrew lifted up through 90°. The concept was also patented in Britain in 1897 and in the USA in 1898. Although it was never patented in Sweden, many Hammesfahr knives were made there. The upper mother-of-pearl example is marked on the tang 'Ahlström & Co Eskilstruna'. The white plastic version was also made in Eskilstruna by O. Andersson. *Top right:* The

shank of the corkscrew has two slots in it on one edge with a pivot between them. When the worm is in the fully open position the lower slot clicks under a small pin across the back of the knife to fix it in the open position. When the hinged worm is closed the upper slot clicks on to the same pin to hold it closed. The blade tangs are stamped 'D.R.G.M.' for Steinfeld's 1897 registration.

If anyone thought that the concept of a double folding corkscrew was an idea from the late nineteenth century, here are older knives to prove otherwise. *Left:* This horseman's knife with antler scales from the mid nineteenth century is well used and has small tools inserted into the end of the body. When the worm and shank are folded flat, the upper side of the shank presents a serrated concave face,

which can grip a small nut for cracking with the hoof hook. *Right:* This is a really wonderful quality old knife with horn scales and excellent decorated steelwork, especially on the bow of the saw and on the edges of the dividers in the body of the knife. A leather punch folds alongside the folding corkscrew. There is a selection of small tools in the end of the knife and two fleams (for bleeding horses) fold from the same end. The silver blade for fruit is hallmarked for George III (1760–1820) but with no date letter.

POCKET AND PROTECTED CORKSCREWS

There has always been a need to carry a corkscrew from place to place, whether it be for a picnic, a coach or train journey or, in the early days, from tavern to tavern, to ensure you were always prepared. Corkscrews have a sharp pointed end, so many solutions were found to stop this damaging the person or their clothes, as well as to protect the point from damage. A cover or sheath for the worm also presented the option to add other tools or to use it for advertising.

As with all corkscrew classifications, there is overlap with other sections. Many pocket knives could be considered as pocket and protected corkscrews but they have their own section in this book (Chapter 3). Similarly, some of the combination corkscrews have a worm that folds into a handle, or a cap lifter as a corkscrew handle with a sheath to cover the worm. This section generally focuses on folding and sheathed corkscrews that do not have significant

A selection of single worm bows. *Top row, left to right:* The elegant slim bow from the late eighteenth century is marked 'TR' (possibly for Thomas Read) and features a nicely decorated hinge, which has a small 'stop plate', allowing the worm to fold through only 180°. The teardrop-shaped bow is marked 'Lund' and has a barrel-shaped hinge with nicks at each side to lock it in either the open or closed positions. The next example is

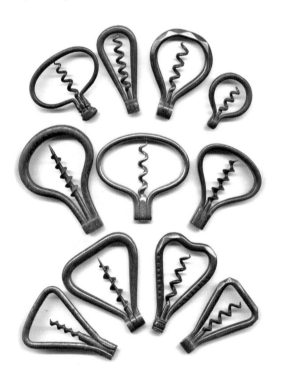

probably the most common size and shape and has a circular hinge with locking nicks. The sides of the bow are marked 'Clements, London'. It has a fluted worm and the faceting gives it a look of quality. Finally *(top left)* a small circular bow with a fluted worm. *Middle row, left to right:* Bows with Archimedean worms are not particularly common and this one has a square section hinge with locking nicks. The friction hinge of the middle example (in plated steel) is stamped 'D.R.G.M.' but the German registration details have not been identified. The last in this row is probably another continental bow with a wide flattened arch, a long square section hinge and bladed worm. *Bottom, left to right:* The origin of this cheaply made bow is unclear. It may be French as the round cross-section of the shank clicks into the concave sides of the neck of the bow. The next example, a simple but well-made bow has an Archimedean worm and circular hinge. You may be lucky enough to be given a heart-shaped bow for Valentine's Day. The corners of this example are faceted, the sides of the bow have dimpled decoration, the worm has a triangular section and the hinge is barrel shaped. The triangular bow is stamped 'R. McQueen & Son'.

other tools extraneously attached to them. *Pocket Corkscrews* by Peters and Giulian is very comprehensive and highly recommended.

Folding bows

Every collection will have folding bows and there are some people who specialize in them. Bows range from the cheap and simple to the complex, elegant

and expensive. Some are marked with the retailer's name or carry advertising. The connoisseur will look at the different types of hinges, of which there are many, as well as the faceting and decoration of the arch of the bow. Faceting is when the smooth round surface of the metal is filed to produce a series of decorative flat faces. The construction of a bow also allowed makers to incorporate more than just a corkscrew and so there are a wide variety of multi-tool bows to be collected.

Right: It is not unusual to find miniature bows, which were made mainly for travelling sets along with other toilet items, and were used to open perfume and medicine bottles. Some have an integral hanging ring and will originally have been hung from a housekeeper's chatelaine (a belt with short chains to carry useful implements). The miniatures are pictured here with a standard common bow for size comparison. *Clockwise from bottom left:* A relatively common design with a fluted worm; standard shape but with decorated edges and a bladed worm; simple circular shape with a triangular section worm; faceted arch, a triangular section worm and rounded hinge; very small gold bow with a friction hinge and a delicate wire worm; three chatelaine bows of different shapes with the heart-shaped one being highly decorated; bow with a flattened arch promoting 'Chr. E. Rothe & Co.'.

Left: These American corkscrews designed for corked bottles of medicines and other liquids provide an interesting group for collecting. They are made of a thin strip of steel fixed with a tubular brass rivet, which also acts as the hinge for the twisted-wire worm. They promote a host of fascinating products. *Top left:* 'Burroughs Wellcome & Co Manufacturing Chemists London', with lots of names of products. Its American origin is indicated (in tiny writing) as 'Clough Pat. 23 84' (the month is obliterated by the hole for the hinge). The day is wrong and it should read 'July 22 84' for 1884. *Bottom left:* 'Scotts Emulsion' and, in smaller letters, 'James M. McDonnel, New York', and 'Patented July 22-84 Made in USA'. The date relates to William Clough's US patent. *Top right:* This is a much less common version as patented by Williamson in 1889. The difference from Clough's patent is a tiny modification to aid manufacturing. It is marked 'Carter's Inks Williamson Co. Newark N.J.' Confusingly, there is also a Clough version advertising Carter's Inks. Bottom right: 'Listerine, Made in USA'. Amongst others you can find are Mary T. Goldman's Grey Hair Restorer, Panopepton, Lung Tonic Cures Coughs, St. Jacobs Oil, Warner's Log Cabin Remedies, Bovinine, The Rawleigh Man, and many more.

These are examples of two-tool bows. The hinge construction and design of the bow allowed manufacturers to add extra tools besides the worm. *From bottom left:* A button hook is a common second tool in a bow (the bow in this example is decorated on the sides and faceted on the arch). It is less common to find a carriage key as a second tool, but it had its advantages for getting into a railway carriage and then opening a bottle of wine for the journey. To have two worms in a bow is unusual and extravagant – one is a simple wire spiral and the other is Archimedean in this continental bow. The next example may look common, but it is not: note the brass washer between the two tools, which reduces friction (the arch, stamped 'Patent No12524', refers to a minor claim in Edward Markham's 1898 British patent). The arch of the next example promotes Charles Heidseick champagne on both sides (the combined blade and cap lifter hook is stamped 'R^d N° 619745' for John Watts' registered design of 1913). The fiendish can opener spike of the next example is stamped 'Patent Appd For', but the documentation has not been found; the arch is stamped 'Made in England', and the circular hinge with a screw head nut through it indicates that this bow is of early manufacture, possibly from the late eighteenth century. The arch of the next bow is marked 'LB B^{te} S.G.D.G.' and shows that it is an example of Jules Leboullanger's Patent No. 97,437 of 1872. The distinguishing features are the concave inside edges of the neck of the bow, which grip the shanks of the worm and button hook. These Leboullanger (LB) bows are usually small; full-sized ones are less common. *Centre.* Although the bow is very plain, it is unusual in having a screwdriver extension (not very practical) opposite the worm.

Multi-tool bows

Once you start collecting bows you need to get a two-tool, three-tool, four-tool and so on. Over a few years and with a little effort it is possible to get a full set up to eleven. But a number of collectors have been waiting so long to complete their 'clock face' that the general consensus is that a twelve-tool bow is not known. However, at least one sixteen-tool bow is known (*see* Watney and Babbidge, page 19). *Top row, left to right:* A

standard three-tool bow with hoof hook, button hook and worm. The four-tool bow is unusual in having a cartridge extractor brazed on to the top of the arch, which is stamped 'J. Nazer 41 Royal Exchange'. The detailed faceting on the next bow (an early flattened bow) is hard to see in the picture but it is a quality piece of steel work and has an auger and an early design of turnscrew (screwdriver). The tightly packed five-tool bow has three gun tools and a carriage key. *Bottom row, left to right:* Most multi-tool bows are of a standard large size but a few were made smaller and more compact. This one has eight tools including a leather punch. The central implement in the seven-tool bow *(centre)* is a cartridge extractor. The arch is nicely faceted and the hinge is a square shape with horizontal decorative lines. With eleven tools, the bow gets quite unwieldy and heavy. This final example is stamped for the retailer 'B.B. Wells'.

Examples of bows with extra functions added. *Top row:* All of these bows have small lugs on them to act as cap lifters. The one on the right is stamped 'D.R.G.M.' for one of Ernst Wahl's German registered designs of 1926. *Bottom row, left to right:* The stem of this bow is shaped as a carriage key. The loop on the miniature perfume bow is probably a glove button hook. Some examples of the bow with a folding cap lifter are marked 'D.R.G.M.' but the registration details have not been identified; this example is only marked with a catalogue number (KN818). The final, very unusual bow is stamped 'Codd's Patent G.F. Hipkins' and is from Hiram Codd's British Patent No. 1,152 of 1881. The vulcanized rubber ball was placed above the concave marble pusher in a Codd bottle to block the flow of fizzy drink before you were ready to pour it. Further Codd bottle openers are shown in the section on combinations (*see* Chapter 9).

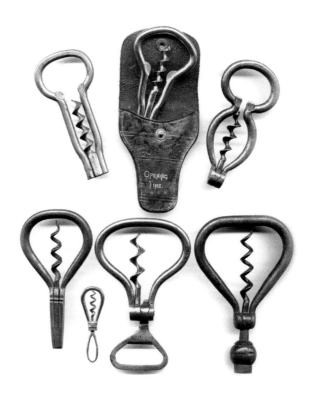

Copley and sheathed bows

The top row shows corkscrews that are often referred to as 'Copley bows' because one was shown in a painting by John Singleton Copley in the late 1760s. They are not common and are characterized by having a long 'neck' with a steel spring at one side, which allows the worm to be folded only one way. *Left to right:* The sides of the neck have ribbed decorations and the top of the arch has three faceted studs on it. The open bow shows the characteristics of the spring and neck of Copley bows. It is stamped 'RS' on the inside of the arch, probably for Richard Singleton who was manufacturing cutlery and corkscrews in Dublin during the second half of the eighteenth century. This silver bow is stamped Singleton on the inside of the arch and has a monogram on the outer side. *Below left:* This ornate silver bow has a fluted worm protected by a screw-on sheath, which is marked on the base 'TR' for Thomas Rush (early eighteenth century). Note that the hinge mechanism is made of steel whereas modern reproductions have a silver hinge. *Below right:* The sheath of this simple eighteenth-century steel bow has a brazed seam to support its authenticity.

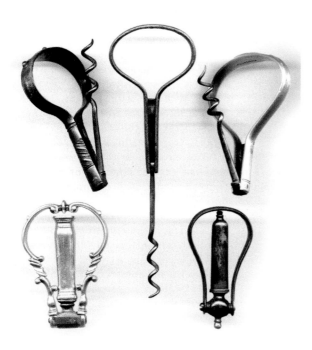

A selection of American bows. *Top left and top:* Both bows are marked 'Pat. Oct 16 77' for George Havell's US patent of 1877. The insides of the neck of the bow are concave so that they snap on to the round shank of the worm. *Top right:* This bow is unmarked and insides of the neck are convex to fit on to the concave sides of the short brass shank. *Centre left and right:* Both bows are marked 'Williamson's'. Bottom: Although this is a European example, a very similar design was patented in the US by Louis Strauss in 1949. The American example has a round-nosed hammer and incorporates a cap lifter hook.

A selection of more unusual bows. *Top left:* This British design was registered in 1878 by George Willetts as 'ornamental design for combined key ring, railway key and corkscrew'. Examples of this design have a registration diamond mark but they are often unclear. *Top centre:* This novelty is a fairly plain bow marked 'foreign', but it comes in a small leather case made to look like a book entitled *Drawing Made Easy* by S.A.

Wenn. This is the old British joke of 'say when' to indicate when enough drink has been poured into a glass – the usual delayed response being 'when!' *Top right:* The tapering bar acts as a cross bar handle for the corkscrew in the 'open' position but carries a rectangular wire clip to hold it in place in the 'closed' position. The end of the narrow bow is a carriage key, marked 'Trade Mark Squirrel' with an image of a squirrel. This was the trademark of Thomas White (late nineteenth century). *Bottom left:* The narrow bow of this French corkscrew can pivot right round over the eyebrow handle. Some examples are marked for Jacques Pérille and derive from his 1885 Patent No. 166,846. *Bottom centre:* This is a beautiful design from the late twentieth century marked 'Made in France, must de Cartier' and a limited edition number. The box is marked 'Marques et Modèle Déposés' (registered trademark and design). *Bottom right:* The slim bow of this French corkscrew folds up and over the horn handle.

Folding 'legs' to protect the worm

By using folding sections or 'legs' to cover the worm when not in use, the point of the worm is protected from damage. With well-constructed hinges that allow only 90 degrees movement, the two legs can form a T-handle for a straight pull corkscrew.

European examples of the folding legs design. *Top row, left to right:* The plated steel example is unmarked but is probably German. The legs incorporate back springs so that they snap down into the closed position. In the next design, the point of the foil cutter blade on one leg locks into a nick in the opposite leg (the hinge is marked 'Ges. Geschützt'). The next design incorporates a carriage key but is unmarked. The final example on the top row is German, with a flattened wire cutter on one leg. *Lower row:* This wishbone-shaped pocket corkscrew is very closely related to Jules Brangs' French patent drawing of 1878. It is unmarked but examples are sometimes stamped 'LB' for the Paris manufacturer Leboullanger. When closed, the two sides of the next example mesh together nicely. It is marked 'Cset-Pat Made in Hungary'. The short shank of the last example in this row is marked 'D.R.G.M. No 54268' for Edmund Jansen's design of 1896. The design incorporates a notch for opening cigar boxes and a foil or wire cutter. *Bottom:* This mid-twentieth-century tool has a can-piercer and D-shaped cap lifter, which close perfectly over the worm. It is marked 'Made in England'.

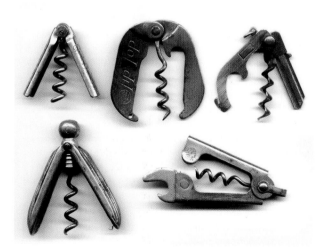

Below left: These are American examples. *Top left to right:* This small folding corkscrew is usually known as the 'Dainty' and the one pictured is stamped 'Dainty Folding Corkscrew Vaughan Chicago Pat Appl'd'. Some examples are marked with advertising. We know no more about the Dainty since Vaughan never obtained a patent. The 'TipTop' is also marked 'Wᵐson Newark N.J.' for Williamson and incorporates a cap lifter on one arm. The last in the row is a real oddity and represents Robert McLean's US patent of 1926 for a combination of a Yale type key, corkscrew, cap lifter and cigar box opener. *Bottom left:* With ribbed brass sides and a tiny clip at the bottom, this corkscrew is usually known as the 'clam shell'. *Bottom right:* The 'upper leg' closes on to the other one and clips in place to protect the worm. It is marked 'Chief Made in USA' and has a trademark of a Red Indian wearing a headdress.

These corkscrews with decorative worm protectors are the ones that everyone wants in their collection and often feature in general articles on corkscrews. The 'Lady's Legs' *(top row)* are German and were registered by Steinfeld and Reimer in 1894, although a British registration preceded this by one year. They come in two sizes and a variety of colours with full stockings, half stockings and no stockings. The sides are mostly celluloid but ivory and wooden versions were made. Known markings include 'Gesetz. Geschützt', 'Registered', 'Registered Germany', and a selection of importers. Contemporary adverts refer to them as 'ballet' or 'can-can' corkscrews. Less attractive modern replicas are known with the half stockings made of ribbed painted bright metal. The celluloid folding girl on the left is marked 'Ges. Gesch'. The sabots are marked D.R.G.M. 82205 for Ernst Steinfeld's design of 1897. Carl Brewer registered the design for the kissing couple in 1898. The example is marked 'Amor Germany D.R.G.M. 105407'. The origin of the aluminium folding 'champagne bottle' is probably British but this corkscrew is not marked.

These modern versions of the 1893 design for 'Lady's Legs' are marked above the worm 'UK Des. Reg. Pat. Pend.' and relate to designs lodged by Universal Housewares in 1996. The cricketer's 'box' is named 'the Leg Pull' and 'the Corkscrew with Character' and marked 'UK Des. Reg. No. 2051565'. British versions were also made as Fisherman, Jockey, Golfer, Rugby Player and Scotsman. There is also an American sports set. A series of footballer corkscrews was released to coincide with the 1998 World Cup. The packaging is marked 'The Footballer Corkscrew®' and apart from Alan Shearer for England, there are five other nations to collect (Brazil, France, Italy, Spain and Germany).

Double-folding corkscrews

Double-folding corkscrews are a clever compact design. Examples can be seen in old trade catalogues from at least 1820 but an engraved example pictured in Giulian's book gives an earlier date of 1769.

Right: **A fancy pipe tamper end – most are plain.**

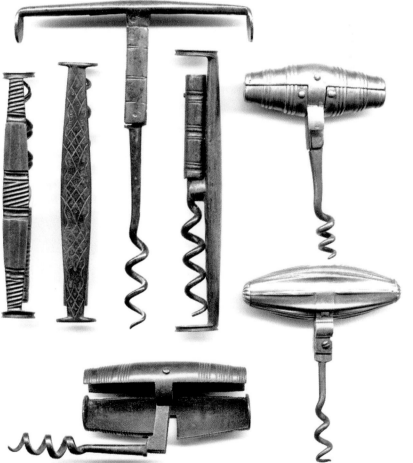

Four examples of the open style are shown and unmarked examples like the unfolded one are relatively easy to acquire. The end pieces are circular and were probably used as pipe tampers. The artistry of early steel workers is apparent in the closed examples, all of which are marked with the maker's name, W. Pardoe (of Wolverhampton). The example on the right is engraved 'Richard Simpson Jnr. 1769'. Silver examples are also known. An even more compact design is where the folded corkscrew is stored inside a small barrel. Brass versions sometimes have red paint on the inside. Silver versions usually have the nice addition of a small, hinged 'door' to cover the slot for the shank when the barrel is closed. Fake copies of these barrels appeared in the early twenty-first century. Details were less sharp and the hinge mechanisms were brass or silver and not steel as in the originals.

Scissor-shaped corkscrews

These scissor-shaped items are for cutting the wires on champagne bottles. *Top left:* The example is stamped 'No 10985' for the 1893 German registered design of Thill and Küll. *Top centre:* The handle incorporates a foil cutter. This one is unmarked but is an example of D.R.G.M. 229956 for Wesche and Ruppelt's design of 1904. *Top right:* This French corkscrew promotes 'Theophile Roederer & Co. Maison Fondée Riems Déposé'. *Bottom:* These small scissors have traces of gold plating and are marked 'Déposé Lefournier J^ne *Champagne*'. The worm is hinged on to one of the arms and folds along the axis of the arm.

Roundlets and cased multi-tool sets

Roundlets are a very neat design with the worm housed inside a two-piece cylindrical case. The worm is then deployed at 90 degrees to the case to form a T-shaped corkscrew. Many roundlets have the worm hinged to a plug that slides inside the barrel. This allows the worm and shank to be almost the same length as the case. The first roundlet to be patented was by Lund and Hipkins in their British patent of 1855, which also included their two-arm lever and London Rack corkscrews. The text in the patent implies, however, that the roundlet concept was older and that they were making improvements.

The standard roundlet has a nickel-plated brass body in two halves which can be screwed together (shown closed below). The shank of the corkscrew is hinged to a brass plug and can be folded out into the slot on one half of the case. There are four sizes of case as shown *(left):* 92mm, 80mm, 69mm and the much less common miniature of 48mm. *Top:* An example derived from Lund and Hipkins' 1855 Patent No. 736 marked 'Lund's Patent Spherical Joint, London' on the case and 'Lund's Patent' on the short flat shank. The novelty is that the shank is fixed to a spherical ball, which acts both as the sliding plug and the hinge. It must have been easy to make, yet examples are not particularly common. This special example is engraved with the poem:

I am the 'screw' of Lizzie Field
All hearts as well as corks must yield
To our united efforts when
I draw the corks, she draws the men.

Right: This roundlet may look the same as the common version but it is stamped round the central band of the case 'Regd Jany 16th 1873'. The design is very similar to Lund's patent with the small addition of a retaining ring. This British design was registered by Wright and Bailey in 1873. *Bottom right:* There is no sliding plug or hinge in this example. The worm just fits inside the case and has a groove on each side of the flat shank, which slides into a slot in the case. The shank is stamped 'Best Steel'.

Left: A selection of less common roundlets. *Top left:* An unusual feature found on better-quality roundlets is a short nickel-plated (or even silver) collar over the shank. The one in the picture is stamped 'Lund Cornhill, London' but other makers' names such as Heeley & Sons are known. *Top centre:* Whistles can be found incorporated into the ends of roundlets. Some examples, like the one shown, have a diamond registration mark for Edwin Sunderland's design of 1870. The design registration was actually for a fancy pattern at either side of the diamond mark and not for the corkscrew. Sunderland, trading as Coney & Co., used this device to add apparent copyright protection to a basic roundlet design. *Top right:* This aluminium-cased roundlet was patented in 1903 by Walter Vaughan, trading as G.F. Hipkins & Son. It is marked 'Pic-nic Patent G.F. Hipkins & Son, Birmingham Patented'. The two parts of the case slide together over the inner steel sleeves. *Bottom left:* There is a bayonet-type fixing on the case of this roundlet, which is stamped 'Buchanan's Black & White Patent Appld For'. The patent has not been found. *Bottom right:* The small brass case may once have been plated and is stamped 'Pat. Applied For'. Again, the patent has not been found.

The case of a roundlet lends itself to ornamentation and there are some very decorative American roundlets (e.g. *right*). The scalloped silver example *(centre)* is hallmarked for London 1904 and has a large monogram. The nickel-plated cases have cross-hatched engine-turned patterns.

American roundlets. *Top left:* At first sight this looks like a plastic body but it is actually made of vulcanized rubber and is lightly stamped 'Goodyear's Patent May 6 1851' for the process of hardening rubber. (It is not a patent for the corkscrew.) *Top right:* This brass roundlet was once plated and is stamped at one end 'Williamson Co. Newark N.J. Patented June 1 97'. The wire worm has a U-shaped bend which fixes it to a sliding slug inside the barrel. The 1897 patent was from William Williamson. *Lower left:* This is a delightful cast aluminium roundlet with a somewhat weedy worm that is hinged inside but does not slide inside the body. The back is marked 'Columbus Corkscrew 1492 Chicago 1892 Pat. Appld For'. The novelty was made for the Chicago World Fair to mark the

400th anniversary of Columbus's landing. The patent has not been identified and was probably never filed. When the worm is deployed it looks as if Columbus is engaged in a more basic pursuit than discovering the New World. *Lower centre:* The three figural roundlets, a bottle and bullets, are all stamped for Williamson's 1897 patent. The bottles are very collectable as they come with different advertising, the one shown promoting Anheuser Busch. *Lower right:* Marked 'The Consolidated Pneumatic Tool C⁰ Lᵈ Boyer Hammer', this is a promotional item for power hammers.

Roundlets with added tools on the end are not common although the case makes a good handle for a cap lifter. *Left:* The worm of this silver-plated roundlet is attached to a standard sliding slug and the inner curve of the cap lifter hook is lined with a 1mm-thick strip of steel for strength. It is stamped 'Asprey London Rᵈ N⁰ 691160' for Philip Rolls Asprey's registered design of 1922. *Right:* This example is marked 'Compliments of Jos. E. Seagram & Sons Limited' and 'Seagram's Whiskies Waterloo Canada'. The end tells us it was made by Ellis Bros.

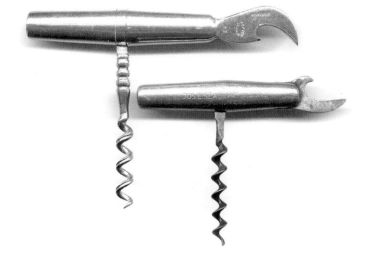

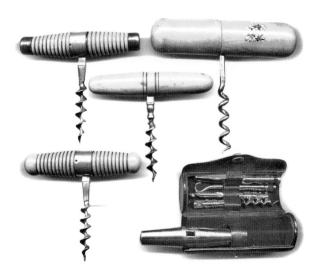

French roundlets. *Left:* These three wooden roundlets are French and the two ribbed ones are marked on the central brass band 'LB Paris Déposé'. The plain one is derived from Leboullanger's patent of 1878 and is marked 'LB Paris Breveté'. It is characterized by having a screw head underneath, which holds an inner metal guide in place. As with all wooden roundlets the wooden thread is prone to damage. *Upper right:* The large wooden roundlet is marked 'B^te S.G.D.G. Made in France' and is an example of André Verpillat's 1955 French patent for a shank with a U-shaped end, which engages with a pin through the body. *Bottom right:* It is not unusual to find this plated brass roundlet containing just the worm without the case and other tools. However, the picture shows what it should be like with three other tools. The cases are often in poor condition with the circular end parts often missing. The roundlet body is marked 'Breveté S.G.D.G. Paris TD' indicating that this is Benoit Thinet's French patent of 1874. ('TD' stands for Thinet Defeu.)

Right: Modern roundlets. The green roundlet is from the late twentieth century and promotes a vineyard. It has a very unusual, and unnecessary, feature of a V-shaped slot in the case so that the flattened part of the shank fits only one way. Both the red and clear roundlets (made in China) were welcome presents inside Christmas crackers.

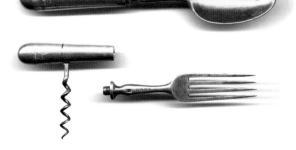

Left: Travelling sets. This gilded silver roundlet is part of a travelling set in which the case forms the handle for a fork. The knife, spoon and fork unscrew from the three handles, two of which have flip-over tops. This allows the two smaller ones to fit inside the larger one rather like Russian dolls. All of the pieces are hallmarked for London 1872.

These are all multi-tool pocket sets in which the two halves of the case screw together to form a handle and house the tools. It is common to find up to five implements inside the cases, but there may be less, and it is up to the seller to make a convincing argument as to whether they are lost or never existed! *Top left:* This is the common version with a single slot into which the double grooved ends of the tools fit. They are held in place by screwing the halves of the case tightly together. The usual tools are a bladed worm, screwdriver, spike, bradawl and tweezers. The cases are usually plain but some have advertising; this one promotes 'Cowborough & C° L^td Leeds – Nourishing Ale for Invalids'. *Top right:* Although this steel case is unmarked it is probably derived from Benoit Thinet's French patent of 1874. The tools have two nicks on them, which fit into slots at opposite sides of the case. *Centre left:* This multi-tool has holes in the case to act as a spanner and even as a cap lifter. It is marked on one end 'Made in England "Bimbo" Regd Trade Mark Pats. Pend.', and at the other end

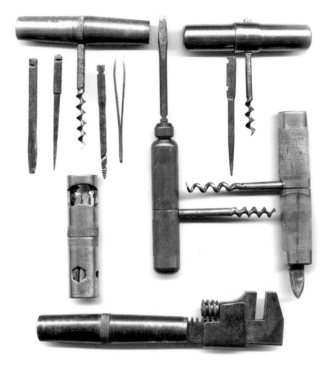

'Beck & Pollitzer'. *Middle:* As well as having the usual central hole for tools, this example has a chuck at one end for a screwdriver. *Centre right:* The blade at the end is held firmly because there is a tube inside the case, which is forced against the end of the blade as the halves of the case are screwed together. It is marked on one end 'TVTO' and a corkscrew logo. *Bottom:* Is this the ultimate multi-tool? It has the usual tools inside but an adjustable wrench on one end, and needs a large pocket.

Hollweg-type corkscrews

These cleverly designed collapsible corkscrews are usually referred to as 'Hollwegs' after Carl Hollweg who patented them in France and the USA in 1891, although the earliest patent was in Britain in 1890 from Robert Culp, who was probably a patent agent acting on Hollweg's behalf. The corkscrews come in four different width sizes: 82mm, 67mm, 56mm and a miniature 39mm (not common). There are also two styles with either three scallops on the inner edge or one scallop. Many are marked 'Made in Germany' 'Patent Applied For', 'Made Abroad', or 'Patent Angemeldet'. Some also promote beer or whisky. *Bottom centre:* A less common American version marked 'The "Handy", Patented Feb 24 1891'. *Lower left:* A different design, marked 'C.T.W.'s Flexible', from the Birmingham firm C.T. Willetts.

Sliding sheath corkscrews

Left: A box section steel sheath with a corkscrew that slides in and out. It is held in the open position by a back spring. One side of the sheath is marked 'G.M. Patent No. 6145', which relates to Edmund Jansen's German patent of 1892. They are usually decorated on the sides with leaf designs but the lower example promotes Christie's Whisky. *Right:* A similar concept with the addition of a cap lifter. It celebrates '1934 Chicago, A Century of Progress' and in small letters has 'Pat. Pend.' It is another neat design and the button on the side is pressed in to push out the hook cap lifter at the first 'stop' and a corkscrew at the second 'stop'. The patent has not been found.

Peg and worm corkscrews

The idea of protecting the point of the worm by pushing a metal rod or 'peg' up the centre of the helix is rather clever and a little counter-intuitive. It can only work with a simple helical wire worm because bladed ones do not have a hole up the centre. The other beauty of the design is that the peg can be put through a hole in the end of the shank to create a cross bar handle for the corkscrew. It is likely that many peg and worm corkscrews were originally from travelling sets and dressing case sets. The peg and worm is the most common corkscrew type in which to find left-handed worms. There is no reason why this should be so, but it is a fact. Rarely does the peg fit into the top of the worm to give a central symmetrical handle but they look good when they do. In some examples, the hole in the end of the worm is slightly tapered to give a tight fit for the peg, and in others the hole and peg are threaded to give a solid fit. One of the attractions of collecting peg and worm corkscrews is the quality of workmanship, such as faceting, found on the ends of some of the items.

A selection of peg and worm corkscrews showing the variety of sizes, types of end and decorative shanks. One example *(upper centre)* has the peg as a bodkin with a handy earwax scoop at the end. There are two left-handed examples in the centre. The one on the left has a hexagonal shank on the peg and is marked 'Stewart's Dundee Cream of the Barley Scotch Whisky' and the pipe tamper end says 'Stewart's Joke', no doubt referring to the left-handed worm, which most people would find impossible to use. The other left-handed example next to it has a small cap lifter hook on the shank and is stamped 'R^d 709401' and advertises Izal on the pipe tamper end. This was registered in 1924 by William Arthur Willetts. Izal was a disinfectant and also the brand name of a somewhat harsh toilet paper remembered affectionately by all British children of the 1950s. A third left-handed example is gilded. The two horizontal examples at the bottom are also British registered designs. The upper one is stamped 'R^d 528199' for Frederick

Sunderland's design of 1908. The lower one, with the angular cap lifter is one of two peg and worm designs from Alfred W. Flint. This example is marked 'A.W. Flint & Co. Made in Sheffield Eng. Patent Applied For. R^d N° 708279', which related to the 1924 design. Flint's British patent was granted in 1924 and in 1925 in the USA.

Sheathed corkscrews

A sheath is a simple way of protecting the worm. Some of the most attractive sheathed corkscrews come from the late eighteenth and early nineteenth centuries. They are not particularly common but are not impossible to find. Some are made of steel and need to be checked carefully to ensure that they are of early manufacture and not twentieth-century copies. The metal working lathe did not come into common use until the early nineteenth century and hardened steel drills were introduced in the late nineteenth century. Before then, sheaths were made from a flat piece of steel, which was rolled into a tube and the gap sealed with a brass weld; a process called 'brazing'. Authentic old sheaths have a brazed seam up them, the circular base is brazed in, and usually the thread inside the top of the sheath is also brazed in as a separate piece. It is often difficult to see the brazed seams due to dirt and

patina or because the artist who made the corkscrew disguised the seam as the edge of a multi-sided sheath. Worms are often replaced – you should check that the worm fixing has not been interfered with, that the length of the worm is just shorter than the sheath, and that it is the correct type of worm – bladed worms are not right.

Silver sheathed corkscrews are also very attractive items to collect. Again, you must beware of fakes or modifications. The sheath can sometimes be a modern replacement – check that the colour or patina of the metal is the same as the top part, that it has the same type of scratches and other signs of wear, that it doesn't look too bright and clean inside the sheath and that decorative patterning is similar. Modern replacements are often quite heavy; the originals were quite light in weight. Again, broken worms are often replaced.

Steel sheathed T-shaped corkscrews are surprisingly uncommon. The one on the left is probably French due to the style of Archimedean worm and the delicate decoration round the shank. The others are English with bone, horn and ivory handles respectively.

Right: Silver sheathed corkscrews are usually attractive pieces of high quality workmanship. The upper row shows four examples with mother-of-pearl handles. The one on the left has a maker's mark 'SP' for the Birmingham silversmith Samuel Pemberton (mid to late eighteenth century). Neither of the two central examples is marked and they may be Dutch. The highly decorative one *(right)* is marked 'JW' for Joseph Willmore, also of Birmingham (early nineteenth century). The lower row shows three different styles from slim to chunky. The one on the left is indistinctly marked 'R&B' for Roberts & Belk of Sheffield. The centre one is by Daniel Field ('DF') and the one on the right is another Joseph Willmore masterpiece.

Left: A selection of other special sheathed corkscrews. *Left to right:* This beautiful late-eighteenth-century piece has an ivory handle and ivory sheath with a perpetual calendar. The gold example, with its chalcedony handle, is possibly French. Finally, a delightful miniature decorated silver example with a pricker that screws into the base of the sheath.

Who can tell whether these wooden handled twisted wire corkscrews with a button were all sold with a wooden sheath or not? You might like to class them as Easers if you prefer. They have an American Clough look to them and the one shown *(right)* with a 'decapitator' on the handle is pictured in a Clough advertisement with a short sheath, as in this example. The handle promotes 'Brubaker's Creamed Pudding Made at Beech Dale Farm, Bird-in-Hand, Penna'. Interestingly, the left-hand end is marked 'WRC Crown Cap Lifter Pat. Mar 1, 1910' ('WRC' stands for William Rockwell Clough).

Sheathed corkscrews with finger pull rings

Top left: The bronze sheath of this early corkscrew shows the dents of age. The ring has an oval seal on the top with the initials 'I.N'. The four other examples are made of steel with different styles of handle. It is not common to find one as small as the

central one, which was probably made for opening perfume bottles. The finger hole on the corkscrew on the right has a circular seal on the top depicting a heraldic device. *Bottom row:* All four corkscrews display high-quality steelwork, especially the one on the left in which the finger hole, the knop above the sheath *(see detail)* and even the filial at the bottom are all delicately faceted. The pointed top of the faceted finger hole of the second one is probably for breaking wax seals on bottles. It is unusual for these types of corkscrews to be marked but the one on the right has a stamp 'TR', possibly for Thomas Read.

Some sheathed corkscrews have a key ring as the finger pull. *Left to right:* The highly decorated brass sheath is an example of Frederick Sunderland's registered design of 1875 for Coney & Co. One of the decorative leaves on the sheath is stamped with a registration diamond. The next example is a very simple corkscrew with a bladed worm and screw-on nickel-plated brass sheath. The steel sheath of the next example has the expected brazed seam. It is rare to find one of these corkscrews *(right)* with a carriage key sheath in good condition. Two small lugs on the shank of the worm fit into two nicks in the thread at the top of the sheath. The upper brass ring then screws down on to it. To the uninitiated, there is a strong temptation to twist the carriage key end in a vice to try to open it, and thus destroy the whole thread assembly.

Wooden sheathed corkscrews like these are derived from Clough's manufacturing process using his wire-twisting machine patented in 1900. These wooden sheaths can form a whole sub-collection as they display a host of interesting advertising. The one on the left is for 'Ross's "Royal Belfast" and "Pale Dry" Ginger Ales' from A. Leech of London, although it clearly states 'Made in the USA'. Note the similar example *(right)*: a more modern example made with a left-handed worm for 'R.B. Hayden Straight Bourbon'. The two centre examples have cap lifters on the wooden sheaths derived from Clough's later patent of 1910. One is marked in small writing 'Made in USA, Pat. Mar 1, 1910 – This Wire Lifts Crown Corks'. The main message, however, is 'Of great service to the busy housewife – a corkscrew, a crown cork opener. Horrocks Warehouse, Ridgway Gates, Bolton.' On some sheaths the wire is sometimes referred to as a 'decapitator'. The second example has a loosely hinged cap lifter hook.

These four pocket corkscrews were cheap advertising items for British businesses and there are many different promotional messages to collect. Those shown are for 'James Dickson Wine Store etc. Dundee', 'T. Britton the Noted Cap & Collar Shop, Ferryhill' and 'Shamrock Whiskey'. The slimmer version below is marked '1492 Hail Columbia 1892' and 'Chicago, 1893' and comes from the World Fair of 1893 which took the 400th anniversary of Columbus's discovery as the theme. The sheath is also marked 'Clough & Maconnel New York Corkscrew Pats No 337309 4411437', which relate to William Crabb's 1886 corkscrew patent and Clough's wire twisting machine that made it.

Silver sheathed corkscrews. *Left to right:* The fairly heavy silver corkscrew is unmarked but is probably continental from the late nineteenth century. Of much more delicate construction, the next example is probably English but is unmarked. The base of the next example, with its fabulous silver sheath, is stamped 'TR', probably for Thomas Rush (first half of the eighteenth century). The last corkscrew, which is a rare, high-quality example, has a large seal on the base of the sheath depicting the arms of a Swiss nobleman. The sheath and handle have high relief silverwork with gold beaten in between them. The fluted ribbon worm is very similar to late-eighteenth-century French corkscrews.

Picnic corkscrews

The concept of the picnic corkscrew was developed around 1800 and examples are found in old trade catalogues of this date. It is a sheathed corkscrew with a hole at the top of the shank. This hole is smaller than finger size and is made so that the sheath can be fitted through it to give a snug fit and form a T-handle. This arrangement gave a very good grip and created a very compact pocket corkscrew. The picnic concept is as popular today as it was in the nineteenth century, with the use of new materials and the almost ubiquitous addition of a cap lifter hook.

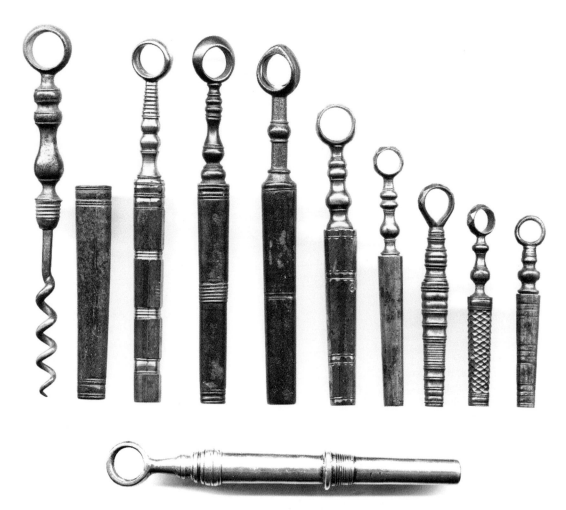

This selection of steel picnic corkscrews is from the early nineteenth century and shows the wide range of sizes and the frequent high-quality workmanship. They range from 126mm in length *(left)* to 61mm *(right)* and they all have a brazed seam on the sheath. Such steel corkscrews are often referred to as 'Georgian picnics', implying manufacturing dates of 1760–1830, a reasonable generalization. Most of the sheaths are just a tight push fit into the top hole, but there are two variations shown. The third left example has a partial thread in the centre of the sheath, which is not just decoration. It matches with a thread inside the top hole and so is solidly held in place for use. The fourth left example has two small springs inside the top hole, which engage with a groove halfway along the sheath. *Below:* A silver example with a thread on the sheath, which matches the one inside the top hole. Surprisingly, silver 'Georgian picnics' tend to be much plainer than the steel versions.

Plated brass sheaths. Examples as shown on the left are ones you will find at any antique or collectors' fair. The sheath snaps on to a small swelling just below the top hole. The sheaths usually bear advertising such as 'Old Parr Antique Scotch Whisky' and 'Robertson's Scotch Whisky' as shown. But the dedicated collector should always look inside these picnics, as there are treasures to be found. The picnic in the centre is a very rare example with a partial worm. The top ring is stamped 'Patent 13644/21', the application number for Francis John Russell's British patent of 1921. The sheath can also hide a left-handed worm *(second from right)*. The picnic on the right has a cap lifter on the end of the sheath and is marked 'Unit D.R.G.M. Germany'.

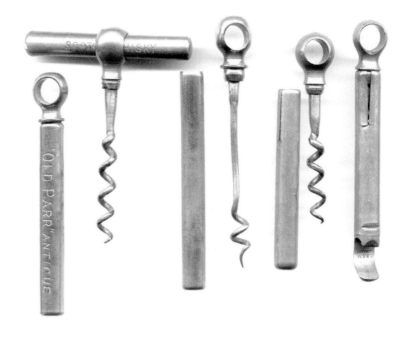

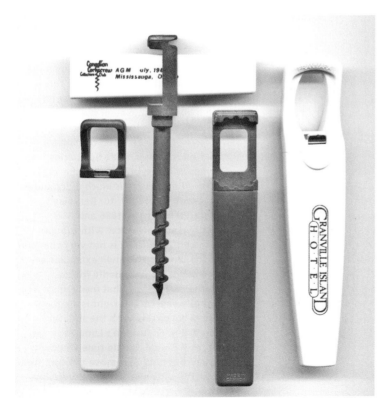

The picnic design has endured well and modern examples can be readily found. A very successful all-plastic picnic, sometimes known as the 'Popit', provides an advertising medium at low cost and has the novelty of having a plastic worm. The yellow example with a rectangular section sheath and cap lifter head is marked 'Made in England Reg. Des.', which relates to David Brian Johnson's 1983 design. A slightly modified design *(second from left)* with a screw-top gripper as the headpiece was used as a souvenir for the 1988 CCCC meeting in Mississauga, Ontario. This one and the blue version are marked 'Rd. 1987 Starline Industries Inc.' The white sheath *(right)* has a truncated oval cross section and a corresponding top hole. It was acquired as a souvenir from the Vancouver hotel where the 2005 CCCC meeting was held.

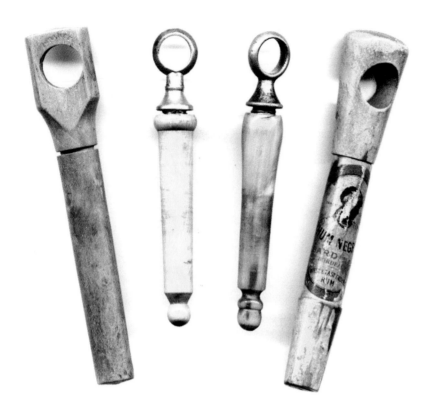

The boxwood corkscrew on the left is marked 'France' and is a classic of its genre with a screw-on sheath over a simple wire worm. The second example also has a wooden sheath but the headpiece is of an aluminium alloy and the worm is bladed. Although very similar in style, the third picnic has a horn sheath, a brass headpiece and a bladed worm. Examples of the style on the right are again made of boxwood. They usually carry advertising and are sometimes marked 'Made in France'. This one promotes 'Rhum Negrit – West & East Indies Rum'.

Wire twisting may have been pioneered by Clough in the USA, but these three picnics are British. The one on the left with a push-on thin steel sheath is stamped 'C.T.W's Universal Pocket Corkscrew' with inch and centimetre scales on it. It was made by Charles Thomas Willetts, probably in the 1930s. The middle example is much older and is stamped 'Rᵈ Nᵒ 46767' for Berkeley's registered design of 1886 and was described as 'Corkscrew with tubular removable handle'. It is not very common and the worms of known examples are often distorted with badly fitting sheaths, suggesting that many were thrown away. On the right is a left-handed corkscrew with the sheath advertising 'Owbridge's Lung Tonic for Coughs & Colds'. By the time you'd worked out how to remove the cork from the bottle of tonic, you were probably better.

Brass picnics can show a lot of variety. The one on the left is relatively plain, has a bladed worm and may well be continental. By contrast the second one has a leafy decoration and although it is not marked, the pattern is the same as on Coney & Co.'s 1875 registered design. The central corkscrew has a tubular cover to the carriage key sheath, which is locked on to the headpiece by a ring. By turning the ring to line up with a slot, the sheath can be removed to uncover the plain worm. The fourth corkscrew from the left is an example of the first registered design for a picnic corkscrew from Coney & Co. in 1871. There are a number of these brass Coney picnic corkscrews in existence, but they all seem to have rather poorly stamped

diamond registration marks that are difficult to read. Some of the diamond marks in fact relate to another Coney design as seen on the whistle roundlet shown earlier (page 70). The corkscrew on the right is American. It is quite small, only 73mm when closed. The head of the larger ring is stamped 'Patd. Jan. 4.76' for F.T. Witte's US Patent No.171,752 of 1876. The patent suggests that the smaller hole is for a key ring.

Coney's brass picnic was the first British registered design for a picnic, but since then quite a number have followed. *Left to right:* The head of this picnic corkscrew is a classic cap lifter with a hole below, so that the sheath can be pushed through it to form a handle. The top edge of the cap lifter is stamped on one side 'Regd Nº 702970' and on the other side 'J.H & S Ld', for the 1924 registration by James Heeley & Sons Ltd. The next example is a very simple design, from M. Myers & Sons Ltd. in 1925, so common that it must have been a great commercial success. The back of the cap lifter hook in the example is stamped 'Regd 717886 Made in England'. These corkscrews are also often stamped 'Regd CANADA 37-7826' for 1927. William Arthur Willetts' 1927 design for a picnic corkscrew (third from left) has a lug which acts as a cap lifter and a support for the sheath when it

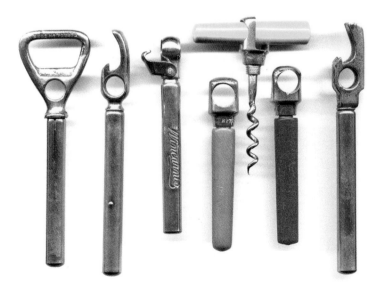

acts as a cross bar. The lug of the example is stamped 'Rd 731702' and it is hinged so that it can be pushed in to prevent it getting caught in clothing. The cap lifter head of Willetts' second design of 1931 for a picnic corkscrew has a very characteristic shape with a distinctive U-shape cross-section. It is normally found with a screw-on plastic sheath in a variety of colours (black, white, green, yellow, red, brown, dark blue). The corkscrews are all marked 'Rd 762004', usually round the neck ring. On the right is another relatively common picnic corkscrew with a cap lifter head made from a sheet of steel folded into a U-shape. The example is stamped 'Regd. Des. 791251 Made in England' as registered by M. Myers & Son Ltd in 1934.

The cap lifter hook on the head (left) has a U-shaped section that is hinged round the hole so that it can fold flat for convenience. It is marked 'Pat. N° 679301 Made in England' for the 1951 invention of Myers & Son Ltd. The next example also has a hinged cap lifter hook, but as a thin steel plate which is stamped 'British Make J.H & S LD' for James Heeley and Sons. It probably dates from the 1930s. The central picnic corkscrew has a screw-on black plastic sheath and is marked 'West Germany' and is therefore from the 1950s or '60s, even though the shape is identical to Christoph Reich's 1930 D.R.G.M. The green plastic sheath of the next example screws on and the cap lifter hook is marked 'Unit', a German marking. With its characteristic S-shaped head *(right)*, this American corkscrew is rather unusual. It is an example of Knud Knudsen's US patent of 1939.

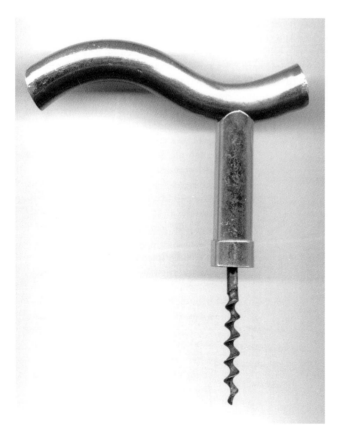

Canes and walking sticks

A cane or a walking stick is very large protective sheath for a corkscrew. Examples do exist, but the collector should beware of fakes. There are many examples of 'square pegs fitting round holes' where it is quite obvious that the corkscrew has been added to an old cane or stick.

This plated curved handle with a corkscrew fits neatly into a black wooden walking stick. Some examples have bayonet fittings.

EASERS

The Easers are one of the most attractive classes of corkscrew. They look good, feel good and there are a great variety available at reasonable prices. They are the ideal starting point for the new collector.

The concept behind the different types of Easer is that once the worm has been fully screwed into the cork, something stops further entry and the turning action of your hand gives the cork a twist in the neck of the bottle. This loosens the adhesion between the cork and the bottle and eases the cork – hence the name. However, you still have to use brute force to pull the cork out. There are four different types: buttons, claws, double helix, and spikes.

Buttons

The very first corkscrew patent in the world was granted in 1795 in England to the Reverend Samuel Henshall, a fellow of Brasenose College, Oxford. His patent states:

> The screw having being introduced in the usual manner through the cork or other substance to be extracted, as far as to get perfect hold thereof, is, according to my new method, to be prevented from penetrating further; and this is done by a cap, or button, or plate, affixed to the upper termination of worm or screw, which cap or button covering the upper part of the cork and being in contact therewith, continues to be turned with the screw, and with it the cork turns also, whereby the resistance arising from adhesion is overcome.

Samuel Henshall's invention was manufactured by the famous Matthew Boulton of the Soho district of Birmingham. These early corkscrews are of very high quality with wooden handles and steel shanks and buttons. The buttons are stamped 'SOHO PATENT ★ OBSTANDO PROMOVES', referring to Boulton's Soho manufactory and the motto 'by standing firm one makes advancement'. Despite their age, there are a reasonable number of 'Soho Patent' corkscrews around, although the collector who aspires to own one may need to seek out specialist dealers to acquire one, and be prepared to pay a serious sum of money. However, these corkscrews are rather 'ordinary' to look at and collectors have picked them up cheaply at antique markets from unsuspecting sellers.

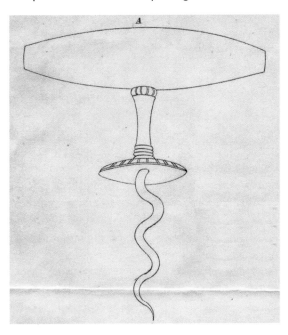

The drawing from Henshall's 1795 patent specification.

Two versions of original 'Soho Patent' corkscrews, both stamped on the button 'SOHO PATENT ★ OBSTANDO PROMOVES'.

Samuel Henshall's concept for the button has been applied extensively to corkscrews from the nineteenth century onwards and they are often referred to as 'Henshall buttons' even if they are unmarked. Most Victorian examples have magnificently decorated steel shanks. They were made by turning on a lathe and often were filed to create cut faces or facets. Somewhat surprisingly, despite the artistry that went into their manufacture, very few bear the maker's name.

The collector will come across a few relatively common shank designs but most will be unique. I have a particular love for Henshall-type corkscrews and have

been amazed at the variety one can find. Handles are mostly of turned wood, but bone and even antler handles are relatively easy to find. The buttons on these corkscrews usually have a plain upper surface and the underside has grooves cut from the centre to the edge – 'radial fluting'. There are variations and some are plain on both sides and some have radial fluting on both sides, for no apparent purpose. In all of these cases the button is a separate piece of metal to the shank. The normal method of construction is for the worm to be screwed into the base of the shank, trapping the button in place like a washer.

Four examples of 'Henshall buttons', which have wooden handles, turned steel shanks and four different kinds of worm. The bottom right example is marked on the shank 'Robt Jones & Son Maker'.

Three examples of 'Henshall buttons' with bone handles. The antler-handled example has a delightful petal-shaped button with scalloped edges.

Corkscrews with Henshall-type buttons were not restricted to steel shanks. There are brass ones as well, usually made of cast brass with an integral button, and most are the same shape. The undersides of the buttons usually have 'orange segment' fluting. Many brass Henshalls probably date from the second half of the nineteenth century, and are often named on the upper side of the button, commanding a higher price premium. Since all of the brass shanks of these Henshalls are identical, apart from the name, it is likely that they were manufactured by just one firm who put different names on them for different clients. Some markings to collect are 'Improved Patent', 'J.F. Lee Warranted', 'Mabson & Labron Birmingham', 'Rodgers & Sons Sheffield', 'Salmon Gough & Bowen Birmingham', 'T. Dowler Manufactr Birmingham', 'Wilmot & Roberts Patent', 'W & R Warranted' and others.

These two Henshalls have the interesting feature of removable worms. *Left:* The collar above the button is marked 'May 14 1847' for the British registered design of William Dray. The button can be unscrewed and the collar removed to reveal the dovetail fastening, which allowed worms to be replaced (*see* close-up on left). The collar is characteristic and can also be found made in brass. *Right:* The central knob is faintly marked 'R^d Aug 18 1851' for the British registration of Joseph Page for a similar removable worm, but this time fixed in by a pin through the bottom knob. Changing the worm was not easy since the pin would have to be drilled out.

In 1892, Rowland Hill Berkeley of Birmingham registered a design for a sleeve to cover the shank of a button corkscrew. This resulted in a series of about ten
very attractive corkscrews, all of which have a brass
collar below the handle marked 'R^d 202169'.

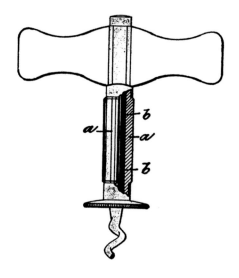

A selection of corkscrews derived from Berkeley's registered design of 1892. *Top right:* **Wooden handle and
sleeve.** *Bottom left:* **Metal handle and black wooden sleeve.** *Bottom right:* **Bone handle and celluloid sleeve.**

These special Henshalls show the quality that can be found. *Left:* This has a decorative impressed sleeve covering the shank, with remnants of a bronzed wash. It shows grapes, vines and ears of wheat, similar to the 'Autumnal Fruits' design of Thomason corkscrews (*see* page 151). Berkeley registered a sleeve cover in1892, described above, but this one is different. *Right:* A very fine Henshall with a decorative faceted steel shank, lacquered handle and silver end caps hallmarked for Chester 1899.

Some versions of button corkscrews have more utilitarian designs as shown. *Left:* Fairly common steel example with an open handle and free button, marked 'Universal' and 'G.F. Hipkins & Son' on the shank. 'Universal' was a trademark of this Birmingham maker. *Right:* This American example with a brass button is derived from Edward Haff's US patent of 1885 for the way the handle is fixed to the thick wire shank. It is marked 'Patent Applied For'.

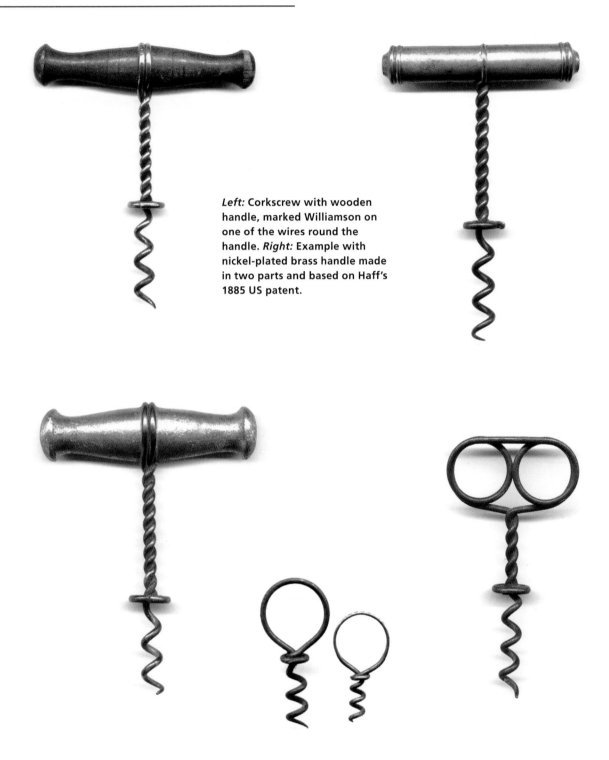

Left: Corkscrew with wooden handle, marked Williamson on one of the wires round the handle. *Right:* Example with nickel-plated brass handle made in two parts and based on Haff's 1885 US patent.

Left: Another with a metal handle (unmarked). *Right:* An example made entirely of twisted wire with two finger holes, probably English. *Centre:* Two small corkscrews for medicine bottles, with the smaller one advertising Listerine on the top of the flattened loop.

Most of the elegant designs of Easers with buttons come from England and there are only a few examples of American corkscrews with simple buttons. However, many American corkscrews made from a single piece of wire feature a small button. The wire forms the worm and is then twisted to give the shank and continues to form a flat spiral to create the button. Many were made by the famous American producer William Williamson after he went into partnership with William Clough, who patented the concept of small wire medicine corkscrews and also invented the machine used to make twisted wire corkscrews.

There is no reason why a button needs to be a slim disc. It can do the same job regardless of its thickness. Inventive designers have created a variety of fat buttons to tempt the collector.

Top left: **Corkscrew with wooden handle and conical shank.** *Top right:* **Example with bone handle and faceted fat button.** *Bottom left:* **Antler handle fixed to balustered shank.** *Bottom right:* **Wooden handle and simple but elegant fat button.**

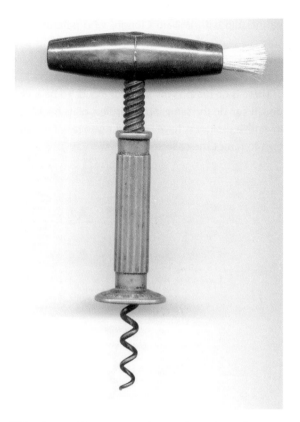

Surprisingly, very few modern corkscrews have been produced with buttons apart from reproductions of antique ones. This plastic one marked 'Hong Kong' is found in a number of bright colours.

This elegant Thomason corkscrew has a large button at the end of a fluted brass barrel. The button is marked 'Thomason P Ne Plus Ultra'. This is derived from Thomason's Patent of 1802, which covers a number of variations, described later in Chapter 8. It has a single threaded shaft, which assists in centring the worm and extracting the cork.

Claws

A more direct way to give the cork a twist to ease it in the neck of the bottle is to use some sort of claw on the base of the shank, just above the top of the worm. There are a variety of designs based on this method, mostly English or French.

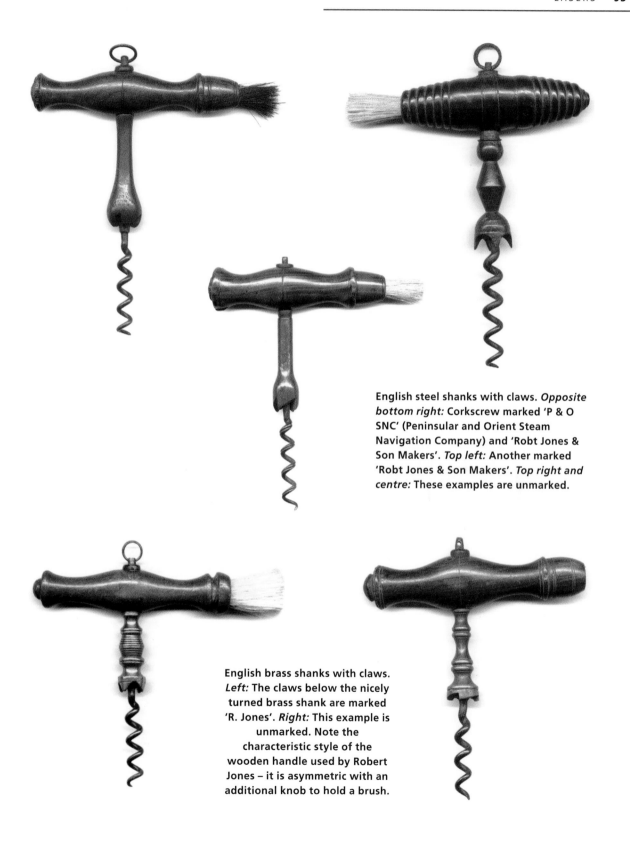

English steel shanks with claws. *Opposite bottom right:* Corkscrew marked 'P & O SNC' (Peninsular and Orient Steam Navigation Company) and 'Robt Jones & Son Makers'. *Top left:* Another marked 'Robt Jones & Son Makers'. *Top right and centre:* These examples are unmarked.

English brass shanks with claws. *Left:* The claws below the nicely turned brass shank are marked 'R. Jones'. *Right:* This example is unmarked. Note the characteristic style of the wooden handle used by Robert Jones – it is asymmetric with an additional knob to hold a brush.

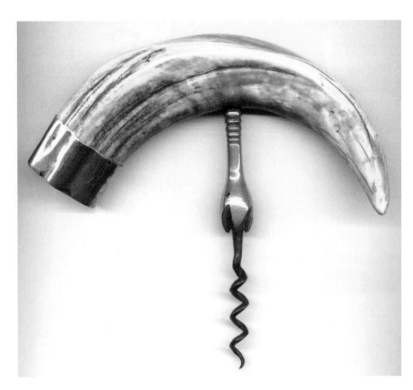

Left: Some very ostentatious corkscrews with claws on the shank have been made and were probably commissioned as presentation pieces, such as the giant boar's tusk example shown. It is a great display piece and has a silver end cap.

French examples with claws. They are typically applied to a small 'bell'. *Bottom left:* The handle has a steel core with a layer of bone and horn on either side. *Bottom right:* The wooden handle has a fancy top nut to hold it on. *Opposite top left:* The four-claw steel 'bell' is fixed like a washer between the worm and the handle. *Opposite top right:* This fine example has bone sides to the ebony core of the handle.

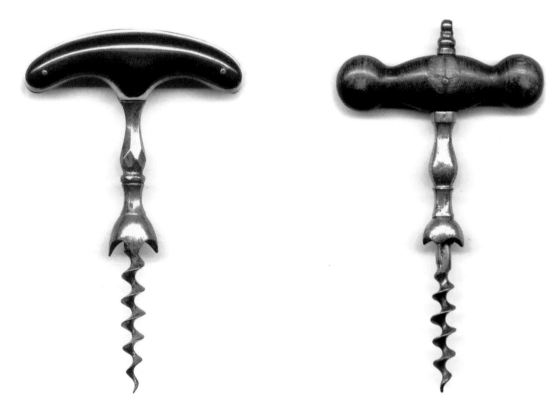

Below left: William Gamble registered a design in 1886 for a corkscrew with two claws. The corkscrew is made from a single flat steel strip for the shank, and the two prongs and the worm are fashioned from it. The shank is marked 'Registered N° 41406 Lever Sheffield' above a wavy line. It is surprising that Gamble called it a lever – it is not a classic type of lever, but the spikes do produce a small twist to the cork. *Below Right:* A twisted wire version of Gamble's design was probably made by Berkeley & Co. It is not marked but bears many similarities to other Berkeley corkscrews such as the 'National' (*see* page 23).

Carl Viarengo, a 'gentleman' of Café Monico, Piccadilly, London, patented a different form of Easer in 1898. His co-patentee was an engineer called Luigi Armanni who is sadly forgotten in the world of corkscrew collecting. It is Viarengo's name that appears on the corkscrews, of which there are a number of variations (*see* Waiters' Friends, page 105). Viarengo corkscrews have two claws above the worm, which are supposed to cut away the centre of the cork, but in practice just act as twisting claws.

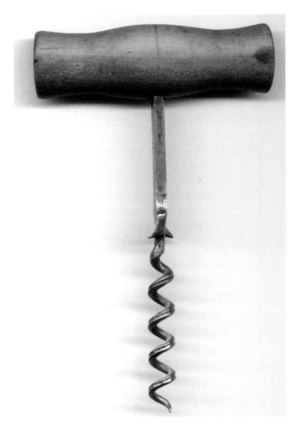

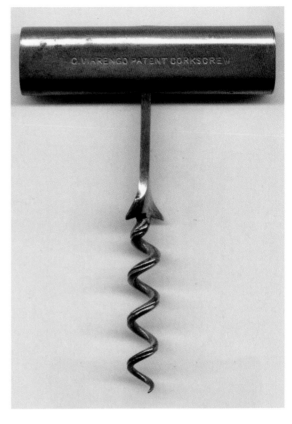

Above: Both corkscrews are stamped on the flat steel shank 'C. Viarengo Patent'. The nickel-plated hollow brass handle of the one on the right is also stamped 'C. Viarengo Patent Corkscrew' for the 1898 Patent No. 10,668.

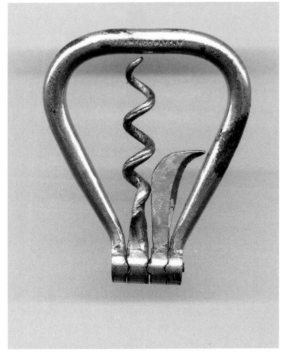

Left: This folding bow is marked 'Viarengo Patent'. This is classed as an Easer rather than a bow.

Double helix

The addition of a second worm may seem bizarre and an unnecessary complication to corkscrew technology. It has nothing to do with the double helix of DNA, the blueprint of life, which was first described in 1953. The double helix corkscrew started life much earlier in an English patent from James Wilson in March 1877 and a few months later in a German patent in July 1877 by Friedrich Schäfer. The action is very similar in principle to the button easer. Once both worms have been screwed into the cork they can go no further, so the cork is twisted to ease the adhesion with the bottle.

Many double helix corkscrews are marked 'S. PAT^T', which probably refers to Schäfer's Patent. They also bear the bell trademark of Brookes & Crookes, a Sheffield manufacturer. Other similar double helix corkscrews without the 'S. PAT^T' markings can be found and the collector should be cautious. Some may be genuinely old, but there are fakes around.

Quite a few American twisted wire corkscrews have a double helix and some carry advertising on the handle for added interest.

Easers are classed higher up the SCReW© Classification than most other corkscrews, so pocket or bow corkscrews that have a double helix are also classed as easers, even though their essence is as a picnic or a bow.

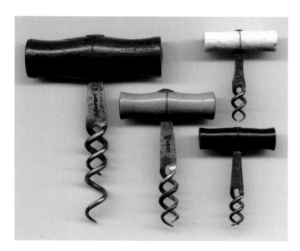

Above: **Four double helix corkscrews, all marked 'S. PAT^T' with a 'bell' trademark. The sizes are: normal (75mm), medium (55mm), and small (38mm).**

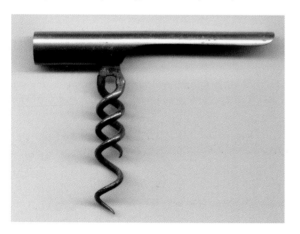

Both these unusual examples are marked 'S. PAT^T' with a 'bell' trademark. *Left:* **A folding double helix corkscrew with a case that has been described as an apple corer, but does not have a sharp edge.** *Above:* **A very uncommon peg and worm, probably from a dressing case set.**

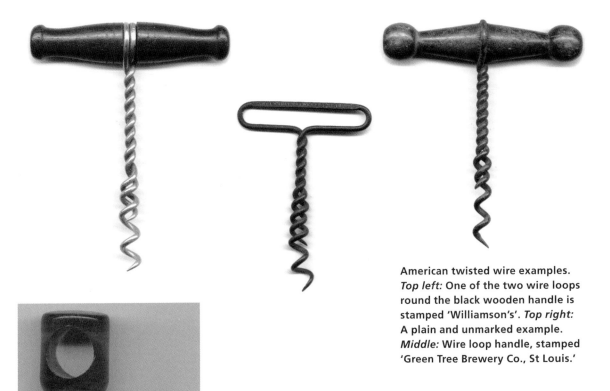

American twisted wire examples.
Top left: One of the two wire loops round the black wooden handle is stamped 'Williamson's'. *Top right:* A plain and unmarked example. *Middle:* Wire loop handle, stamped 'Green Tree Brewery Co., St Louis.'

Left: This modern Swiss corkscrew with a double helix is fairly common and is made of bright plastic in a picnic style with a folding cap lifter. It is usually marked 'Maxram Swiss Made', but there are German and Russian versions to collect as well.

The double helix concept was also applied to pickle forks with long handles. Do not confuse them with corkscrews unless you want to retrieve a cork from a jar of gherkins.

Below: Pickle forks – the bone-handled example is marked 'PAT^{T}' with a 'bell' trademark for Brookes & Crookes.

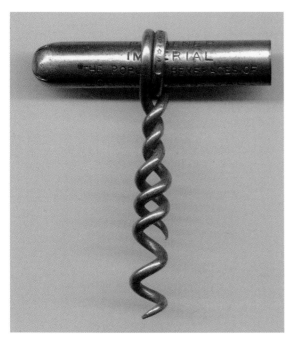
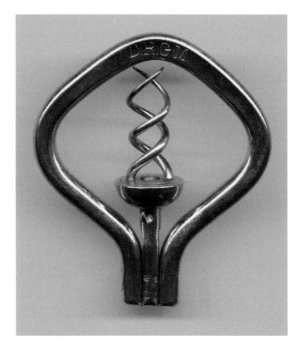

Left: An American picnic marked 'Williamson' on the top loop, with advertising on the sheath for a Pilsner Imperial beer. *Right:* A folding bow marked 'D.R.G.M.' from the 1926 German registered design of Christian Usbeck.

Spikes

There are relatively few examples of this style of easer and the collector will either have to be very lucky or have good contacts to add these to their collection. The concept behind them is that as the worm is screwed into the cork, one or more spikes enter the cork as well and eventually give a solid turn to the cork to ease it.

The first British registered design for a corkscrew was for an easer with two spikes. It was registered in 1840 by Robert Jones & Son of Birmingham. Many people see this corkscrew as being 'mechanical' as it has a threaded shank, but it provides no mechanical advantage for removing the cork. The cleverness of the design lies in the two spikes and the brass button, which ensure that the worm is positioned correctly before starting to screw it in. The pitch of the threaded shank has to be the same as that of the worm, otherwise the helix will rip out the centre of the cork. Once the worm is fully inserted, the button and spikes give the cork a twist and loosen the adhesion. Withdrawal is down to brute force, but afterwards, turning the handle anti-clockwise removes the worm from the cork, which is stuck on the spikes.

There is no doubt that Robert Jones had an affinity for spikes as shown in his second design registration in 1842. This 'Jones II' was really just a more complicated version of his earlier design, but it is a highly regarded expensive corkscrew for collectors to dream of owning.

Another spiked easer was described by William Robert Maud in England in two patents in 1894 and 1895. There are a few variations in design.

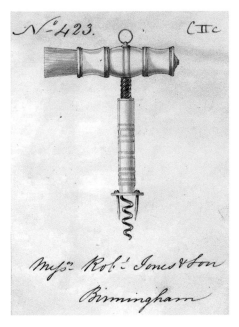

The 'Jones I' example is marked 'Robert Jones & Son Makers 105 Cheapside Birmingham, Reg. No. 423 8th Octr 1840' with 'VR' and a crown on the edge of the button. Some examples are not marked with the address or 'VR' (Victoria Regina).

The barrel of the Jones II has an impressive diamond registration mark for 1842.

Middle: The earlier Maud example has a freely rotating steel button bearing three stubby spikes. It is marked 'Patent' on the steel shank for the 1894 Patent No. 12,529. *Right:* The later version is much more complex. It has a thin steel collar with three spikes, which is free to rotate inside an outer collar, which acts as a type of clutch, which makes the spiked collar turn once the worm is right into the cork. It is marked 'Maud's Patent' for the 1895 Patent No. 10,211.

LEVERS

'Give me a place to stand and I will move the earth,' Archimedes allegedly said, based on his studies of levers. A lever can be arranged to provide a very large mechanical advantage and, in its simplest form, is a solid bar pivoting about a fixed point known as a fulcrum. A see-saw is the simplest example; by pushing down on one end it makes the other end go up. By moving the fulcrum away from the half-way point to a third of the way along it creates a system that provides a two-fold mechanical advantage. If you press down on the longer side, which is twice as long as the shorter side, the opposite end will push up with twice the force applied to the other end. It is a very useful concept for removing a cork from a bottle and there are a good variety of lever corkscrews to collect, from the very cheap to the highly expensive. Almost everyone owns a 'Waiter's Friend' – the pocket tool with a fold-down arm that rests on the edge of the bottle's neck. That is a simple lever.

Mechanically, there are three basic ways to arrange the fulcrum and the push and lift forces on a lever. Many corkscrew levers have an arrangement whereby the fulcrum is between the push and lift forces (like a see-saw); the differences being in the length of the lever at either side of the fulcrum. When you have the fulcrum at the end of the lever, there are two other arrangements possible (*see* diagram). However, of these two options, corkscrews always have the lift in between the fulcrum and the push (this is the way Waiter's Friends are arranged). The third arrangement is not known in the corkscrew world, as it offers no mechanical advantage.

There are five major classifications of lever corkscrews: Single Levers, Double Levers, Compound Levers, Lund Levers, and Waiter's Friends. The Lund Levers and Waiter's Friends are actually Single Levers but are so characteristic that they deserve to be considered separately.

Waiter's friends

Karl Wienke was granted a German patent in 1882 for what was to become probably the most widely manufactured corkscrew. The key to the invention was to have the fulcrum at the end of the lever arm, at the top of an arm that rests on the edge of the lip of the

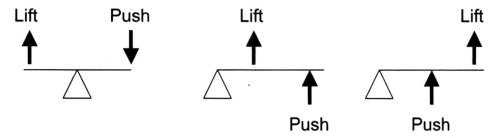

Lever and fulcrum arrangements.

bottle's neck. The worm was hinged at about a quarter of the way along the body, giving a three-fold mechanical advantage. The other key to making this design so popular was that both the fulcrum arm and the worm could be folded up to lie alongside or even inside the body. The now ubiquitous crown cap for soft drink and beer bottles was patented by William Painter in the United States in 1892 and manufacturers soon realized that the fulcrum post of a Waiter's Friend could easily be adapted to open crown caps by adding a hook close to the hinge. This compact design of corkscrew and cap lifter made it perfect for keeping in a pocket, especially for waiters – hence the name. In France they are often called *limonadiers*.

The corkscrew was also patented in Britain, France and the USA in 1883. Examples have been found bearing patent marks for the German and US patents, but not the British or French ones. A very similar corkscrew was patented in the United States by David Davis in 1891 and it is very surprising that it was granted, as it has no innovative advantages over Wienke's patent.

Left: **Wienke's patent marked 'Patent N° 283,731 USA' and advertising A. Wellmann, New Orleans. The 1883 US patent was lodged by Wienke's agent Rudolph Dolberg.** *Centre:* **This German example is marked 'D.R. Patent No 20815' for 1882 with a wire cutting blade.** *Right:* **An example of Davis's version marked 'The Davis Corkscrew, Pat. July 14, 1891'. None of these examples has a cap lifter, suggesting that they are early models from before 1892.**

Since 1882, numerous Waiter's Friends have been made in a variety of novel designs. It is a good area for collectors with some bargains available, as well as more expensive rarities. *Left:* **French bottle shape with plastic scales promoting Cherry Rocher. The blade is from Thiers and the fulcrum arm is marked 'A.S. Made in France'.** *Top:* **A German example marked 'Paul A. Heinkels' near the cap lifter and promoting the Italian sparkling water Acqua S. Pellegrino. There are many similar Waiter's Friends promoting Italian wines.** *Bottom:* **Moulded plastic scales that advertise 'Liqueur Cointreau'.** *Right:* **Uncommon novelty corkscrew with the celluloid scales moulded as a mermaid. The fulcrum post is marked 'Germany Ges. Geschützt'. Versions are also known with wire cutter blades. Apart from the mermaid, all of these examples have cap lifters.**

Variations on the Waiter's Friend concept. *Top:* This uncommon French corkscrew with a leopard's head at one end is marked 'Express J-P Paris Bté S.G.D.G. Déposé J-P', for the 1899 patent of Jacques Pérille. *Centre:* This small folded steel French lever has a cap lifter hook and is stamped 'Débouchoir "Ajoux" Bté S.G.D.G'. It derives from Georges Roux's French patent of 1922. *Bottom:* The fulcrum arm of this British corkscrew has a serrated cutting edge and broad yoke to fit on the neck of the bottle. It is wide so that it can cover the special worm, which has two claws on the shank, as this is a Viarengo corkscrew, as described in Chapter 5. The Waiter's Friend bears the markings 'John Watts Sheffield Estb 1765 Viarengo Patent Corkscrew Sheffield England', and 'Rᵈ Nº 504185', showing that it is derived from John Watts' registered design of 1907.

These corkscrews may look complicated but they are still Waiter's Friends. *Left:* This promotional tool with cap lifter and blade is marked 'Orangina Gazéifiée à la Pulpe d'Orange, Made in France A.S.', for A. Sarry of Thiers. *Right:* The tool has additional grippers for easing champagne corks and promotes 'Champagne Delamotte P&F'.

Lund levers

In 1855 William Lund and William Edward Hipkins were granted British Patent No. 736 for 'Improvements in the manufacture of corkscrews'. Hipkins was listed as being Lund's foreman. Unusually for a patent, it described three completely different types of corkscrews. One of these was a simple lever with a central fulcrum and this has come to be known generically as a 'Lund Lever'. The creative element of the design was that it was in two parts with a lever and a separate corkscrew. The worm was first screwed into the cork. The lower static arm of the Lund Lever had an open ring, which was placed over the top of the neck of the bottle, and at the same time the hook on the upper arm was inserted into a hole in the corkscrew. By simply squeezing the two arms of the lever together the cork was lifted.

The Lund Lever was an unqualified success, as judged by the number that are still around today. The concept was also copied and adapted by other makers and inventors, creating a rich field of collectable items. The classic Lund Lever has a triangular plate fixed to the lower arm, and its upper point acts as the fulcrum for the upper arm. This triangular plate was

A Lund Lever in use, as shown in a catalogue of about 1865.

A classic Lund Lever, marked on one side 'Sold by the Patentee 24 Fleet St & 57 Cornhill London / Lund Patentee London.' The matching worm is marked 'Lund Patentee & Maker 57 Cornhill & 24 Fleet St London'. The addresses of 57 Cornhill and 24 Fleet Street in London relate to Lund's manufactory and wholesale outlet respectively.

used as a badge for promoting the various patentees, makers and wholesalers, and there is a multitude to collect. The corkscrew was the other crucial part of Lund and Hipkins' invention and it has a hole just above the worm, into which fits the hook on the upper arm of the Lever. The corkscrews are also found with different markings and it is obviously good to find one that matches the triangular badge on the lever. It is, however, quite common to find unmatched pairs, but that should not necessarily worry the collector. There is evidence from trade catalogues that the worms were sold separately from the levers and mis-matches were created when worms broke or bent and had to be replaced. There are stories that a line of wine bottles used to be set up before a grand meal, all with Lund worms already inserted into the corks. A butler would then use one lever to open them as required.

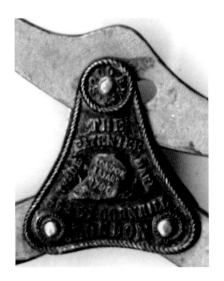

A much less common badge shows a 'Milestone' marked 'Sold by the Patentee Trade Mark 56 & 57 Cornhill London / Lund Patentee London.' The milestone is marked London Estabd 1796, which probably relates to the business bought by Thomas Lund, William's father.

A selection of badges found on Lund-type Levers. *Left:* 'The Patent Lever' (marked on both sides) with an 'h' in a circle, often referred to as the 'Gothic H'. Just above the badge, the impressed mark is 'JH&S', suggesting that the manufacturer was James Heeley & Sons. Their much rarer badges also show their trademark of a cockerel. *Centre:* An interesting hand and lever badge that is not easy to find. *Right:* The badge is marked 'Improved Lever for Drawing Corks' on both sides.

The biggest problem in Lund and Hipkins' design for their lever was how to keep the worm vertical as it was being lifted by the upper arm. The locus of the hook on the end of the upper lever is a curve and not a direct vertical pull. As a consequence, Lund Levers do not have a fixed fulcrum pivot on the upper arm, but there is a small slot along which the fulcrum pivot slides. This thus allows the worm to stay vertical as it is pulled upwards.

An alternative solution to this problem was made by Edwin Wolverson who developed a clever three-part hinge design that was marketed as the 'Tangent Lever'. Wolverson's design was registered in 1873 and was a commercial success.

Left and above: The oval hinges of Tangent Levers are usually stamped and bear a variety of markings. Ones to look out for are 'The Tangent Lever', 'Registered Nov 4th 1873' and 'Edwin Wolverson'.

Right: Wolverson's original drawing of his lever did not give any clear indication of the worm he intended to go with it. However, three years later in 1876 he registered a design for the 'Lever Signet', which makes a satisfying match for the collector.

Top: The Holborn Lever is marked on the other side 'Patent 6793' for the 1885 patent of Henry Arthur Goodall, whose address was in the Holborn district of London. It has a rod that passes through a swivel stud in the upper arm and allows the hook at the end to move vertically. The matching worm is also marked 'Holborn Lever'. *Bottom:* This is the Hampton Lever, named on both sides of the hinge, which has a vertical rod fixed to the top lever, but is free to slide through a hole in the lower one. The worm is attached to a collar on the upper arm. The oval hinge is so like the Tangent that it suggests that it was made by Wolverson.

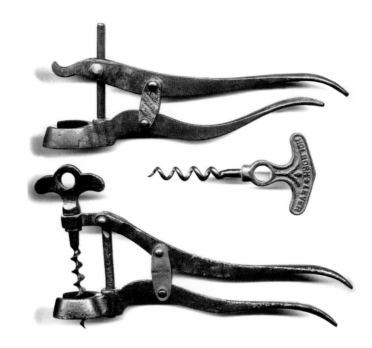

Top: Although this is marked 'Coney Patent', the patent has not been found and the name is probably a marketing ploy. *Bottom:* The 'BB Lever' was patented by Henry Seward Bowles Goodall in 1889, No. 13,314, and uses two sliding slots to achieve a vertical lift. He was the son of the inventor of the Holborn Lever.

A number of other levers show how creative minds solved the problem of the vertical lift. These are not particularly common, but there are sufficient around for the determined collector.

The Lund Lever is a particularly British corkscrew and there are very few others around. Some very rare examples from the early 1850s, before Lund and Hipkins' patent, are derived from the 1852 Belgian patent of Levaux-Lemaitre or the 1854 British patent of Edmund Burke. Early French and Belgian examples are often marked with the manufacturer's name, Dordet, and have a worm that is fixed within a slot in the upper arm. In the second half of the twentieth century, a similar, but less attractive, lever was produced in Argentina.

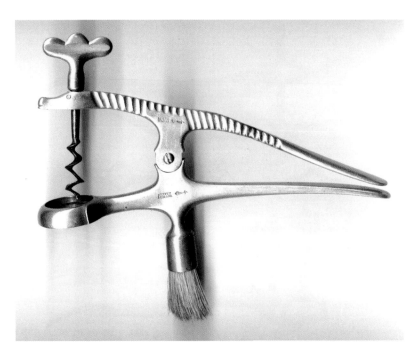

A fine plated lever marked 'Levaux a Namur, Brevet di 15 Ans', with small crown and dagger marks and 2031 on the back of both parts of the lever. The 1852 Belgian patent has not been found, and Burke's 1854 patent looks identical to the example, apart from the decorative snake's head.

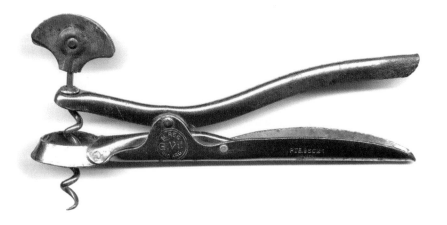

Top: The Dordet-style lever has a decorative head to the worm and a 'dolphin' head at the end of the upper arm. *Bottom:* The plated steel lever is marked 'Industria Argentina Pte. 96521 M.Reg. GVi Ind.Arg.'

Single levers

There are relatively few single levers that are not classified as Lund types or Waiter's Friends. However, most are very desirable collectors' pieces and hence prices tend to be relatively high.

Simple pivots

A very characteristic design has a ring to fit over the top of the bottle neck. Integral with the neck ring is an upright arm with a fulcrum pivot on the top. At one end of the lever is a handle and at the other is the corkscrew worm. There are two problems for the designer to solve with this type of corkscrew. One is how to ensure that the cork is pulled up vertically, since the end of a lever moves in an arc, not in a straight line. The simple solution is to hinge the worm to the end of the lever.

The second problem is how to turn the worm to get it into the cork. Designers have come up with two solutions. John Burgess and Albert Fenton presented their idea in 1874 in British Patent No. 3,004, in which the worm is free to rotate in a small collar which is itself hinged to the end of the lever. Their patent also covered the second solution in which the worm is fixed in line with the lever. Their concept was simplified by William Tucker and by Alfred Sperry in two US patents of 1878. In their designs the worm is held either in an 'in-line' or in a vertical position by a back spring.

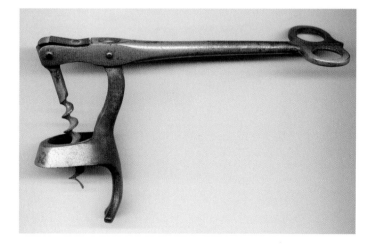

Top left: **Burgess and Fenton's Lever is marked 'Patent Lift / J.B. & Sons'.** *Top right:* **Sperry's version is marked on the back of the plated brass arm 'Pat^d May 23, 1878'.** *Bottom:* **Tucker's patent is marked on the handle 'Pat'd Sep 3 1878'.**

There is a very good selection of French corkscrews that use the single lever principle with the worm at the end of the lever and the fulcrum in the centre. Many of them were created by Jacques Pérille and are highly collectable. Pérille corkscrews are marked with his initials, often in a circle. The mark looks as if it is 'JHP' but it is just 'J-P' with a connecting line.

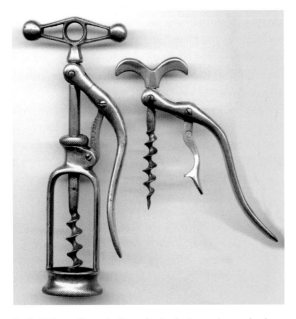

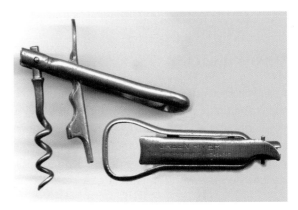

A relatively common, and hence economically priced, American corkscrew was patented by Harry Noyes in 1906, Patent No. 824,807. Many examples advertise 'Green River – The Whiskey Without a Headache'. Examples are lightly marked under the handle 'Universal June 27 '05 July 3 '06'.

Left: This well-made French single Lever is marked 'Le Presto' and 'Paris J-P Déposé' for the Jacques Pérille Patent No. 291,691 of 1899. A much later version is known as the 'Lesto'. *Right:* Another Pérille example, named the 'Subito' in his catalogue, is marked 'Déposé J-P Paris'.

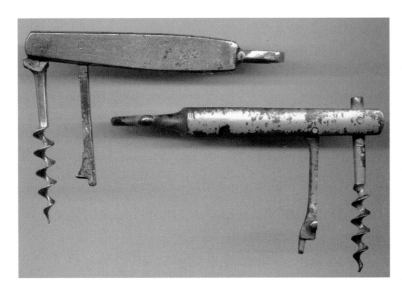

Left: This is marked 'Béchon Morel Breveté S.G.D.G.' on the lever, for the 1877 French Patent No. 118,056 of Rémy Béchon-Morel. It folds up into the case and has an open two-finger steel handle. *Right:* This is marked 'Déposé' on the lever for Sosthène Menneret's French Patent No. 101,871 of 1874. The lever has two side pegs that slot into notches on the case. The worm has to be turned through 270° from the closed position, forcing the two arms of the case apart, so it is quite complex to use. The steel handle is a single-finger loop with two side finger supports.

Cam action single levers

Another group of corkscrews, which tend to be expensive, are constructed so that the fulcrum of the lever is not fixed but moves as a curved cam arm turns.

The 'Royal Club' is an example of this and is one of the most elegant of all corkscrews with its sinuously curved handle. Charles Hull patented this corkscrew in 1864, Patent No. 480, and there are 'roller' and 'non-roller' design variations. The badge on the front of them all is a statement of Charles Hull's pride in his products. Variations are all marked 'Sold by B.B. Wells'.

Hull's Royal Club has a pressed brass badge stating 'C. Hull Patentee Birmingham Royal Club Corkscrew'. There are three basic versions: one with rollers and a two-part sleeve through which the shank slides, as in the example shown; and also a solid sleeve version and a non-roller version, as in the close-ups. A design closely related to that of Charles Hull's was patented in the United States by Russel in 1862 and has a large D-shaped cam that acts on the top of a relatively thin brass barrel (*see* O'Leary). There are very few examples known.

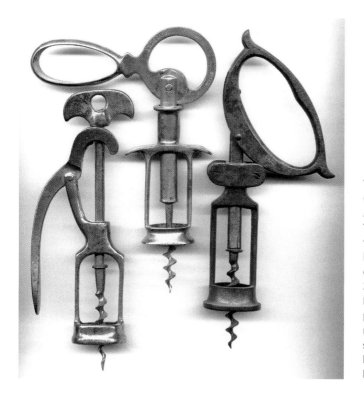

There are also very desirable French and German single levers with cam actions. *Left:* The 'Rapide' has an open forked cam. The handle is marked 'JH Déposé' in a star, for Jules Hurel who made corkscrews between 1878 and 1897. *Centre:* An example of the 1902 French Patent No. 323,030 of Fernand François, marked 'Ultra Rapide Bté S.G.D.G.' *Right:* The 1882 German patent of Valentine Rasch described a large rocking cam handle with rollers on either side. This example is marked 'DRP 20803', but they are often unmarked, and are also known without the rollers.

Rack and pinion action single levers

This is a very select group of corkscrews in which the lever arm turns a pinion gear, which acts on a toothed rack attached to the worm. In one type, exemplified by the 1905 French patent from Victor Rousseau, the worm is driven into the cork, which pushes the single lever arm upwards. To withdraw the cork, the arm is pushed down. It is essentially a single lever version of the common modern household Double Lever described later. With the second type the whole corkscrew is turned to insert the worm into the cork. The lever arm is then raised to lift the worm and extract the cork.

Above: **This example of Rousseau's 1905 French Patent No. 352,411 is marked 'Bté S.G.D.G. Paris A.C.' The shank is free to rotate inside a sleeve to which the rack is fixed.** *Centre:* **A British corkscrew marked 'Lever-Rack Patent G.F. Hipkins & Son', from William Edward Hipkins' 1879 British Patent No. 3,167.** *Right:* **This plated steel lever rack is marked 'Traifor Bté S.G.D.G. Fr. Et. Dep Made in France' for the 1949 French Patent No. 951,926 of Arsène Jean Grandfils. There are modern unmarked brass reproductions available.**

Above: **This hefty piece is marked 'Torpille Breveté Bruxles'. It is based on the 1913 German Registered Design of Heinrich Fuckel and was manufactured by Rechnagel in Germany and sold in Belgium as the 'Torpille' ('torpedo'). It is also known as the 'Gasoline Pump' for obvious reasons. It has an ornamental bottle grip at the bottom.**

Double levers

One of the most common household corkscrews is an example of a Double Lever. Such corkscrews have two lever arms as the name suggests. By using the two arms together it halves the force required to pull out a cork. The worm is screwed into the cork and the levers on either side rise up. By pushing down on the two lever arms the cork is withdrawn easily. Well, relatively easily – these common corkscrews often have Archimedean worms, which tend to rip a hole out of the centre of the cork if too much force is used.

Cam action double levers

The first description of a Double Lever corkscrew was in the 1880 British Patent No. 2,950 of William Baker. Corkscrews derived from it are colloquially known as 'the Baker patent' and their construction used similar parts to the slightly later 'Heeley A1 Double Lever'. It is the only fairly common cam action Double Lever and both bronze-washed and nickel-plated versions are known.

Double levers with pivot hinges

The second example of a Double Lever corkscrew was described in Britain by Neville Smith Heeley in his Patent No. 6,006 of 1888. He was the grandson of James Heeley, who started the firm that continued well into the twentieth century. These corkscrews are relatively common and for the collector of details, there are three slightly different types showing different markings and lever arm construction, as well as either bronze-washed or nickel-plated finishes. The two lever arms are connected directly to a large 'washer' through which the shank can rotate when the worm is being screwed into the cork.

Just two years later in 1890, Neville Heeley patented a second Double Lever, known as the 'Empire', in which the two arms lock together with a satisfying click. Since the worm sticks out from the bottom of the body, it can be screwed into the cork quite easily

The 'Baker patent' is marked 'James Heeley & Sons Patent Double Lever / A1 Patent'. The two lever arms are fixed to the frame, but are free at the top.

without the encumbrance of the arms lifting up. Only then are the arms unlocked and the cork withdrawn. A very nicely designed modern example of the Empire was registered in 1996 and marketed as the 'Bull Pull'.

The double lever concept was taken up in continental Europe with a variety of designs. The heavy brass Italian patent from Gropelli is another easy-to-use corkscrew, as the whole unit can be screwed into the cork before lowering the two arms. An alternative design from Placido Vogliotti is less easy to use, as the arms rise as the worm is screwed into the cork. It does, however, have a useful feature in that the ring at the bottom of the frame can be folded in half to cover and protect the point of the worm.

Above: The bronze-washed corkscrew is marked 'The Empire J. Heeley & Sons Patent' on both sides, for Patent No. 13,320 of 1890. It was also produced with a nickel-plated finish. *Below:* The modern version was registered by Mark Holden, Universal Housewares, in 1996 and is marked 'Bull Pull'. The box states, 'The design of this beautifully crafted corkscrew was inspired by the original "Empire Double-Lever" of 1890.'

The earliest versions are marked 'James Heeley and Sons 6006 Patent Double Lever/A1 Patent'. Later examples are marked 'A1 Heeley's Double Lever' (with or without 'James Heeley & Sons'). Less common versions bear the name of a retailer such as Stacy or promote Big Ben Scotch.

Left: The brass Italian corkscrew is marked 'Brevetto Gropelli'. *Centre:* Both arms are marked 'Brevetti Vogliotto Torino' for the 1910 Italian patent. The neck ring is shown closed covering the worm and making a nice pocket corkscrew. *Right:* The French version of the Vogliotti, without the folding base, is marked 'Practic Boy-Scout Marque & Modelle Déposé', with an image of a boy scout on one of the arms. The name comes from the manufacturer Alexandre Boy of Lyon.

Below: A fairly compact corkscrew was patented in France in 1920, No. 512,657, by Léo Debeaurain and is marked 'Le Désiré B^te S.G.D.G.' The production model differs from the patent drawing in that it has a thin steel handle joining the two lever arms. This handle was dumb-bell shaped and was prone to break; consequently, repaired versions are not uncommon. This design was also produced for the British market and is marked 'The Butler/Made in France.'

Above left: The 'Tyr' is from France and has a long plated double lever with a pin that slides up a slot in the frame, which helps to equalize the force applied to each lever arm. It was patented by Henri Paraf in 1927 with a modification in 1929 from his widow Marguerite. It is marked 'B^te S.G.D.G.' *Above Right:* Moët & Chandon commissioned a heavy variation of the 'Tyr' to promote their champagne. It is marked 'Champagne Moët & Chandon Made in France Déposé.'

Rack and pinion action double levers

This is an area with a multitude of examples ranging from Murray and Stalker's British patent of 1894 to plastic examples of the current day. The basic designs are all the same, and they suffer from being awkward to use because, in some, the lever arms must be in the 'up' position before screwing in the worm; in others the arms rise as the worm is screwed into the cork. In all of them the shank has a series of slots cut into it – the 'rack'. To engage with the rack, the end of each arm has a 'pinion', a partially toothed gear. In many examples the top handle is made as a crown cap lifter. As this design of corkscrew has 'two arms and a head', creative designers, especially in Italy, have come up with some delightful people-shaped corkscrews. There is a Homer Simpson, Wallace, and even a Bugs Bunny double lever!

Rack and pinion double levers have been developed into the likeness of an owl. Some are relatively common and many Spanish ones are marked 'BOJ'. Modern ones can be bought in Spanish shops today. *Left:* **This version, probably from the mid twentieth century, is marked 'Magic Lever Cork Drawer' and 'Pat. Appl^d For', but the patent record is not known. It also promotes Shaw Brothers, 81 Bold Street, Liverpool.** *Right:* **This, the ultimate and very desirable bronze 'owl' is the 'Hootch-Owl' and was copyrighted by Richard Smythe in American Design Patent No. 2,115,289 of 1938. It is marked on the square rack 'Pat. App^d For' and on the opposite side, the two screw heads of the pivots give the impression that the owl has its eyes closed. The wings act as bottle cap grips and have cap lifter hooks.**

Left: Examples like this unmarked Italian basic brass double lever with a cap lifter handle can be found in many kitchen drawers. *Second left:* This Argentinean example has a closed barrel marked 'Industrai Gaumen Argentina'. *Third left:* Wladyslaw Chudzikowski of Lwow patented this uncommon double lever in Germany, Patent No. 205,952 in 1908. It is marked 'Fora' and 'Patent' and is very easy to use because cork insertion starts with the two handles in the 'up' position. *Right:* This uncommon plated-steel British corkscrew was patented by John Thomas Murray and John Joseph Stalker in 1894 and is stamped on one of the arms 'Patent No. 234.'

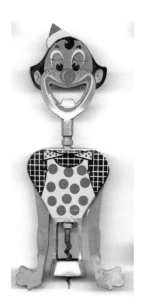

Two jolly Italian corkscrew people: 'Lulu' promotes a variety of drinks and the clown has 'Good Luck' and 'Cheers' in a number of languages on the back. They have four black painted friends to collect as well: two called 'Barmaid Opener' and two called 'Barman Opener.' They are based on Carlo Gemelli's Italian and American Design Patents of 1959.

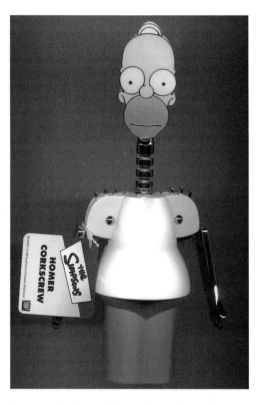

Above, Left: This modern Italian classic design is from Alessandro Mendini (Alessi) and is known as 'Anna G.' *Centre:* The 'Sommelier' is also from Italy. *Right:* The familiar figure of Homer Simpson, Trademark and Copyright 2000 Fox Film Corporation, marked 'Matt Groening'.

Compound levers. *Below, Top left:* This uncommon six-arm version is marked 'Patent Weir's Patent 2804 25 Septr 1884 Heeley & Sons Maker'. *Top right:* The common ten-arm corkscrew is marked Patent / Weir's Patent 12804 25 Septr 1884 J Heeley & Sons Makers'. Bottom left: Heeley's catalogue refers to this design as 'lighter for ladies' use'. It is marked 'Made in England J.H.S.B Wier's Patent No. 4377'. *Bottom right:* This corkscrew, marked 'The "Pullezi" Heeley's Original Patent 4307' is moderately common (4307 is the catalogue number for the bronzed finish and 4324 is for nickel plated). Note that spelling is 'Wier' on the patent and some of the corkscrews and 'Weir' in the Heeley catalogue and other corkscrews. 'JHSB' is probably an abbreviation for James Heeley & Sons Birmingham.

Compound levers

Sometimes known as 'lazy tongs', compound levers comprise an even number of simple levers joined together to give a large mechanical advantage. By pulling the top handle 25cm (thus extending the criss-crossed set of arms) you can lift the worm and cork 5cm to give a five-fold mechanical advantage. The first description of such a corkscrew was in the 1884 British Patent No. 12,804 from Marshall Arthur Wier. The patent describes only the basic ten-arm design (six connected levers plus four struts) but the manufacturer, J. Heeley & Sons, made five different designs with either two lever arms or six lever arms.

Left: This extraordinary design is known as the 'Double Wier's' and has two sets of ten arms separated by spacers and a small wooden handle at the top. It is a compact tool but the maximum extension is only 10cm lifting the worm only 2cm. The five-fold mechanical advantage is good but it will not withdraw a cork very far and the whole extended corkscrew then needs a good tug to get the cork fully out of the bottle. Such exertion would have led to many of these corkscrews being damaged, hence their scarcity today. Examples are marked 'Double No.4283 Wier's Patent J H S B'.

Below: Wier's patent was followed in 1902 by two British patents, No. 354 and No. 10,595 from Henry David Armstrong, with the key difference being in the way that the worm was fixed to the lowest lever arms. His second patent shows drawings for corkscrews with six arms (two levers) and eight arms (four levers). *Left:* The six-arm version is fairly common but examples are rarely an attractive collector's piece due to the poor quality of the painted steel. This six-arm example is marked 'H.D. Armstrong Patt Appd For' but they are also found marked 'H.D. Armstrong Patent'. *Right:* The eight-arm version is extremely rare and is marked 'H.D. Armstrong Patt Appd For'.

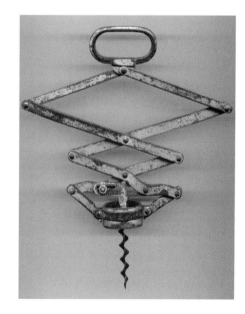

The vast majority of compound lever corkscrews are French. There are numerous examples and they have a variety of names including: 'Perfect' (six arms, two levers); 'Débouchtout' (six arms, two levers); 'Idéal' (eight arms, four levers); 'Le Polichinelle' (eight arms, four levers); 'Rapid' (eight arms, four levers); 'Éclair' (ten arms, six levers); 'Yprim' (ten arms, six levers); 'Zig-Zag' (ten arms, six levers); 'Souplex' (ten arms, six levers); 'Kis-Ply' (eight or ten arms). Of these the 'Idéal' is a relatively common corkscrew but is unusual in that it is one of the few examples of having eight arms (four levers).

Top left: A French six-arm corkscrew marked 'Perfect Breveté S.G.D.G.' with a floppy folding handle, patent not found. *Top right:* The 'Idéal Breveté' also has a floppy folding handle, patent not found. Both the Perfect and the Idéal were believed to be made by Ernest Martenet in the late 1920s. *Bottom:* This has double lower arms and is marked 'Débouchtout'/Bté S.G.D.G. Marque et Modele Déposés France et Etranger'. This is a 1929 addition to Patent No. 503,957 of Jules Bart.

Below: The Compound Lever was so successful that modern versions with spring-loaded handles like the Zig-Zag have been made in the shape of fish, frogs, scorpions and many more. This goldfish is marked 'Lazy Fish Made in England' and is from a 1992-registered design from Mark Christopher Hughes and Janusz Lucien Holland.

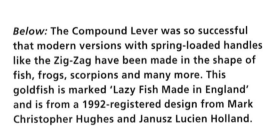

Above, Left: The 'Kis-Ply' has a spring-loaded handle to return it to the closed position and is marked 'Kis-Ply Paris'. It was patented by Jean Thomas in 1932, Patent No. 723,604. The name derives from *qui s'plie (qui se plie)*, meaning 'that which folds'. *Right:* The plated steel Zig-Zag was patented in France by Jules Bart in 1919, Number 503,957, and also has a spring-loaded handle. It is still made today. This example is derived from Bart's later patent of 1928, Number 649,209 and has cap lifter hooks added on the upper arms. It is marked 'Zig-Zag Brevetés. G.D.G. Marque et Modèle Déposés France et Etranger'. Examples can be found made of folded sheet steel.

SELF-PULLERS AND PARTIAL PULLERS

For those users who don't really think about what is happening when they use one of these corkscrews, their action seems like magic. By simply screwing the worm into the cork and continuing to turn, the cork climbs up the worm and out of the bottle. But it's not magic – it is just that the turning helix converts rotary motion into linear motion. It is the same as when you screw the top on to a drinks bottle; the top moves from one end of the thread to the other.

The key to success for a self-puller corkscrew is some sort of frame to limit how far the worm and shank can travel into the cork. Once the frame hits the top of the bottle, the only option for the cork is to climb up the worm. How far the cork moves out of the bottle depends upon the length of the frame and the length of the worm. For some, like the modern Screwpull®,

the frame is long enough to allow complete extraction. Springs can help to pull the cork out. At the other extreme, the classic American 'bell' allows only a short movement but is sufficient to loosen the cork in the bottle significantly and to pull it out a little way. For this reason they are usually referred to as partial pullers.

Self-pullers with full-length worms

These are mechanically the most effective because there is no hindrance to the cork climbing up the worm until it is completely withdrawn. In my opinion

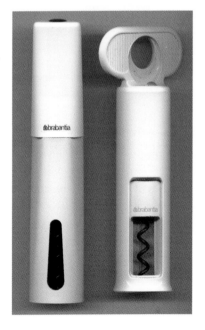

Left: **These versions of the very successful Screwpull are both marked 'Patented Screwpull® Pat. Pend.'** *Right:* **These two corkscrews, which are registered designs from Brabantia, are known as the 'Obelisque' (1995) and the 'Cork-mate' (1984). One of the problems that had to be solved for using these corkscrews is how to get the cork off the worm after extraction. The solution was to put linear grips inside the frames or barrels to hold the cork stationary whilst the worm is unscrewed. They can just be seen inside the frame of the brown Screwpull®.**

Left: 'Alessandro' is marked 'A. Mendini 2003 Alessi' and is available in a variety of colours and designs. *Right:* Betterware, the homeware company, produced this unmarked chef corkscrew.

the Screwpull®, and derivatives of it, are the most efficient corkscrews of all, as long as the cork is not well and truly stuck in the neck of the bottle. The Screwpull® was invented by Herb Allen; he went through numerous prototypes before coming up with the final designs, patenting them in 1981 and 1983. Somewhat sadly, but rightly, the patent was challenged by the Brabantia company. The challenge was successful and, as a result, generic versions of the Screwpull® rapidly came on to the market. They have certainly

allowed designers to demonstrate their creativity, and a wide variety of self-pullers became available, including figurals. The patent challenge was on the basis that the self-puller concept was not new; indeed, it goes back to John Loach's British patent of 1844 and Charles Chinnock's US patent of 1862. Allen's other inventive claim was for a worm that was coated with non-stick Teflon® so that the cork slipped easily up the worm. This claim was also discredited because this was seen as an obvious property of Teflon®.

British patent self-pullers. *Left:* This example of John Loach's British Patent No. 10,176 of 1844 is one of the most desirable corkscrews. It has an Archimedean worm hidden within the brass barrel and two spikes right at the top of it. The shank is free to move up and down in the neck, and the idea is that the cork is drawn as usual, climbing up the worm. It then gets impaled on the spikes and the action of turning the handle anticlockwise removes the worm from the cork. The badge on the barrel is marked 'Loach & Clarke's Patent'. Clarke was a partner with Loach in the manufacturing company. *Right:* The frame of this uncommon corkscrew is marked 'Handee' and the handle, shank and worm are separate from it. The corkscrew is derived from the 1901 British Patent No. 8,711 from Alfred Baumgarten of the USA. Surprisingly, he did not patent it in his own country.

These British self-pullers with brass frames are referred to as 'Preston's Improved Power Corkscrews' in Edward Preston's trade catalogue of about 1900. A version of the loop-handled one is also known with a short, half-length frame.

Left: Carl Blombach's 1897 British Patent No. 185 was registered three weeks earlier in Germany in December 1896. The arms of the frame are hinged to allow partial movement and to close over the worm when not in use to protect it. The arms are marked 'Express D.R.G.M. 70026 Made in Germany Engl. P. 815/97'. *Centre:* W. Sommers' German design was registered in 1897 and is marked on the handle 'D.R.G.M. 84075'. The corkscrew is often referred to as a 'duckbill'. *Right:* This unusual pocket corkscrew, found with a variety of markings, has a ring that can be swivelled through 90˚. The steel frame has a partial Bakelite insert between the two sides, and the ring can be slid up it to create a good partial puller. This example is marked 'Bonsa Registered', but it is also found marked 'D.R.G.M. 118056' for David Everts' German registration of 1899. Bonsa was the trade name of the exporters Böntgen and Sabin. A possibly earlier version (in which the sides are riveted together, without the Bakelite insert) is also known, marked 'Andree D.R.G.M. 118056'.

Self-pullers from the Willetts family of Birmingham, England. *Left:* This design registered by George Willetts in 1884 was very successful, judging by the number of these corkscrews that can be found. It is marked 'The Surprise' and 'Registered 13185'. *Centre:* A variation was registered by George Willetts' son, William Arthur in 1922, with a cap lifter at the end of the handle marked Reg. No. 692453. *Right:* A second related design from William Arthur Willetts, with a central cap lifter and eyebrow (Reg. No. 790035), was from 1934 and was advertised as having 'lugs for extra pulling power'.

Self-pullers with ball-bearings. The ball-bearings on top of the frame reduce friction between the handle and the frame. *Left:* This relatively common German self-puller is marked 'D.R.G.M. Monopol' from G. Usbeck's Registered Design No. 397282 of 1909. A similar design, but with the ball-bearings hidden, is named 'Solon' (D.R.G.M. 152004, from Ernst Scharff in 1901), and is shown on the box on the right. A British version is known as the 'Fagan'. *Centre:* A fancy version marked 'Monopol Universal D.R.G.M. Germany D. Peres Germany. *Right:* This very uncommon and early version of the Monopol marked 'D.R.G.M.' is also regarded as being from Usbeck's design of 1909. Rather than having ball-bearings to ease the friction, it has four small rollers, which are unique to this corkscrew.

Left: An unusual compact design in which the frame is also the handle. It is from the 1905 British patent of William Plant and is marked 'Plant's Patent Magic No. 12140' and 'Farrow Jackson' (the manufacturer). *Centre:* The 'Little Joker' is less effective as the base of the frame is only one third of the way down the worm. It is therefore not possible to lift a normal cork completely out of a bottle. This corkscrew was also made as 'The Pet'. *Right:* This uncommon German corkscrew is marked 'D.R.G.M.' and is from the 1897 Registered Design No. 90904 of G.H. Volkmar.

Self-pullers with a straight shank above the worm

The beauty of a full-length worm in a self-puller is that the cork climbs right up the worm. There were however, many self-pullers made with a shank above the worm and they are less effective. Either the extraction process is blocked part way or the cork is forced to split.

Above: One of the earliest descriptions of a self-puller was from Charles Chinnock in his US patent of 1862. *Left:* This example is marked 'Chinnock's Patent May 27, 1862'. The characteristic brass barrel has oval cut-outs so that, after extraction, the cork can be grasped for unscrewing the worm. British versions of this corkscrew usually have more curvaceous handles and more decorative barrels. Some are named 'Apollinaris', the trade name of a bottled water established in 1892. *Right:* This open-framed version of Chinnock's concept is British.

Above, Left: This sliding frame version of Edwin Wolverson's 'Signet' is not common and is marked with just a registration diamond for 1876. This example strays from the design drawing, although the Signet handle is the same. All examples seem to have an Archimedean worm. This feature makes it a very ineffective self-puller because the worm bores a hole through the cork and it does not climb up the helix. (No wonder they are uncommon.) *Right:* A rare German corkscrew from Louis Öhring's design registration of 1893 which is indistinctly marked 'D.R.G.M. 13585'. The legs are hinged to accommodate different sizes of bottle necks.

Above, Left: A German corkscrew marked 'Record' and 'D.R.G.M', based on Theodor Kampf's design of 1926, having a ball-bearing race (a groove or channel into which the ball-bearings fit) fixed to the sliding shank. *Centre:* An Italian self-puller that has a brass frame with detailed decoration. *Right:* An unmarked corkscrew, probably German, with a frame and ball-bearing race and a cap lifter handle.

Self-pullers with springs

As a worm is turned into a cork and the base of the frame hits the top of the bottle, an upward force can be applied to the cork by using an appropriately positioned spring. Emil Dunisch and Wilhelm Schoeler realized in their 1883 German patent D.R.P. 27175 that by putting a spring on the shank above the frame, this force would squash the spring and ultimately result in an extra upward pull on the cork. There are a host of variations of this basic concept.

The problem with using many self-puller corkscrews is how to get the cork off the worm after extraction, as mentioned for the Screwpull®. The German designers tackled this problem vigorously and came up with many solutions to get all, or part, of the impaled cork out of the frame or barrel, so that it could be grasped by the hand. Many of these corkscrews were either patented (DRP) or registered (DRGM).

Left: **This is one of the most common corkscrews to be found in antique markets, usually marked 'Hercules', although this less common example bears the patent number D.R.P. 27175 for the 1883 patent of Dunisch and Schoeler.** *Centre:* **A miniature perfume screw of the same style and a steel-handled version.** *Right:* **A 1950s white polyethylene plastic frame with a painted wooden handle, marked 'Foreign' on the shank.**

Left: **Rather than having the spring on the shank, Carl Ulrich's 1895 German registration had springs on the sides of the frame. This example is marked 'D.R.G.S.' on the top of the frame.**

Above: **Different types of spring.** *Left:* **The conical spring is fixed to the circular top of the frame of this unmarked corkscrew.** *Centre:* **This fancy corkscrew with models of children forming the steel frame has a volute or rolled spiral spring on the shank. Plain versions are named 'Germania' and collectors should be wary of examples that are not named.** *Right:* **This example has a concealed spring inside the long neck of the frame and is marked 'Gesetzl. Geschützt' from C.Ch. Neues' German registration of 1893.**

Self-pullers with split frames

Above: The 'Columbus' corkscrew was patented in Germany in 1893 by Eduard Becker. It may have been given the name to commemorate the 400th anniversary of the great adventurer's voyage in 1492, or as a promotional aid in connection with the 1893 Chicago World Fair, which had the Columbus anniversary as the theme. *Left:* The Columbus is characterized by having a hinged split frame held together by a steel ring. When the frame is opened, the cork can be grasped and removed from the worm. There is a spring on the shank and the shoulder of the frame is marked 'Columbus' on one side and 'D.R. Patent No. 70879' on the other. *Centre:* This smaller-sized version with a bone handle is marked exactly the same as its big brother. *Right:* It is much rarer to find the fancy version, which on this example is marked 'Columbus' on one side and 'D.R.P. No. 70879'.

Below: There are many variations on the Columbus theme and they are found named 'Original', 'Original Bacchus', and 'Gerveo Traube', as well as unmarked examples and some with decorated frames. *Left:* One side of the frame is stamped 'D.R.G.M. 354,940' and refers to Gustav Twellsiek's 1908 German registration for making the split frame from sheet metal. *Right:* The Monopol 117 has a ball-bearing race on the neck of the frame and a full-length worm to create an effective self-puller. This is G. Usbeck's 1909 registration, DRGM 405,690.

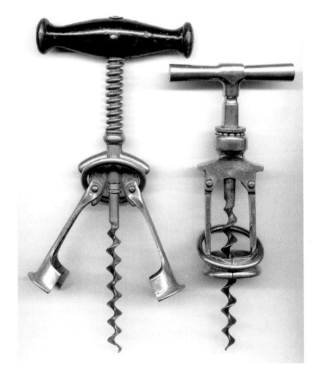

Self-pullers with locking devices

Left: The wooden handle is lightly marked 'D.R.G.M. 114369' for W. Sommers' German design of 1899. The spring frame is free to slide up and down the shank but can be locked in position for screwing the worm into the cork, using a type of 'paper clip' with a pin that passes through a hole through the shank. *Centre:* This is an unmarked example of D.R.G.M. 596751 from 1914 although the registrant's name, Gotlieb Giessler, is written under the handle. The spiral on the shank can 'climb' up and down the shank on a small pin that can be seen part way down it. The advertising is for Lauchstädter Mineralbrunnen. *Right:* The marking 'D.R.G.M. 152293' on the handle shows that this is Johan Wolters' design from 1901. The half sleeve is hinged to the shank and can be folded down flat to it. This allows the upper collar to be pushed down on to the top of the spring frame before inserting the worm into the cork.

Bottom, Left: The sleeve on the shank has a bayonet-type lock to fix it in the 'down' position. The spring frame can then be released to remove the worm from the cork. Although unmarked, this is a version of Georg Giessler's design, D.R.G.M. 96377 of 1898. *Centre:* The sleeve of this example is fixed to the spring frame and has two spiral slots with bayonet ends. The concept was registered by Richard Recknagel in D.R.G.M. 109374 in 1899. *Right:* Thanks to two slots on the base of the neck, the steel barrel can be locked in the 'down' position or released. It is named 'Neue Hercules mit Kork Austosser' ('with cork expeller'), marked 'D.R.G.M. GERMANY' and is derived from D.R.G.M. 1246839 of 1933 from Georg Usbeck. An export version is known as the 'Bacchus' and has a cap lifter slot cut into the barrel.

Left: An unmarked example of D.R.G.M. 184844 from Georg Usbeck in 1902, which was for the two U-shaped hooks that fit over the top of the frame to lock it in place. *Centre:* A crossbar on the shank is free to swivel and locks into slots on the upper part of the sides of the frame. It is marked 'D.R.G.M.' but the registration has not been identified for certain. *Right:* It is hard to see in the picture, but there is an 'umbrella-style' clip on the shank, which locks the frame in the 'down' position. There is a ball-bearing race above the frame and it is marked 'D.R.G.M.' for the 1934 registered design from the widow of Adolf Menz.

Left: The frame on this uncommon corkscrew is marked 'Meteor D.R.G.M. 263041' for the 1905 design of Louis Kummer. The sleeve round the shank contains a spring to assist the removal of the cork and a slot that allows it to be locked in the 'up' position for screwing the worm in. *Right:* Although not visible in the picture, the ring of the frame is not complete and this allows the frame to be swung out of the way to remove the cork from the worm. This example is marked 'D.R.G.M. No 206878' for the 1903 design of Wilhelm Neues.

Self-pullers with bells

Whilst frames and springs were being used in Europe, the Americans came up with a different concept known as the 'bell'. In 1883, William Bennit conceived a small inverted cup or bell, fixed to the shank above the worm. It works in a similar way to Henshall's button in that it eases the cork once the bell hits the top of the bottle. The advantage is that, being hollow, there is room for the cork to be drawn up into the bell and be partially removed. There are numerous American bells to collect, from the fairly common mass-produced corkscrews of Edwin Walker and William Williamson to the rare patents. The handles often carry advertising for beers, drinks and other goods. It was only later that the Europeans also started using bells, and there are few examples.

American bells. *Left to right:* **The first American patent for a bell was from William Bennit and the corkscrew is marked 'Pat. May 15th 1883'. Versions are also known marked 'Magic Corkscrew'. The next example uses the design of Thomas Strait (patented just one month after Bennit's design), who invented a conical bell that was threaded to the shank. The bottom of the bell has a slightly sharp edge designed to cut wires. It is not exactly clear why it has the threaded shank – perhaps so that you can screw the bell upwards and free the cork after extraction. It is marked on the bell 'Pat. June 12, 83.' Thomas Curley also had a solution for freeing the cork by using a left-handed spiral slot in the neck of the bell. The bell could be released by a left-handed twist. His corkscrew is marked on the steel band round the handle 'Pat. Apr. 22, 1884 T. Curley, Troy, N.Y.' There are several Curley variations and collectors will pay top prices for them. The fourth US patent for a bell was from Charles Griswold for a bell with a long neck that is free to slide on the shank. The construction seems to serve no purpose as the long neck is pushed up hard against the handle during cork extraction. This example is not marked but some have the patent date (July 22, 1884) stamped lightly on the handle.**

Walker bells. *Left:* **Edwin Walker's patent number 501,975 of 1893 was his first of three for bells. This is an unmarked example, with a blunt knife edge to the base of the bell and the wooden handle fixed by a pin through the end. These are features that help to identify Walker corkscrews, the knife edge apparently being for cutting wires.** *Centre:* **Walker's second patent number 579,200 of 1897 added a wire cutter spike to the bell. Examples tend not to be marked and this one is named 'Champion' on the shank.** *Right:* **With the advent of the crown cap in 1892 and its success in subsequent years, Walker introduced a cap lifter hook to his bell. This example is marked under the handle 'Walker's Patents – Do Not Pull – Turn Cork Out', with advertising on the handle. It is an example of his third patent number 647,775 of 1900. Examples can be found with handles made of silver, bone, or huge tusks, sometimes carved or with silver end pieces.**

Williamson bells. *Left:* William Williamson was a great rival of Edwin Walker and eventually bought his factory after Walker's death. Williamson's first patent for a bell was in 1897, number 587,900, with the key innovations being a small washer between the top of the bell and the 'stop' above it; either a sleeve round the shank or a split pin. This example has the pin through the front of the handle and a flat edge to the bottom of the bell. Markings under the handle state 'Need Not Pull – Keep Turning.' These features are typical of Williamson. It is also indistinctly stamped on the end of the handle with Williamson's details and promotes 'Pabst Milwaukee'. *Centre:* Williamson's patent drawing also showed the addition of a steel-plated wire cutter and cap lifter hook above the bell. This example is stamped 'Williamson's' down the shank and 'Williamson Co. Newark N.J. Patented Aug. 10 '97.' *Right:* The Williamson Novelty Company eventually became part of ETAMCO and this corkscrew is the last of the 'Williamson' bells. ETAMCO Industries was granted a design patent in 1976 for this double cap lifter bell, which is marked 'Pat. Pend.' on the shank.

Right: **European bells.** *Left:* This bell has a hole in it and is marked 'Caplifter' above it. It has the look of a 1930s German corkscrew, but could be British. *Centre:* The markings, 'L'Hercule B^{te} S.G.D.G.', impressed into the handle show that this is a French corkscrew. It is from the late twentieth century and the plastic handle is mainly red but with a white core. *Right:* This silver-plated corkscrew with a fixed conical bell is from the early twentieth century and is stamped 'Dixon' plus a trademark. James Dixon & Sons was one of the biggest Sheffield cutlery manufacturers, known for their plated wares. The trademark shown on the corkscrew was granted in 1890.

Left: This small British corkscrew with a cap lifter handle was promoted as the 'Power corkscrew, self-pulling corkscrew with cap remover'. It has a flat base to the bell, typical of Williamson corkscrews. Examples often have a wooden sheath over the worm, which makes it more comfortable when using it as a cap lifter, but the covers often got lost. *Centre:* This delightful German corkscrew is an example of D.R.G.M. 6050 from Eduard Müller in 1892. It was marketed as the 'Viktoria' and it is rare to find a marked one. *Right:* This 1894 German design, D.R.G.M. 35052, is from Wilhelm von zur Gathen and promotes Küpper Bier. The worm and the bell, with its two cap lifter slots, fold out of the handle for use.

MECHANICAL CORKSCREWS

Most corkscrew collectors have a fascination for mechanical corkscrews. Beginners have ambitions to own a Thomason, a King's Screw, a Perpetual, a Farrow & Jackson and others. Established collectors will probably have examples of these but will always find a new variation, or a twist to a well-known concept, or have their ears open for rumours of a rare patent turning up somewhere.

This section on mechanical corkscrews includes items in which the mechanisms provide a mechanical advantage to the withdrawal of the cork. They nearly always have screw threads and a cunning device to convert rotary motion into a vertical lift for removing the cork from the bottle. These devices include fly nuts, wing nuts and crab pieces. There are also a few examples included that do not provide any mechani-

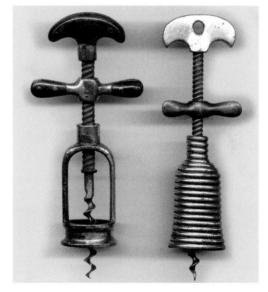

Free fly nut

Left to right: The corkscrew has a three-winged free fly nut, although the third one is hardly visible in the picture. The three-wing fly nut is very characteristic of French corkscrews. There are a variety of top handle types to collect, such as this cap lifter version; this example is unmarked. The next example is a classic French piece named 'Aero' on the fly nut and marked with Jacque Pérille's 'J-P' logo on the frame. The 'Le Français' corkscrew is different in having a very wide and deep thread on the shaft. Most of the plating on the fly nut has worn off from use showing the brass underneath. It is marked 'BF Déposé', probably for Baptiste Fedrici. The next example is an unmarked but upmarket version of the Aero with horn dressings to the handles. It is German, was probably made by the Monopol firm and was also made in a bone or ivory version. The coiled wire bee-hive barrel of the last corkscrew gives no mechanical advantage, only aesthetic pleasure. It is stamped with Boué-Deveson's logo of JB in a multi-pointed star.

cal advantage but still convert one motion into another, such as direct pressure or ratchet mechanisms. I have not followed the SCReWcode© classifications exactly, but discuss them by basic structure. *Mechanical Corkscrews* by Ferd Peters is highly recommended to fill in the multitude of details that cannot be covered here.

It should be noted that three other chapters in this book (Chapters 6, 7 and 10) also include pieces with varying degrees of mechanical advantage.

Free fly nut

This is a particularly French genre, although there are good British and Italian examples. They all have a top handle on a right-hand threaded shaft with a lower handle, the free fly nut, which rides on the threaded shaft. The fly nut is a nut with flat side wings. The worm is screwed into the cork with the top handle and then the free fly nut is turned whilst sitting on top of the frame. When the free fly handle meets the unthreaded frame, turning this handle clockwise causes the shaft to rise and pull the cork.

Fixed fly or wing nut and top handle

The free fly nut concept described is a very successful mechanism, and works because the fly nut acts on the top of the neck of the frame. There is no real advan-

Above, left: **Known as a 'coffee grinder', this Italian corkscrew has a modified fly nut to act as a crank handle and enhance the mechanical advantage. Turning the handle clockwise causes the shaft to rise and pull the cork. Collectors should be aware that there are fake versions of these corkscrews. There are also late-twentieth-century versions that are attractive but show little signs of age.** *Right:* **This most desirable French corkscrew has a frame that can pivot and swing out of the way to make it easy to remove the cork from the worm. It is stamped 'J. Pérille Bte S.G.D.G.' for the 1931 Patent No. 715,085 of Estienne Bizet. It was marketed as 'A Déclenche'.**

Below: **In a field populated by continental corkscrews, it is surprising that the British made few examples.** *Left:* **This corkscrew marked 'The Victor' has a bronze wash finish. Examples sometimes promote 'The Athenaeum, Birmingham'.** *Right:* **The heavy brass frame of this example strongly suggests that it is an Italian corkscrew.**

This fine English example carries the Thomason badge marked 'Thomason Patent Ne Plus Ultra'. This refers to the 1802 British Patent No. 2,617 of Edward Thomason, which lists a number of variations. This has a bronze barrel and a varnished wooden handle that is not attached to the barrel. At a first glance this looks like a Thomason variant, described later, but the handle is effectively a free fly nut.

tage in having the fly nut attached to the neck of the frame, but some manufacturers tried it. Wing nuts, with raised side wings, were also fixed to the frame. There are relatively few examples of fixed nuts, but the 'Hélice' is the most quintessential French corkscrew of them all.

Fixed wing nut without top handle

Some very high quality nineteenth-century British corkscrews have a double wing nut that is fixed to the

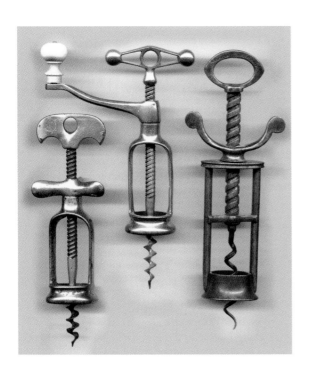

Left: Pérille's 'Hélice' has a triple-wing fly nut that is fixed to the frame but can rotate (the third wing can only just be seen in the picture). The example shown is marked 'J. Pérille Déposé Paris' on one side of the handle and 'Hélice J-P Déposé' on the other. It was described in Jacques Pérille's 1876 Patent No. 112,465. *Centre:* Pérille modified the design to turn it into a very elegant 'coffee grinder', which is highly prized with its bone topped winding handle. It is marked 'Déposé J-P Paris' and sold under the name 'à Manivelle'. High-quality reproductions of this corkscrew have been made but with ugly modern worms. *Right:* This unmistakable British example has a lovely patinated steel construction and an elegant wing nut fixed to the frame. The top handle is stamped for the retailer 'B.B. Wells 431 West Strand' (in London).

frame but can rotate. There are, however, two subtle variations: ones with a left-hand thread shaft and those with a right-hand thread.

Those with a right-hand thread are probably earlier in design but harder to use. Examples shown in early catalogues (*see* Giulian) are right-handed. To use one of these corkscrews, the cross-bar or plate that slides up and down the frame has to be at the bottom of the frame before inserting the worm. It is impossible to insert the worm clockwise by holding the wing nut handles because that just pulls the cross-bar up the frame. The whole frame has to be held in your hand to screw the worm into the cork. Only then can the wing nut handle be used in an anticlockwise sense to withdraw the cork.

The left-hand threaded versions are much easier to use because the cross-bar can be screwed right down and the worm inserted into the cork using the wing nut handles. Turning the wing nut anticlockwise will then remove the cork.

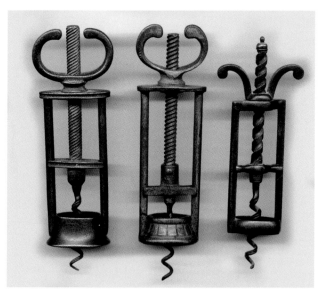

Right-hand thread

Left: With its curved handle, this corkscrew from the second half of the nineteenth century must have been quite popular as there are a reasonable number around for the patient collector. It is, however, rare to find them marked. *Centre:* This example is probably from around 1900 and has a decorative skirt and remains of its bronze wash finish. The skirt and the pillars are cast in one piece unlike the earlier versions where the pillars are riveted to the lower ring. *Right:* This elegant British steel corkscrew is from about 1800 and once had a sheath that screwed on to the thread above the worm. Examples like this are not common.

Left-hand thread

Left: This is one of the classic British corkscrews and is usually referred to as a 'Farrow & Jackson' because examples appeared in their catalogue from around 1870. However, a catalogue of Charles Hull from the period 1860–65 also shows the design. The example shown is marked 'Farrow & Jackson Ltd' on the wing nut and they can also be found marked 'FJ' or 'Farrow & Jackson London & Paris', and even more opportunistically, 'Patent App. For'. Marked examples are fairly uncommon. They are usually plain brass or occasionally plated. *Centre:* One of the handles of this patinated steel corkscrew is stamped 'Farrow' and is obviously from an earlier date. *Right:* With a bladed worm and heavy brass construction, this is probably an Italian version.

Locking fly nut and related mechanisms with right-hand threaded shafts

The concept described earlier of having a top handle and a free fly nut can be simplified by combining the functions of the top handle, which drives in the worm, with a fly nut that draws out the cork. Mechanically and design-wise these corkscrews are much more complex and some inventors have gone to extreme lengths to create new locking and unlocking mechanisms.

Left: **One of the most common locking devices, the 'heavy nose', was patented in Germany by Heinrich Ehrhardt in 1891, Patent No. 60,662. The collar swivels round the cylindrical handle and, in the locked position, the top of the threaded shaft butts up against it. As the worm is inserted into the cork, the 'heavy nose' hits the neck of the frame and is swivelled so that a hole in the collar allows the threaded shaft to pass through it. Continued clockwise turning withdraws the cork. This steel example is stamped 'J.A. Henckels, Solingen' with their 'twins' trademark.** *Right:* **This heavily constructed corkscrew, shown in the locked position, is marked 'Cyclope 243', and was shown in a 1928 Pérille catalogue.**

They all have a right-hand threaded shaft with a free-floating threaded handle that can be locked to the top of the shaft. To insert the worm, the handle is locked. Once the worm is completely inserted into the cork, the handle is either automatically or manually unlocked as it hits the top of the frame. Further clockwise turning pulls the cork.

Before the invention of the automatically deployed 'heavy nose', similar corkscrews were fitted with a 'swivel-over collar'. The collar on the handle can swivel through 90 degrees to lock or unlock the handle.

Left: **This decorative brass corkscrew with a 'heavy nose' is probably German from the mid twentieth century.** *Right:* **The 'heavy nose' construction is still being developed as shown by the 1993 registered design from Y & H Industrial Ltd, Hong Kong. The novel feature of this plastic frame corkscrew is that the 'heavy nose' is spring-loaded and automatically locks on to the top of the shaft.**

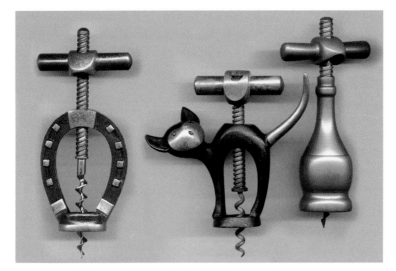

Figural versions of the 'heavy nose' mechanism have also been made, as illustrated by the lucky horseshoe, cat, and Chianti bottle. These are from the second half of the twentieth century and the bottle is Italian.

Below, left: The American version of the Challenge is marked 'R. Murphy Boston'. *Right:* This aluminium corkscrew is named 'Korkmaster JR'. It was made by the same company as the Korkmaster rack and pinion corkscrew, the subject of McDowell's 1948 US patent described later (*see* page 156).

Above, left: Perhaps the best-known British example with a 'swivel-over collar' is 'The Challenge'. It has an identical frame to the 'Victor' described earlier (*see* page 137). Occasionally the manufacturers made mistakes in assembly and the real collector 'nerds' will treasure examples with the wrong name on them. *Centre:* This is an elegant Italian version with a black composite handle and a brass frame with decorated skirt, which was once plated. *Right:* Jacques Pérille patented the 'swivel-over collar' in France in 1884 in Patent No. 160,949. The production model is marked 'Bague J-P' and has a characteristic hanging ring which also helps to swivel the collar.

Other locking devices

Left: This British corkscrew is named 'Wulfruna', which is the old name for Wolverhampton where the manufacturing firm of W. & J. Plant was based. The other side is marked 'Plant's Patent No. 5549' for the 1884 patent of Stephen Plant. The top of the handle has a keyhole-shaped hole and a slot in which a steel plate can slide to lock the handle to the threaded shaft, using the protruding screw head. Later models, which are not marked, do not have the screw head for moving the plate; they have a much more elegant and simple L-shaped plate. Examples are found with a bronze wash as shown, or plated. Some are marked with a retailer's name such as Farrow & Jackson. *Centre:* The plated corkscrew with a locking handle is marked 'Jdeal' (Ideal) and derives from Otto Voigt's German 1895 Registered Design No. 36,019. In this design, the handle is locked to the threaded shaft by screwing

in a pin down the centre of the handle. The German registration also covered a rubber ring in the base of the frame to protect the bottle neck. In many examples this has petrified or is missing. The corkscrew was also patented in France in 1895 (No. 244,993) and in Britain in 1897 (Number 201). *Right:* There are three versions of the Bodega, which has characteristic hinged handles curving upwards. They are marked 'Bodega 1', 'Bodega 2' and 'Bodega 3'. Versions 1 and 2 are very similar in size and the differences are very small; however, version 3 is larger. Some examples are also marked 'D.R.P. N° 113367' for Ernst Scharff's 1899 German patent. The inside ends of the heavy handles automatically cover the top of the threaded shaft and lock it for insertion into the cork. When they hit the top of the frame they are forced upwards and allow the shaft to pass between them and raise the cork. The concept was also patented in Britain in 1900, No. 113,367.

Left: Etienne de Gounevitch filed a patent for a very complicated handle locking device in France in 1912, Patent No. 447,625. The handle can be locked to the shaft as the worm is screwed into the cork. Then, the small lever down the side of the neck of the handle hits the top of the frame, is forced outwards and unlocks the handle to allow the threaded shaft to rise up inside the neck of the handle. The corkscrew was also patented in England and Germany in 1912 but it never caught on and examples are hard to find. *Right:* In this uncommon German corkscrew, the worm is first inserted into the cork and then the small lug at the base of the handle assembly is pushed outwards by the bevelled top of the frame. This unlocks the handle from the threaded shaft and further turning pulls the cork upwards. The example is marked 'Graef and Schmidt Germany 107' and is from Theodor Kämpf's 1930 German Patent No. 545,647.

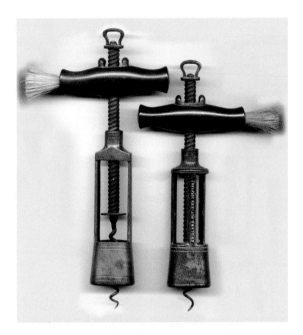 

George Twigg's 1867 British Patent No. 2,851 described a mechanism for locking the handle to the threaded shaft by means of a swivel catch on the top. Three versions of this classic corkscrew are known. *Left:* This bronze example has a wooden handle that glides along the thread and has two pillars to the frame marked 'G. Twigg's Patent' on both sides. *Second left:* The three-pillar version is made of steel and bears the markings 'G. Twigg's Patent – England October 10th 1867 – U.S. America Jany 21st 1868'. *Third left:* The steel-handled version is probably the most common and is marked on the frame 'Twigg's Patent – England October 10th 1867 – U.S. America Jany 21st 1868'. It has a bronze wash finish. *Right:* Hyde Bateman patented another solution to locking the handle a year earlier than Twigg in December 1866, British Patent No. 3,162. He introduced a small swivel plate that covers up the top hole in the handle. Examples are rare, probably because so much pressure is put on the pin that holds the plate that many were damaged. The frame is marked 'H. Bateman's Patent' on both sides.

Whilst slightly different from the above examples, Wilber Woodman's US Patent No. 344,556 from June 1886 used a similar principle of locking the handle whilst inserting the worm into the cork and then unlocking it for extraction. To lock the worm and handle, the steel ring is hooked over a small spur on the handle, and the whole unit can then be screwed into the cork. Then, by releasing the hook, continued turning removes the cork. 'Woodman's Patent' is cast into the handle and on the other side, the *wrong* patent date ('Patd Jan.y 6. 1886').

Fixed handles to left-hand threaded shafts

The concept of a fixed handle and a left-hand threaded shaft is good, but anyone who tries to use a Mabson soon realizes the problem that has to be solved to make this type of corkscrew effective. By screwing the worm into the cork, the base of the barrel or frame hits the top of the bottle neck and further right hand turning withdraws the cork. This procedure only works if the barrel or frame can be prevented from sliding down the threaded shaft.

Left: John Mabson's 1869 British Patent No. 527 described a number of mechanisms of which only one seems to have been manufactured. The early example shown is very difficult to use and the neck of the barrel has to be grasped at the same time as turning the worm into the cork. It is marked 'Mabson's Patent Sole Maker James Heeley & Sons'. It has a disc inside the barrel to keep the worm centralized. *Right:* The more common example also has an internal disc, usually marked 'T. Dowler Manufacturer Birmingham'. Dowler added three springs, fixed into corresponding slots in the disc, which press against the inside of the barrel to stop it slipping. This creates an effective corkscrew. Examples often have one or more of the springs missing, as can be seen by 'empty' slots.

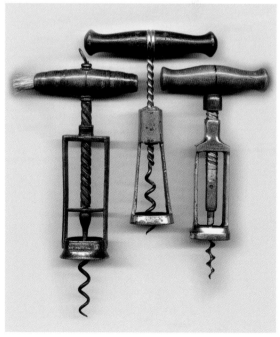

Left: This English example is marked 'Underwood' on the skirt for the retailer and is from the early nineteenth century. The action is good because the cross-bar grips the frame quite tightly, the threaded shaft is stiff in the neck and so the frame does not slip. *Centre:* This American corkscrew is known as the 'Power Cone' and is marked on one of the wires round the handle 'Patented Feb 1 1876'. This refers to William Clough's 1876 US Patent No. 172,868, which was acquired by Cornelius T. Williamson. The left-hand twisted wire shank acts through a plug of lead, which was poured in when molten into the centre of the neck. It is a nice idea, but lead creates a very slippery surface and the frame slides down easily. *Right:* Another problem of these left-hand threaded shaft corkscrews is that the cork is twisted as it is pulled out of the bottle, rather than being pulled straight. This French corkscrew, marked 'Déposé Perfect Automatique', solves this by having a clutch mechanism in the lower part of the shaft that disengages the worm when an upward force is applied. This mechanism is often broken.

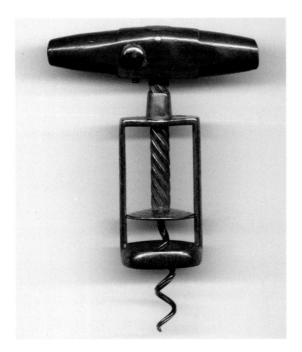
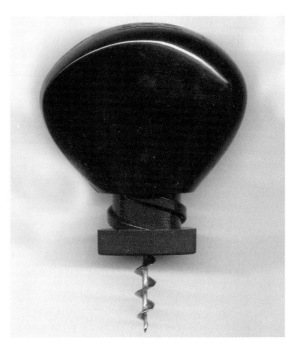

Left: The first British corkscrew patent, Samuel Henshall's Patent No. 2,061 of August 1795, described his very successful button (as covered in Chapter 5). It is often forgotten however, that the patent also covered a mechanical corkscrew, of which very few examples exist. The handle is locked on to the top of the frame by a small catch, which can be released using the steel button. Above the worm is the typical Henshall button marked 'Obstando Promoves Soho Patent'. *Right:* The 'Sieger 600' is a very effective corkscrew and the plastic handle and threaded shaft are held in place using an internal spring. The concept was patented in Germany by Gunther Pracht in 1983 (Patent No. 3,346,414C1) and in the USA in 1986.

The ultimate way of solving the awkwardness of having a left-hand threaded shaft, and consequential slipping and sliding of the frame, is to separate the threaded shaft and the worm. The first patent for this idea was from Jean Picard in his 1875 French Patent No. 106,849. There are very few examples of his corkscrew known and they look unwieldy to use. *Left:* A much simplified design, and one that has been copied in many guises, is faintly marked 'The Club, Made in France'. This boxwood corkscrew is probably from the late nineteenth century. *Right:* A mid-twentieth-century painted wood version advertising Burrough's Beefeater London Dry Gin, with Australian and South African sherry on the back. In the USA this type of corkscrew is often referred to by the Copex brand name, introduced in 1945.

There are countless examples to collect with advertising and with decorative and carved barrels, made in a variety of materials. *Left:* A shiny moulded plastic example. *Right:* A chunky plated Italian example with open four-pillar frame, marked 'Brevettato'.

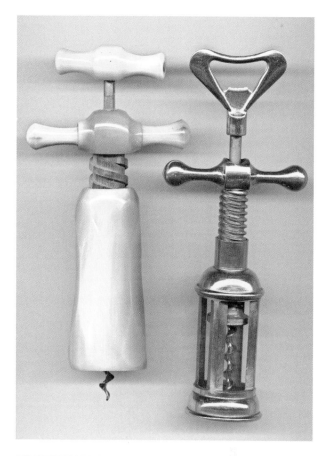

The 'Valezina' corkscrew works on the same principle. It was made of aluminium with anodized coloured finishes in red, blue, silver or gold. The bases of the threaded inner section are variously marked, including: 'Made in England Reg. Design No. 857383' and 'Canadian R.D. No. 112-17645'. These details relate to the 1949 British registered design of John Bagwell-Purefoy and the 1950 Canadian Industrial Design. The German registered design number D.R.G.M. 1,614,301 was obtained in 1950. The instruction leaflet in the box describes it as 'The Valezina "Butterfly" Corkscrew': 'VALEZINA is the name of a beautiful variety of the English Butterfly – the Silver Washed Fritillary – and this picturesque name has been chosen for the most colourful and efficient variety of the common corkscrew yet produced. The VALEZINA is an up to date version of the old wooden corkscrews used in France since wine was first bottled. The Masters who designed it found this the ideal way in which to withdraw a cork without in anyway disturbing the sediment.'

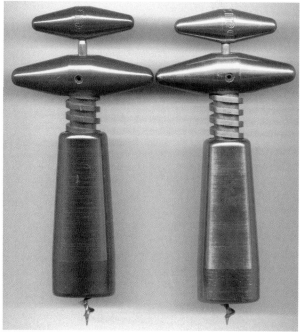

Fixed handles to right-hand threaded shafts

In one of the early British patents, No. 1,811 of 1854, John Coney described a right-hand threaded shaft with a clutch mechanism above the worm, which engaged the handle, shaft and worm for the insertion phase, and then disengaged for the upward pull to prevent the cork twisting. This uncommon example is stamped on the steel skirt with a crown plus 'VR Patent' ('VR' referring to Victoria Regina).

Below right: Several interesting British corkscrews follow the Coney concept and solve the cork-twisting problem in different ways. *Left:* The steel corkscrew with bone handle is unmarked, but the swelling above the cross-bar hides a Coney-type clutch. *Right:* This handsome British corkscrew has a mahogany handle and a brass frame and shaft. The brass button, which is firmly fixed to the worm, rides up and down the sides of the frame but is only loosely connected to the shaft. The shaft is free to turn but does not turn the button.

Left: This French corkscrew is marked on the nickel plated brass button 'L'Excelsior A.G. Bte S.G.D.G. Paris' and is the 1880 French Patent No. 138,887 of Armand Guichard. Bone-handled versions are also known. *Right:* German catalogues in the 1920s showed this style of corkscrew. This example is marked 'Charles Lueftner Prague', although many are unmarked.

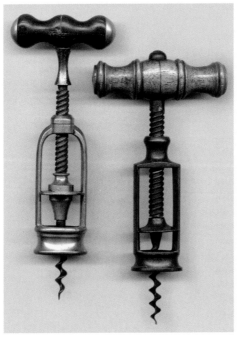

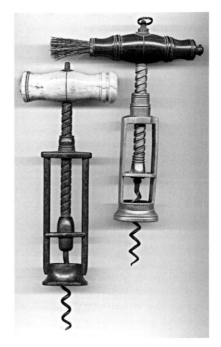

Corkscrews working on this principle are relatively common in Italy and are usually of very heavy construction. They often have Archimedean worms. *Left:* The steel handle is stamped 'Sighicelli'. *Right:* This unmarked corkscrew weighs a massive 340g (¾lb).

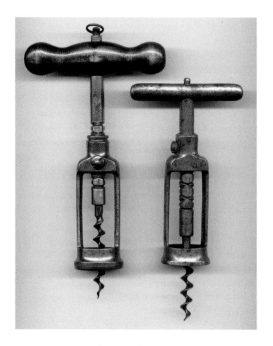

Perpetual corkscrews

These German corkscrews have a very cleverly designed cross-over thread on the shank; one being right handed and one left handed. The worm is turned into the cork by turning the handle clockwise as usual, but at the end of the thread, a small swivelling pin flips over to the left-hand thread so that continued clockwise turning pulls the cork upwards. The pins get worn with repeated use and they can sometimes be accessed via a screw on the front of the frame *(left)* or the side of the neck *(right)*. Some quite elegant German versions were made with ornate barrels.

Edwin Cotterill's registered design of 1842 is one of the 'Great British Corkscrews'. The corkscrew is heavy and solid with an ebony handle and a brass barrel with a large badge surmounted by the Royal Coat of Arms. The badge states 'Edwin Cotterill's – Patent – Self-Adjusting'. Inside the long brass neck, the steel shank has cross-over threads as found in the later 'Perpetual'-style corkscrew. Turning the handle clockwise produces both up and down movement due to a clever clutch mechanism, which disengages the worm on the 'up' part of the sequence. Inside the barrel there is also a button with two small pointed studs that engage the cork. These hold it whilst the worm is removed by turning the handle anticlockwise after extraction. It is a complicated but extremely well made and elegant machine.

Threaded sleeve that interlocks with the handle

The French 'Diamant' is the most common example of this limited, but cleverly designed type of corkscrew. *Left and centre:* The two versions with metal and wooden handles show the plain shank above the worm, which slides freely through the long neck of the frame. The neck itself has a left-handed thread and a threaded sleeve rides on it. To use these corkscrews, the sleeve is turned to its lowest position and the worm is screwed into the cork. There are two small claws underneath the handle and when these catch on to corresponding ones on the top of the sleeve, continued clockwise turning lifts the sleeve on its thread upwards, thus withdrawing the cork. The frames are marked 'Diamant J-P Paris B^te S.G.D.G. 24 Oct 1887'. The mechanism is another of Jacques Pérille's inventions, Patent No. 186,560, and examples were also made with a bone handle with nickel end caps. *Right:* This early version of the Diamant is unmarked and has lost most of its original plating.

Below, left: This is a complex corkscrew but works on a similar principle. It has a free moving sleeve with a left-hand threaded slot cut into it. This rides on a pin through the back of the frame. As the worm is inserted into the cork, two small claws under the handle engage with ones on the top of the sleeve and twist it. Continued turning withdraws the cork. An added feature to this design is four cork grips at the bottom of the sleeve. The example is marked 'R.G.M.' (should be D.R.G.M.) for the 1904 German registered design by Louis Kummer. It

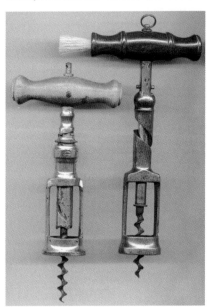

was marketed as the 'Mauser'. *Centre:* This more simple design has a collar above the frame with a long sloping face that is a partial left-hand thread. The free sliding sleeve above it has a matching face and the two engage once the worm has been screwed into the cork to create an upward pull. This concept is sometimes referred to as a 'snail face', though it does not look like any snails I know! The frame is marked 'D.R. Patent FK' for Friedrich Kummer's 1880 German Patent No. 14,531. *Right:* This example is a well-constructed modern corkscrew working on the same principle with two multi-toothed rings to lock the plain shaft to the left-hand threaded sleeve. It is marked on the handle 'Etain' (pewter), suggesting a French origin.

Right, left: The first example of a crab piece was in Twigg and Bateman's 1868 British Patent No. 956. This fine example has a bronze frame and crab piece that locks on to the neck of the frame with the two lugs. The frame is marked 'G. Twigg's Patent' on both sides. The corkscrew is also known with a bronze-washed steel frame. *Right:* This is marked 'The King' and 'Patent 6064', for the 1904 British Patent of Frederick Sunderland, trading as Coney and Company, and John Cox. This example has a brass frame but it was also made in bronze-washed and plated steel.

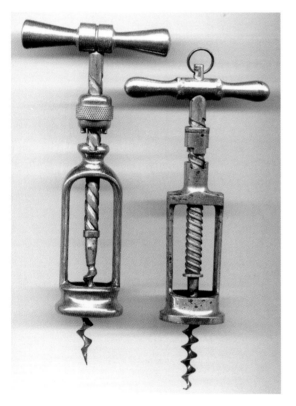

Above, left: this French corkscrew is marked 'L'Extract J-P Paris' and is an example of the 1877 Patent No. 112,465 of Jacques Pérille. Unusually for Pérille, it is a poor design, because the crab piece is so heavy and loosely fitting that it will not stay at the top of the shaft – it runs down the thread and stops the worm entering all the way into the cork. *Right:* With a much lighter crab piece and shallower-pitched thread, this unmarked French corkscrew is much more user-friendly.

Crab pieces

A 'crab piece' is a threaded collar that rides on a left-hand threaded shaft. The action starts with the crab piece at the top of the shaft and when it comes into contact with the top of the frame, it locks, and further clockwise turning causes the shaft to rise and pull the cork.

Thomasons

Thomason corkscrews are among the most desirable and elegant corkscrews and are highly appreciated by both collectors and non-collectors, who can all see that these are objects of quality and beauty.

Edward Thomason of Birmingham obtained the second British patent for corkscrews, Patent No. 2,617 in 1802. This shows a corkscrew with two shafts and a complex but elegant, well-engineered mechanism. The inner shaft is right-hand threaded and fixed to a right-threaded worm – turning this shaft clockwise inserts the worm. The outer shaft is right-threaded on the inside and left-threaded on the outside (a hermaphrodite shaft). Once the inner shaft is all the way into the outer shaft, further clockwise turning causes the outer shaft to rise and pull the cork.

Thomasons were very popular corkscrews in the nineteenth century and are quite easy to come by. The most highly prized are obviously Thomason corkscrews carrying the Thomason badge, stating 'Thomasons Patent' and his logo 'Ne Plus Ultra' ('none better'). The badge also carries the Royal Coat of Arms, with lion and unicorn and motto 'Dieu et mon Droit', and the motto of the Order of the Garter 'Honi Soit qui Mal y Pense' (Thomason was knighted in 1832). The patent describes a number of variations (*see* Wallis), and a few examples are shown here. Many other manufacturers made these with their own badges after the patent expired, including Coney, Cotterill, Dowler, Heeley, Rodgers, and Wilmot & Roberts; these are all very collectable. You should

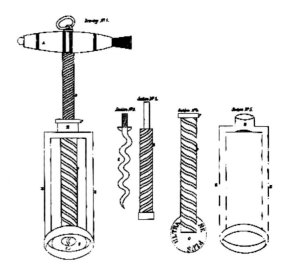

Patent drawings from the 1802 British Patent No. 2,617 of Edward Thomason.

make sure the badge is original and hasn't been soldered on recently to an unmarked barrel, changing the patina of the barrel. However, it may have dropped off and been replaced.

Thomasons

Left: This is a basic Thomason with a bronze barrel with the Thomason badge and 'Ne Plus Ultra' motto. *Right:* This bronze barrel is cut away to give four supports and 'windows' – this is known as 'fenestration'. The barrel is not marked but the button at the bottom of the brass outer shaft is marked 'Thomason Pt Ne Plus Ultra'. Variations can be found with differing numbers of windows or with pillars.

Thomasons with decorative bronze or brass barrels are highly prized. There are variations of both these designs. Some more recent examples are made of much thinner brass and are poorly cast, so the collector needs to consider the balance between price and quality. *Left:* The 'Autumn Fruits' design in impressed bronze with grapes on the front, and with 'Improved Patent' on the back amongst foliage and ears of wheat. *Right:* The 'Gothic Windows' or 'Cathedral Windows' design in impressed bronze.

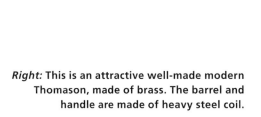

Above, left: A fine, rare, bronze example with the Thomason badge and a simple impressed 'Grapes' design on both the front and back. *Right:* A rare lacquered or japanned example with golden grapes and vine leaves on a black background.

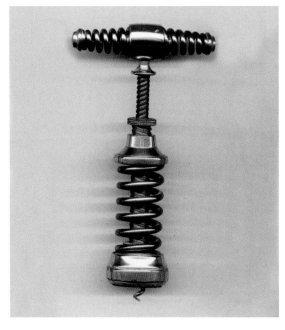

Right: This is an attractive well-made modern Thomason, made of brass. The barrel and handle are made of heavy steel coil.

Thomason Variants

Thomason Variants are not specifically covered in the 1802 Thomason patent and in fact the mechanism is very different, using two handles, one of which is fixed to the barrel or frame. The cork extraction process begins with the right-threaded worm/inner shaft attached to the upper handle in the 'up' position, the outer shaft in the 'down' position and the barrel positioned over the bottle to centre the worm. Clockwise turning of the upper handle inserts the worm into the cork. Clockwise turning of the lower handle, which is fixed to the barrel but can be turned, causes the right-threaded outer shaft to rise and pull the cork. The button at the bottom of the brass outer shaft has two grooves that move up two ridges inside the barrel, keeping the worm centred.

King's Screws

These are classic elegant corkscrews, prized by collectors and admired by all. There is a resemblance to the Thomason corkscrews and although King's Screws are often marked 'Patent', there was no patent, probably because Edward Thomason covered the principal mechanism in his 1802 patent. They originated in the early nineteenth century when there was a king on the throne, before Victoria started her reign in 1837. King's Screws have a rack and pinion design and two

Left: **This is a classic Thomason Variant with a bronze barrel and the Thomason badge with 'Ne Plus Ultra' motto.** *Centre:* **A less-common Thomason Variant with the Thomason badge on the cut-away bronze barrel. The button at the bottom of the brass outer shaft is marked 'Thomason P^t Ne Plus Ultra'.** *Right:* **The ultimate, and very rare Thomason 'Serpent Variant', with a partly gilded serpent with an attachment for a brush at its mouth. The bronze barrel carries the Thomason badge and the handle is decorated with a lion and a unicorn and the rather indistinct words 'Dieu et Mon Droit', and surmounted with a fine crown.**

Left: This is a classic King's Screw with a bronze barrel carrying a badge marked 'Dowler Patent' for the maker. It has two bone handles. *Right:* An example with parts of the bronze barrel cut away, bearing a 'Ne Plus Ultra' badge, which is not quite the same as the standard Thomason badge and is probably pretending to be a Thomason. These are both wide racks, and the pinions of both are exposed. The pinion handles can match the top handle but often are made of steel, as shown.

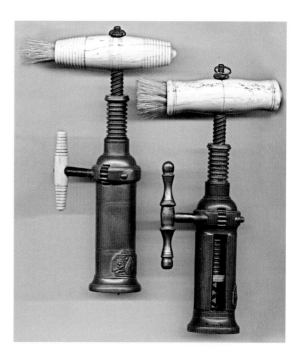

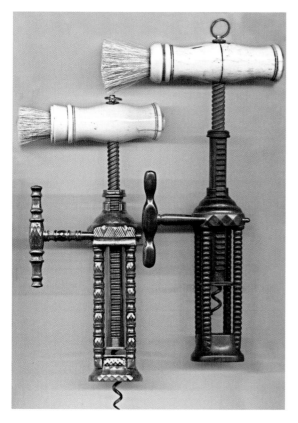

Above: These two very decorative King's Screws both have narrow racks, and the pinions are hidden in the top part of the barrel. The pinion handles both match the pillars in material and decoration. *Left:* Highly faceted pillar decorations in shiny plated steel. *Right:* Decorative pillars in dark patinated steel.

Right: This is an unusual German King's Screw, made in steel with a narrow rack. It has four claws at the bottom of the outer shaft. It is unmarked but may have been made by Louis Kummer in about 1900.

Above: This matching pair of King's Screw and Thomason are both made by William Dray and carry a brass badge stating 'Registered May 14 1847, W Dray, Patent. This refers his design for a dove-tailed fastening allowing broken worms to be replaced (*see* page 89). The badge of the King's Screw on the left also states 'London Bridge', the location of his premises.

Left: This is a classic example of a London Rack. The steel collar under the handle is marked 'Lund's Patent London Rack' and the steel frame is marked 'Lund's Patent London', referring to British Patent No. 736 of 1855, assigned to William Lund and William Edward Hipkins, who was Lund's foreman. There is a notch at the top of the frame, which catches a small pin at the top of the rack. Later plated examples are marked 'Lund Maker Cornhill' on one side of the frame, and 'Fleet St London' on the other. *Right:* An unmarked example with a bronze barrel, which has a notch cut into the barrel to catch a pin on the shaft. It is also found in plated versions.

handles. They have an inner right-hand threaded shaft, like the Thomason, but the outer shaft is a rack with horizontal bars. On the side there is a small pinion or cog with teeth, fixed to a small handle. Turning the top handle rotates the inner shaft and inserts the worm. The side handle engages the rack on the outer shaft to pull up the cork. The most common examples have a narrow rack fixed to a smooth outer shaft. Less common are those with wide racks that cover the whole outer shaft. Some carry badges of the makers, which include Coney, Dowler, Heeley, Rodgers, and Wilmot & Roberts.

Racks

Other corkscrews used a rack and pinion mechanism similar to the King's Screw, but with a different, simplified design. The inner threaded shaft was eliminated and a single shaft was used with a rack going all round. The earliest example was the London Rack, but they were also made in France, Germany and the USA.

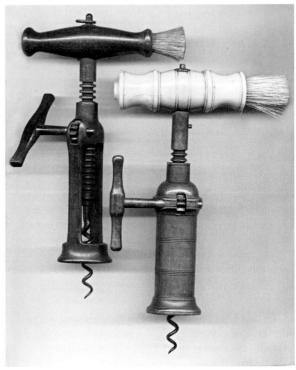

Thomas Lund's 1838 British Patent No. 7,761 covered a design of corkscrew with springs on the frame to act as bottle grips. They were attached to quality Thomasons and King's Screws and, after 1855, to London Racks, which were patented by his son William. The bottle grips were made of tempered steel and there are versions with three or four springs. Sadly they were often broken, so complete examples are rare, and you can sometimes find frames with just the remnants. *Left:* Bronze-barrelled King's Screw marked 'Lund Patent 57 Cornhill'. The three springs of the bottle grips are marked 'The Queen's Patent', 'Granted', and 'To T. Lund London', and each has a

large crown at the top. *Right:* The steel frame is marked 'Lund's Patent London' and the top of the frame is marked 'Lund's London Rack' and has the small notch at the top. The three springs are marked 'Lund', 'Patentee' and 'London', and there is a crown above 'Lund'.

Left: This classic French rack, with a single ratchet wheel at the front of the frame, is an unmarked version of Jacques Pérille's 1879 Patent No. 112,465 known as 'Crémaillère'. *Centre:* This example with two ratchet wheels, one on each side of the frame, is marked 'Modèle Déposé' with 'JB' inside a multi-pointed star for Jean Boué, founder of the firm Boué et Deveson. *Right:* This version of Pérille's 1879 patent, marked 'J-P', has a single ratchet wheel at the side of the frame.

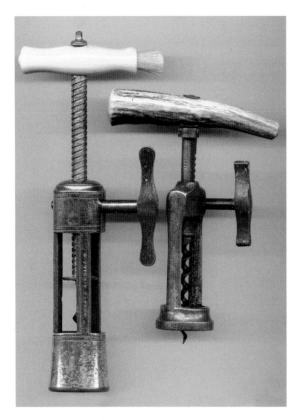

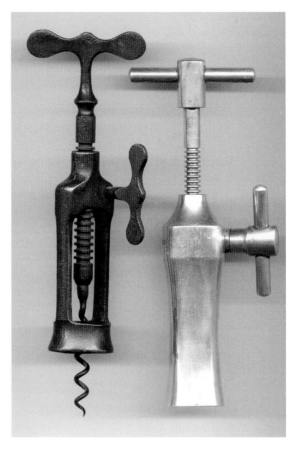

Above, left: This fine silver-plated piece is marked 'G. Twigg's Patent' on each of the three pillars, for George Twigg's 1868 British Patent No. 2,851. This showed a number of variations with locking devices described earlier, but the 'Twigg IX' showed a toothed pinion and side handle. This is described as a lifting jack in the patent. The shaft has a right-handed thread, not a horizontal rack, and the button at the bottom has small chequered grips to cling to the cork. The pinion on the side engages with a horizontal pinion hidden inside the barrel, and the rotation of this makes the threaded shaft rise and lift the cork. *Right:* This German rack is fixed to a plain inner rod marked 'J.A. Henckels' with number 19 and 3 on the steel frame, which shows remnants of a bronze wash. It is based on Edwin Sunderland's 1870 British Patent No. 2,841.

Above, Left: An old English steel rack, unmarked. *Right:* An aluminium American rack marked 'Korkmaster, Trademark, Pat Pending', for Marshall T. McDowell's 1948 US Patent No. 148,810, made by the Korkmaster Company.

Ratchets

Ratchets have sets of teeth on the edge of a bar or wheel which engage to ensure motion in one direction only. They were used as devices to allow handles to be turned without having to change grip.

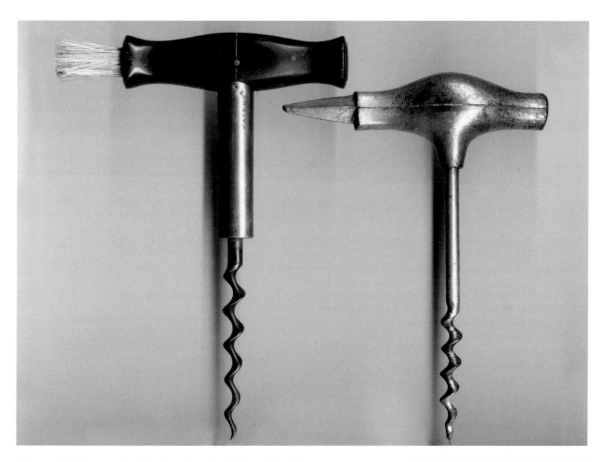

Above, left: Newton's ratchet mechanism is found in this example, marked 'Patent', for Alfred Vincent Newton's 1856 British Patent No. 2,230. The ratchet is inside the handle. It may have been manufactured by Charles Hull in Birmingham, as the handle and barrel are very similar to the van Gieson and Presto corkscrews which were made by Hull and are discussed below (*see* page 158).
Right: Walter Dickson patented a ratchet corkscrew in the USA. This nickel-plated steel example is marked 'Pat. Aug. 2 1870'. The heavy handle is made from two cast halves and has a handy ice pick.

Direct pressure

In this type of corkscrew, downward direct pressure pushes the threaded or grooved shaft through some mechanism that turns the screw, thus inserting it into the cork. Once that is done, the cork has to be pulled out vertically using the usual straight pulling action, but there are some mechanically assisted combinations.

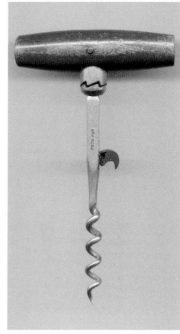

Right: This English ratchet is marked 'Prov. Pat.' but is not believed to have been patented. It has a hook on the shank, which was the subject of the 1912 British Reg. Design No. 596,671 of William Arthur Willetts.

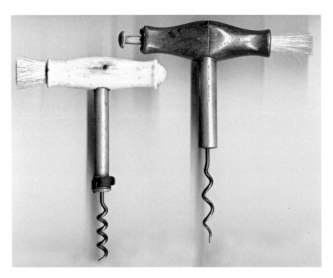

Left: The 'van Gieson' has a brass barrel and is marked 'Patent' in tiny lettering underneath the small coiled spring, which presses a pin in a notch at the upper end of the threaded shaft. This refers to the 1867 US Patent No. 61,485 of W.H. van Gieson. *Right:* The 'Presto' has a brass barrel marked 'C. Hull's Patent' and has a locking device on the end of the wooden handle. The brass end cap on the handle states 'Chas Hull's Patent, Presto Corkscrew'. There is no patent assigned to Hull, and it is believed that Hull manufactured the van Gieson corkscrew before it was patented. Hull considered the 'Presto' to be just a variation of the van Gieson, and the two were often advertised alongside each other in trade directories.

Below, left: An unmarked Qvarnström example with the typical speed worm, which drops down to reveal a long plain shaft. A.L. Qvarnström, a Swedish inventor, obtained three patents for a direct pressure corkscrew in Sweden between 1892 and 1895. It was patented in Britain in 1893. The patents were possibly sold to Julius Slöör of Stockholm and are sometimes marked as 'Slöör Patent'. *Right:* This is an unmarked example of Edward Brailey Hatfield's 1904 British Patent No. 17,920. The bladed worm drops down to reveal a tubular shank with a spiral groove, which meshes with a hard steel ball inside the shank.

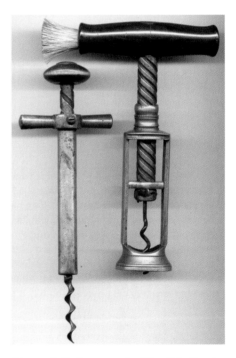

Above, left: An unmarked English direct pressure screw without a locking device. It has a brass barrel and handles and a wooden knob at the top. *Right:* This is a combination of van Gieson's 1867 US Patent with a brass-framed threaded shaft. It is marked 'Patent' underneath the spring at the bottom of the shaft. It was shown in Farrow & Jackson's 1875 catalogue as the 'Despatch Corkscrew'. The threaded shaft helps to extract the cork.

Unclassified

This section includes a variety of difficult-to-classify but innovative ways to remove a cork, including pulleys and windlasses, jacks, hydraulics, and electric power. It also includes finger power, as demonstrated by the Whelan corkscrew.

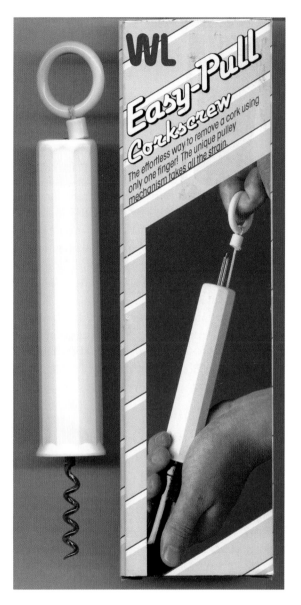

Right: The 'WL Easy-Pull Corkscrew' in cream or black plastic, with an intriguing pull string mechanism. It was invented by Frenchman Bruno Desnoulez for his wife and had a European Patent Application No. 80401103.9. The 1986 copyright was assigned to William Levene Ltd. of London, hence 'WL'.

Left: Frederick Astley Whelan was granted Patent No. 2,642 in 1881 for his elegant finger-pull corkscrew. The bronze-washed example is marked 'Patent' and 'G.F. Hipkins and Son' for the Birmingham manufacturer. The worm is inserted and the cork is then removed by pulling up with the finger and palm of the hand, not an easy task.

COMBINATIONS

A large proportion of all corkscrews carry one or more features or tools to carry out secondary functions other than withdrawing corks from bottles. Indeed on some items, it is the corkscrew that is the subsidiary tool. Combination corkscrews, as described in this section, provide no mechanical advantage to withdrawing the cork, but have extra functions for other jobs.

In terms of categorizing corkscrews, combinations come low in the order of things. It will be appreciated that most Waiter's Friends have cap lifters incorporated into their designs, as do many double levers.

Knives usually have a multitude of functions as do many pocket and protected corkscrews. For the sake of organization and simplicity, mechanical corkscrews with secondary tools and functions will not be considered here and most knives, pocket corkscrews and figurals are also excluded.

Despite missing out all these, there are still a multitude of combinations and the author has a diverse collection of well over four hundred. The SCReW© categorization system uses a hierarchical series of tools and functions to tag and sort combinations. This section will essentially follow this system.

Straight pulls with a blade or a spike on the handle

Left: The quintessential 'corkscrew with spike' has a horn handle and, usually, a square shank. This example was made by Christopher Johnson & Company and bears their 'flag' trademark on the shank. They were also made by Lockwood Brothers who marketed them as 'Adelaide' corkscrews. Another mark to look out for on the

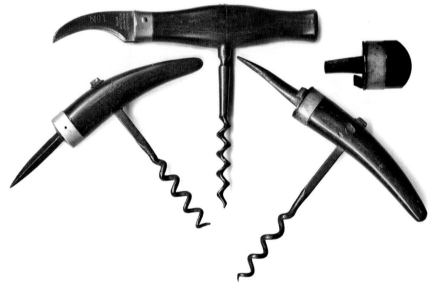

shank is for the shipping line P&O. *Centre:* This much rarer horn-handled corkscrew has a blade stamped 'No. 1 Wade Wingfield Rowbotham Sheffield' (number 2 does not have the blade). *Right:* Variations on the basic horn handle and spike are much less common. This one combines two features: a flattened curved spike from the 1886 registered design of Christopher Johnson & Company, No. 42353, and a small cap lifter lug (shown magnified) from the Australians, George Gustav Kemter and Gordon Bell, in their 1913 British Patent No. 954. Another design with a triangular spike was registered by Lockwood Brothers in 1904, Reg. No. 437760.

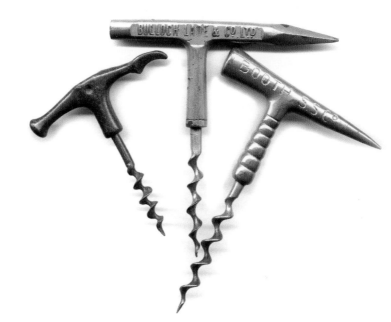

Left: **This small corkscrew is probably French and has a curved wax- or wire-cutter on the steel handle.** *Centre:* **There are a variety of British steel corkscrews of this basic design. They often bear advertising like this one for Bulloch Lade & Co. Ltd. and Extra Special Gold Label (on the other side).** *Right:* **Steel corkscrews with a conical handle and spike are ice hammers. This example promotes 'Booth S.S.C°'. If you ever find one with a diamond registration mark on it, then it is the 'Wenham Ice Hammer', a registered design from James Henry Stone of 1879 (*see* page 168).**

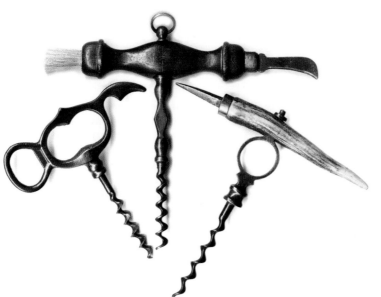

Left: **This steel corkscrew is designed for four fingers and features a curved blade at one end and a D-shaped cap lifter at the other end.** *Centre:* **The long wire-cutter blade has a serrated edge and the corkscrew is probably American.** *Right:* **Antler handles with spikes are not very common. This one has the added attraction of a 'signet' finger hole.**

Can openers

This is an area in which there is a real problem of where to begin and how much to include. There are all sorts of can openers and many have a corkscrew attached to create a kitchen gadget to open almost anything. The first one I bought was less than a pound in a junk shop and it lay almost forgotten in a drawer until I realized that it was a British patent. Since then, my collection has grown to over a hundred different can openers – many being examples of patents or registered designs. There are a few British patents but it was the Americans who were really inventive. This sub-section can present only a few of the more significant can openers.

Early British can openers. *From the top:* William Sykes was the first to register a design for a can opener and this delicate nickel-plated example is marked with a registration diamond for his design of 1875. It was also made in steel.

The next example is an early bronze-washed can opener, marked 'H.A.K. & Co' on the nose above the blade for the manufacturer H.H. Knox. The fish is from Frederick Sunderland's design of 1875 and is marked with an indistinct registration diamond on the gill. Not all examples are marked. The original documents for these old items often describe them as a 'metal case opener' or a 'sardine box knife', as this was before mass canning started. Although the bottom example is marked 'Pat. Apld. For' on the blade, the documentation has not been found. It has a cap lifter hook just behind the blade, which dates it after 1892, the date of the crown cap patent.

Below, top: The 'Chandos' is one of at least three names that Frederick Sunderland (Coney & Co.) gave to his registered can opener design of 1914. It is also marked 'Reg^d N° 633376' on the blade and 'Made in England' on the handle. Other names were 'Anzac' and 'Waratah' (the floral symbol of New South Wales). *Centre:*

Sunderland also took out two patents for can openers in 1909 and 1916 and this is an example of the second one. It features twin cap lifter hooks on the handle, which are marked 'Crown Cork Opener'. The handle is stamped 'The "Super British" Coney's Patents 11360 & 7659/16' (the application number for 1916). This item should really be marked 102580 because patent number 11360 actually refers to the 1909 patent, the 'British', which has only a single cap lifter hook. *Bottom:* Saunders and Collins registered this design in 1924 for a combined tin opener, corkscrew, crown cork opener and bottle stopper. It is stamped 'Reg^d Pat Appd For Best Steel R^d 707111 British Make'. The rubber stopper has perished on many examples and is often missing.

American can openers. *From the top:* Although this is not the first US patent, this is one of the earliest that the collector will come across. The can openers are very prone to breakage of the curved lips above the blade. The example is indistinctly stamped on the blade 'Pat. Aug 16 1898' and is from William Browne's 1898 patent. There are two ways of opening cans with the next tool: a standard blade and 'nose', plus a spike and sliding blade. Frank White and Fred Winkler's patent number 765,450 of 1904 also incorporates a cap lifter hook and is marked 'No 35 "Sure-Cut" Can & Bottle Opener with Cap Lifter (Pat. 7-19-04)'. Wooden-handled versions are also known. The third example is a well-known tool named 'King'. It has a crown logo and is stamped 'Made in USA' and 'Pat. June 11-95 & AUG 18-08'. These dates relate to the patents of The Browne & Dowde Manufacturing Company, although the earlier one did not include the corkscrew. These openers are found with a variety of advertising. Harry Vaughan's can opener from the 1929 patent *(bottom)* is one of the most common, but it carries a wealth of information. The blade states 'Tempered Steel' and the cap lifter

above it has 'USA Pat. No. 2,018,083' (for this lug patented in 1935). The handle is stamped '*Vaughan's* Made in USA' and the attachment, which is hidden on the other side in the picture, has 'Hand Guard Pat. In USA June 4-1929'. Even the fold-out can piercer is stamped 'USA Pat. No. 1,996,550', for the 1935 patent for this part.

Complicated can openers. *From the top:* Whilst it is not the prettiest looking domestic tool, it was certainly a successful design as judged by the number of examples that exist. The tool has ten functions as described in an advert for 'The "Utility" No 9 Combination Tool'. The small slots are apparently coin testers as well as glass snappers. Examples are marked 'Regd 689051 British Make U.M.C° Ldn' for The Utility Manufacturing Company's design of 1922.

The 'Quintuplet' *(second from top)* was patented in Britain and USA in 1955 by Joseph Cahil. It has a butterfly handle on the opposite side to turn the toothed wheel that grips the edge of the can, and the fifth tool is the lid pry at the end. The handle is lightly stamped 'The Quintuplet Kitchen Utility Reg. U.S. Pat. Off. Pat. N° D-100469 Others Pend'. This US Design Patent number is for July 1936 when the headpiece was originally described (without a corkscrew). The third example must be the ultimate combination tool. It was patented by Erik Nylin in the USA in 1909 and is marked 'Pat 09'. The black paint is usually in poor condition and there are a few variations around. The patent lists twenty functions and Fred O'Leary challenges the collector to spot them all. You should check whether the sliding can opener blade is present if buying one. The last example is a delightful, delicate little tool with a folding fork and, sometimes, a folding cap lifter on the same hinge. The American patent was from William Moore in 1918 and judging from the advertising, it was designed for opening cans of fish, and then eating the contents. This one is marked 'B.M. Shipman Importer New York Bon Accord Herring Bon Accord Mackerel'.

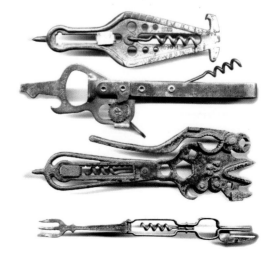

International can openers. *From the top:* The 'Pathos Profit' is from Germany and has a swing blade can opener at one end and a knife sharpener at the other. It is also marked 'D.R.G.M.' for the 1930 registration of Richard Weilputz. A similar example, 'Pathos Privat', is shown later in the knife sharpener section. The next tool is Spanish, from the mid twentieth century, and bears the details 'Patente N° 27116' with the trademark 'BOJ'. It has a swing blade and a sardine can opener. Also with a sardine can opener, the next gadget is French, and is marked 'Déposé' and 'magasins j.' It has a can piercer, fixed blade and stud can opener plus a saw-toothed edge.

The folding side arm of the next tool *(second from bottom)* is a knife-sharpening steel. It is an uncommon 1910 German registration from Bewer, marked 'D.R.G.M. ANG'. The last, wooden-handled can opener has a twisted wire corkscrew in the end derived from William Clough's US patent of 1900. It carries an advert for Walz Hardware Co.

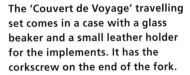

The 'Couvert de Voyage' travelling set comes in a case with a glass beaker and a small leather holder for the implements. It has the corkscrew on the end of the fork.

Eating implements

Folding knife, fork and spoon sets, which also include a folding corkscrew, come into this group. They are often found in a case with a glass or metal beaker. The separate parts are often found on their own on antique stalls and the collector must decide whether to buy the individual piece or be patient and wait for the whole set.

The most common type is with the folding worm on the fork, hinged either in the centre or at the end. To have the worm on the knife or the spoon is less common.

Right: The mottled plastic scales of this set suggest that it is from the mid twentieth century, but there are no clues as to its country of origin. The worm is hinged on the knife and it all comes in a brown leather case with a glass beaker.

Below, left: This is a picnic tool with everything: a knife, fork, spoon, can opener and corkscrew. The tang is stamped 'American Muse Japan'. *Right:* The stem of the fork is stamped with Russian marks and a hammer and sickle and the scales are imitation mother-of-pearl.

Below: These are different examples where the three pieces slot and slide together using pins on the outer parts, which insert into the keyholes in the central handle. *Left:* The outer scales are in patterned etched blue steel, and the worm is on the spoon. The engraved name 'Carlsbad' on the spoon suggests a German origin. *Right:* This is a very high-quality set with tortoiseshell scales. The fork and spoon are silver and the latter is hallmarked for London 1803 and the steel blade is stamped 'Nowill'.

This stylish set is the 1885 British Registered Design of Frederick Shaw. The knife blade and fork fit into slots on the opposite handle and the spoon's handle fits into a slot above the knife blade. The shank of the fork is marked 'R^d 24169'.

Funnels

Top left: The hammered silver funnel is marked 'Sterling 999' and the sheath of the corkscrew can be put into the stem of the funnel from either side, either for storage or to create a cup. *Bottom left:* The top part of this small American cocktail shaker can be used as a funnel for pouring out the drink. The worm is pushed into the spout of the funnel on the inner side and the small cap put on for storage. The base is marked 'Napier Silver Plate Pat. Pend.' *Right:* This plated funnel is part of a travelling set comprising three cups with coloured sides. The funnel fits inside the other cups with the corkscrew and sheath the other way round to what is shown in the picture. The leather strap passes through the cap lifter. All of the items are marked 'Made in Germany' and the cap lifter bears a pentagonal trademark for Müller and Schmidt of Solingen.

Funnels

Corkscrews can easily fit into the stem of metal wine funnels. This provides protection of the worm and also allows the funnel to be used as a drinking cup by blocking up the orifice. The corkscrew and funnel combination is often found in a case or sometimes inside expensive cocktail shaker sets, some of which are amazingly shaped as zeppelins or aeroplanes.

Glass cutters

This is a niche area for collectors and these are predominantly American tools for the handyman. Many of them have patent markings even though the original patents did not usually show the tool in the way it was manufactured. They all have a small glass cutting wheel and slots for snapping glass. There is usually a knife sharpener (a steel strip with V-shaped slots at either side) that is sometimes missing. Most have a pointed blade that has variously been described as a putty knife, ice pick, can opener, lid pry or cigar box opener, but in a British registered design document it is referred to as a 'sardine knife'. The worms are often fairly thin wire (they do not stand up to much use) and are hinged to swivel in the plane of the tool. The American tools also usually have little feet on one side (the opposite side to the pictures). This was a clever arrangement so that the tool could be placed on a bench at a 45 degrees angle for sharpening knives. Many of the tools have markings that relate to the three main patents which introduced these tools: S.G. Monce 1869, Pat. No. 91,150; Frank R. Woodward 1875, Pat. No. 166,954; and Benjamin F. Adams 1880, Pat. No. 229,228. Fred O'Leary has written an excellent article on these tools in the *Quarterly Worme*, June 2006.

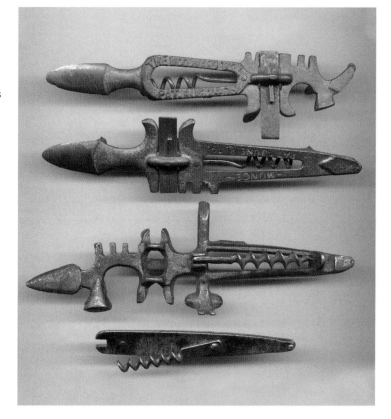

Top to bottom: 'The Woodward Tool' is marked 'Pat. Aug 24. 75'. The protrusion close to the glass wheel is a small tack hammer. Almost identical tools are found marked 'The Andress Tool Pat. Aug. 24.75' and 'The Artisans Tool /AT. July 22 1874' (this is a bogus marking as it is '/AT' rather than 'PAT'). The tool marked 'Monce Pat. June 8. 69' *(second from top)* was made without the tack hammer. The next example is a very uncommon tool, probably British, with a bronze wash typical of the late nineteenth century. The bladed worm folds out from the body of the tool. It has a conical tack hammer, a screwdriver or lid pry (the upward-pointing rod) and a tack-removing claw. The knife-sharpening strip is missing. The German registration for the small glazier's tool *(bottom)* was in 1904 from Max Melchior. It is made of two strips of steel riveted together and lightly stamped 'D.R.G.M.' It has a cutting wheel at one end and glass snapping slot at the other.

Ice picks, hammers, and choppers

There are various examples of vicious implements to smash ice.

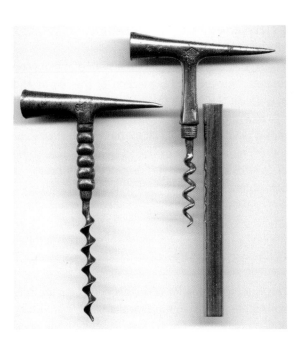

The 'Wenham Ice Hammer' was a British Registered Design from James Henry Stone in 1879. These examples show the diamond registration mark. *Left:* The more common unsheathed version with multi-knopped shank. *Right:* The sheathed version as in the design drawing, with replaceable spike.

Jiggers

Every home bar needs a measure for spirits and mixers for that cocktail party. Many were designed to incorporate the other tools necessary for the job – a cap lifter and corkscrew.

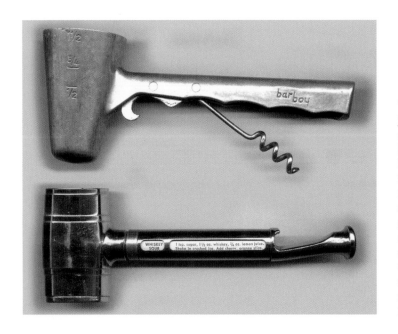

Top: The 'bar boy' is an American jigger made of aluminium from the mid twentieth century. It has a cap lifter hook underneath and is marked inside the handle 'Pat. Appld For 3 Newton New Haven', but the patent has not been found. *Bottom:* There are many American jiggers of this general design in which the handle unscrews from the 'head' to reveal a second-rate worm. This example is fun because the handle has a rotating sleeve that shows eight cocktail recipes. It is marked on the base 'Mr. Bartender Products'.

The dark green plastic handle unscrews from this double jigger to reveal a good bladed worm. The larger jigger is marked 'PHV&Co EPNS Made in England'. P.H. Vogel & C°. Ltd. was a Birmingham manufacturer of plated objects including novelty corkscrews.

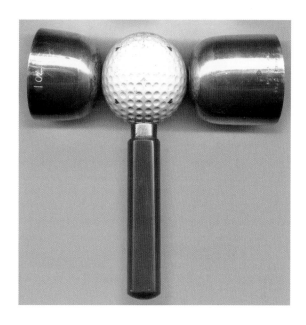

Knife-sharpeners

One type of knife sharpener has already been described in the section on glass cutters. It has a steel strip with a V-shaped slot at either side. There are two other types: a pair of interleaved wheels that create a V-shaped slot between them, and the classic sharpening steel. Not surprisingly for a kitchen tool, they were sometimes fitted with corkscrews.

V-slot and double wheel sharpeners. *Left:* This small uncommon tool is from Wilhelm Hartmann's 1887 British Patent No. 9749A. Some examples are marked 'Patent'. *Top:* The 'Pathos Privat' is from Germany and has a D-shaped cap lifter at one end and a knife sharpener at the other. Although not marked 'D.R.G.M.', this design is from the Richard Weilputz registration of 1930. A similar example, 'Pathos Profit', is shown on page 164. *Centre and bottom:* Two views of the 'Wizard Knife Sharpener', an American tool with a cap lifter hook at the opposite end to the knife sharpener.

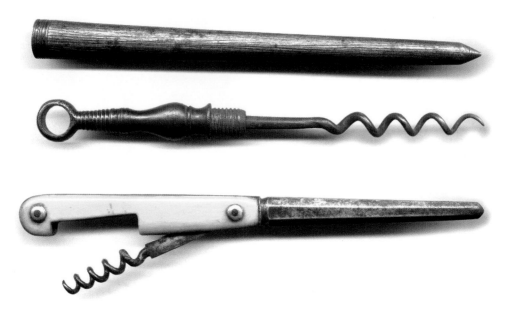

Sharpening steels. *Top:* The sharpening steel acts as a sheath for the corkscrew worm and can also be used as a cross-bar handle as in a picnic corkscrew. They come in a variety of lengths, including a massive 38cm. *Bottom:* This very uncommon steel has a folding worm and a bone handle with fixing rivets of a style suggesting the early nineteenth century.

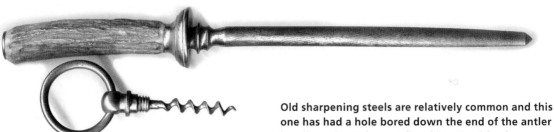

Old sharpening steels are relatively common and this one has had a hole bored down the end of the antler handle and a corkscrew fitted into it with a brass threaded fixing. There are a number of these in circulation and they are attractive and very well made, but the marriage only dates from the 1990s when they appeared in a Midlands antique centre.

Cap lifters

Once the crown cap had been invented and commercialized in the 1890s, corkscrew designers started adding crown cap lifters to corkscrews (or was it the other way around?). Only relatively simple corkscrews with cap lifters are described here.

Cap lifters on handles. *From bottom left:* One of the most common corkscrews with a cap lifter handle is this one marked 'R^d N° 713438' for the design of Coneys Ltd. from 1925. It comes in two sizes, 65mm and 43mm wide. The smaller size should come with a snap-on sheath, though this is often missing.

The next example is an unmarked simple corkscrew with added 'ears' to create a four-finger pull handle. Edward Marwood & Co., cork merchants of Liverpool, registered the design for the double cap lifter corkscrew in 1916 *(top)*. It was made as a novelty promotional item and is marked on the handle 'E^d Marwood & C° L^{td} Reg^d 656515' with 'Liverpool' on the back. The eyebrow corkscrew with a cap lifter is a lovely design and advertises Apollinaris, the name of a bottled water established in 1892. The addition of the extra lug to a standard four-finger pull *(right)* creates a useful cap lifter. This early-twentieth-century corkscrew is unmarked. *Bottom:* Harold Robert Smyth and George Duncan Mackay patented this cap lifter corkscrew in Britain in 1898. There are two versions and this one has a small lug to engage with the bayonet-like slot on the carriage key sheath, which was easily lost. The other version has no lug and therefore no sheath. All are marked 'Patent N° 9509' with a variety of advertising. This one promotes Cantrell & Cochranes Club Soda.

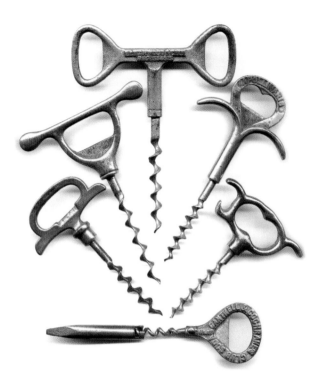

Cap lifter hooks on shanks and handles. *From bottom left:* The handle of this corkscrew is solid aluminium and has a deep slot cut into it. It is not marked and probably dates from the mid twentieth century. The straight pull with a C-shaped cap lifter on the shank is stamped *'Corinthian'* and *'Regd. Design.'* It probably dates from the 1950s but the design details have not been found.

The square shank of the next example *(top)* is stamped 'Henry Boker Made in Germany'. Boker was an American importer. William Arthur Willetts registered a design in 1912 for a cap lifter hook on the shank of a straight pull corkscrew. The hook of this example *(top right)* is marked 'R^d 596671' but they are not always marked. The fixing for the hook is relatively weak and the hook is often twisted as a result. The other corkscrew with a cap lifter on the shank *(bottom right)* is stamped 'Walker' under the handle. It was advertised in a 1905 J.W. Edgerly & Co.'s Iowa catalogue as 'Walker's Waiters and Hallboys Corkscrew'. It may be derived from Walker's 1897 patent.

D-shaped cap lifters with a folding worm. *Top:* This classy, late-twentieth-century French cap lifter had a wood-look handle and spring-loaded hinge for the worm. The cap lifter is marked 'L'Atelier Du Vin'. *Left:* The large steel tool has a lid pry at one end and a large cap lifter hook at the other. The hook is marked 'B&C', for Beaton & Cadwell Manufacturing Co., Connecticut. *Centre:* This is a German registered design from Kirchner in 1928, marked 'D.R.G.M.' It is relatively common to find ones marked with advertising. *Right:* In this mid-twentieth-century example, the plastic scales of the handle imitated bone and the base of the cap lifter is stamped 'Pfeilring Solingen', with a pentagonal trademark.

Hook-type cap lifters with a folding worm. *Top left:* The *'Nifty'* is a common corkscrew in the USA but is rarely found in Europe. It was patented by Harry Vaughan in 1916 and countless numbers have been made, many covered in advertising. The one pictured is marked 'Made & Patd in USA Vaughan Chicago'. There are a number of small variations to collect, relating to how the point of the closed worm is protected. The British produced very similar little tools with a variety of names: *'Nappy'*, *'Nippy'*, *'Pop'* and *'Puck'*. *Top right:* The British also added a nail file to the basic Nifty and this one is marked 'Made in Sheffield England'. Centre left: The basic Nifty was also modified in the USA as shown by this tool marked 'Four in One Pal Made in U.S.A. Made By Robt. H Ingersoll Inc. New York. *Centre right:* This handy pocket tool has a cap lifter hook at one end and the worm folds out on a double spring that holds the shank in place. One side is stamped 'Pat. Apl. For J.E. Mergott Co., N.J.' The patent was granted for Mergott & Co. in 1929. *Bottom:* This unusual curved tool has a cap lifter at one end and a flattened section at the opposite end. It is designed for removing ice trays from old-fashioned refrigerators, as made by Stewart Warner, the name on the tool.

Cap lifters with sheathed worms. *From bottom left:* This simple unmarked example has a lid pry and a push-on steel sheath. The next cap lifter is one of many souvenir corkscrews with a sheath promoting the 'Empire State Building, World's Tallest New York City Height 1,472 Feet'. The corkscrew is a simple piece of thick wire folded in a tight U-bend over the neck of the thicker cap lifter. This design is usually referred to as Williamson's 'Flash'. There are many silver or silver-plated corkscrews with sheaths. This sizeable one has a bladed worm and the sheath is marked 'Sterling'.

The next example is my favourite advertising on a corkscrew: 'For Constipation Tryalax – Laxative Chocolate for Adults and Children'. The simple worm is twisted wire, as made in the thousands by Clough under his patent of 1900. The wooden sheath carries other promotional information but also the detail 'Pat. Apr. 30, 1901', which refers to John

Baseler's patent for the hook at the end. The patent does not show a hook of this type but covers the small point that punched a hole in the top of the cap that was being removed, so that it could not be used again. The next example is wooden sheathed with twisted wire corkscrew inserts. It is British and promotes LMS Hotels ('LMS' stands for the London, Midland, and Scottish Railway Company, which became part of British Railways in 1948). The last example is a silver sheathed corkscrew from the 1924 Norwegian patent of Paul Skarsten. The two ridges on the sheath allow it to be used as a 'saddle' to fit under the upper curve of the cap lifter for pulling out the cork. Examples are often richly decorated. This example is marked 'Pat. 38570' on both the cap lifter and the sheath.

Cap lifters with can piercers. *From the left:* These 'Probus' tools come with different coloured handles including cream, yellow, brown, blue, red and brick red. The metal head is stamped 'Brit. Pat 1575063 Made in England Probus Reg. Des. 980867', which refers to the 1977 design of Gill-Mentor Limited of Probus Works.

The tool with a lid pry at one end bears the markings 'Pat. No. 222093 Foreign', but the patent has not been identified. It is, however, identical to the Japanese patent 38-009768 from 1963. Tools named 'Oasis' *(second from right)* are fairly common and are made from a punched strip of steel. All examples are marked 'Oasis R.D.N° 888,293' with an address 'H^Y. Squire & Sons Ltd Willenhall Staffs. Made in England'. The 1958 design registration was from Henry Squire. This useful American tool *(right)* comes in a number of colours and has a can piercer, cap lifter and corkscrew housed in its plastic body. It is marked 'Pat. No. 170,999 *TapBoy* Vaughan – Chicago 24 U.S.A.' on one side and '*Vaughan's TapBoy*' on the other side. The markings refer to the 1953 Design Patent for Vaughan Mfg. Co.

Can piercers

These all have a can piercer, a triangular blade with a lever action.

Codd bottle openers – Marble pushers

Hiram Codd lodged a series of patents in the early 1870s relating to the bottle that is generically named after him. Codd was not the first to invent bottles with internal seals to hold fizzy drinks, but his idea of using a simple glass ball was introduced in a British patent in 1870. Codd's later 1872 patent extended the idea by describing how a ledge on the inside of the bottle neck would catch the glass marble and stop it blocking up the neck once the bottle was opened. Of course, the development, success and popularity of the 'Codd bottle' necessitated the need for a tool to push the marble down to open the bottle and break the seal. Hiram Codd was the first to describe such a tool in combination with a corkscrew in his 1876 registration, which he followed with a very different design described in his 1881 British Patent No. 1,152.

10,874. **Perkins. M.** Aug. 2.

Corkscrews; opening internally-stoppered bottles. — The stem and part of the handle of a corkscrew are made tubular as shown, and the tubular end of the handle is provided with an india-rubber washer, so that the instrument can also be used when required as an opener for aërated water bottles.

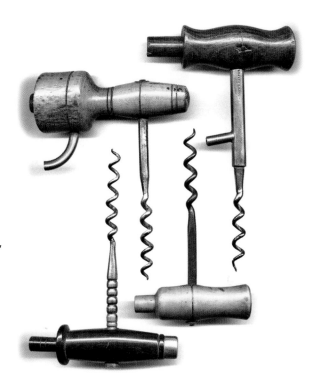

Corkscrews with 'marble pushers' used to break the seal in a Codd bottle. *Top left:* The bulbous end to the wooden handle is fairly typical. It acts as a 'cowl' to fit over the top of the bottle. The central marble pusher can just be seen and in this example it has a hole through it to allow the beverage to be pushed through the brass outlet tube. *Top right:* Although this is marked 'Coney's Patent', it was in fact patented by Matt Perkins in 1884, Patent No. 10,874, but was made by Coney & Co. The brass outlet tube is fixed to the side of a hollow shank and the patent diagram shows how it is supposed to work. *Bottom:* These two simple Codd openers have horn and wooden handles.

Left to right: This wonderful boxwood corkscrew has two bulbous ends, one with the Codd bottle opener and the other with a fluted inner metal liner for gripping and opening bottle tops. It is marked 'Patent No. 7451', but the patent has not been identified. The simple boxwood example *(centre)* is marked 'No. 1837' for the British Registered design of J&W Roper. This was an illegal marking as the registration was only provisional. The final Codd bottle opener shown here has a hole in it and a brass outlet tube for the liquid. It is marked 'W Vaughan R^d 15930' on the brass sleeve of the opener for the 1884 British Registered Design of Walter Vaughan. It can come with a cork sleeve over the wooden marble pusher.

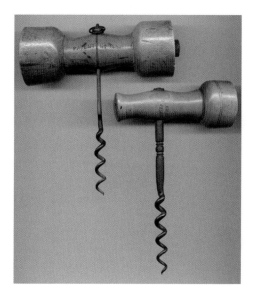

Steel Codd bottle openers. *Left:* This vicious-looking bent tool was patented in Britain by Sydney Flowers in 1900. It is marked 'Patent 3347 D.R.G.M. 130884', which refers to the British patent and the corresponding German registration. The marble pusher is the bent lug on the end, which doubles as a cap lifter. A long slot in the handle (not visible in the picture) is for twisting the rectangular grip of glass stoppers. *Centre:* This is an unlikely device that apparently opens everything imaginable. A few examples do exist – some missing the wooden marble pusher. It is marked 'Pat. No. 128450 21/6/19' although the patent from William Glen Ward was granted on 31 July 1919. The three slots are for gripping bottle stoppers to give them a twist. *Right:* Hiram Codd took out British and US patents in 1881 for a corkscrew that would also open his bottles. This example is marked 'Codd's Patent' and 'G.F. Hipkins'. There are two other versions (one has a hanging hole; the other is a folding bow – *see* page 63), but none of the three is common. *Bottom:* This pair of plated steel cork grips with two handles has a Codd marble pusher on the hinge. It is marked 'Aston Bottling Co.', a company active in Birmingham in the early twentieth century.

Spoons

Included here are medicine and cocktail spoons, but not eating spoons, which have been described previously as eating implements (*see* page 164).

Medicine spoons. These two spoons have worms that fold into the bowl. They both promote the same Burroughs Wellcome Co. products. The difference between the two is that the lower one has decorative curly writing. The advertisements are as follows: 'Tabloids of Compressed Drugs, Hazeline Cream, Kepler Extract and Essence of Malt, Kepler Solution

of Cod Liver Oil, Digestive, Demulcent, Strengthening, Hazeline Beef, and Iron Wine.' The upper one is also stamped 'Patent' and the lower one 'Patented'. They are examples of Cornelius Tunis Williamson's 1882 US Patent No. 264,391 (1892 British Patent No. 18,819). The collector should be wary of some silver spoons that were sold in the mid-1990s; these were a marriage between old hallmarked spoon bowls with unrelated corkscrew worms.

Cocktail spoons and a knife. The three American cocktail spoons are excellent promotional items and advertise a liquor store, a music shop and a tool company. The lower one even has the name 'Ope-An-Stir'. They are marked respectively 'Pat. Apld. For', 'Des. Pat. Pdg.', and 'Pat Pend.' None of these patents has been found. The cocktail knife for that impromptu wine and cheese party of the late '50s and early '60s has an imitation antler

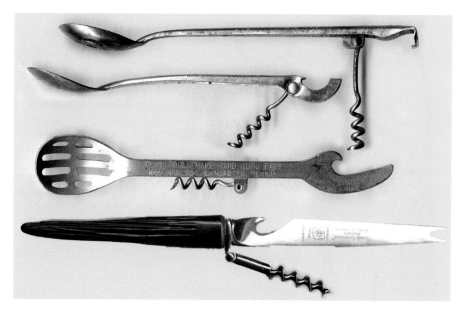

handle and a stainless steel blade marked 'Soiree Companion Stainless Sheffield England Reg. Des. 878771'. It is also marked 'Monogram Cutlery' with an intertwined ISD trademark. These knives are relatively common but it is rare to find one marked with the registration number for I.S. Dearsden and Sons' 1955 design.

Wall-mounted cap lifters

Wall-mounted cap lifters are an American genre and were probably designed for motel rooms.

Left: The plated steel wall-mounted cap lifter has a razor strop hook. The worm fits into a small lug near the top. It is marked 'Brown Mfg. Co. Newport News, VA Patd. Apr 25' and 'Made in USA' on the back. Raymond Brown's patent was actually granted in 1935 and the 1925 reference is to an earlier patent of Thomas Hamilton, which was acquired by Brown. Variations are sometimes marked 'Starr Brown', and Coca Cola ones are very collectable. *Centre:* This cast aluminium wall mount has a razor strop hook marked 'Zip'. The back is marked 'R.S. Products Corp. Phila. Pa. Pat. Pend.' The patent has not been found. *Right:* The back of the aluminium casting of this cap lifter is marked 'Corbin S 8582 22'. This wall mount is also known with a razor strop hook.

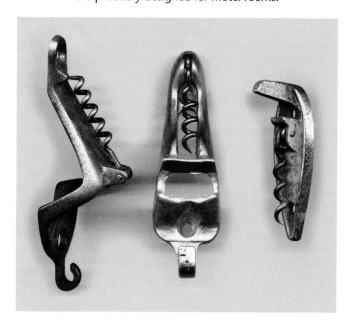

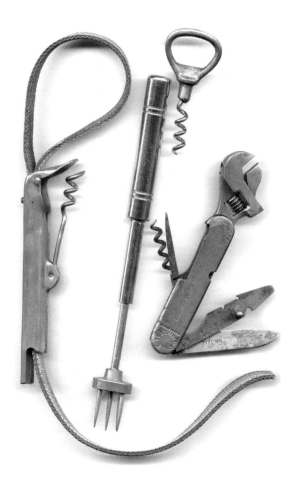

Unclassified

The problem of classifying combination tools is that the nature of the functions are only limited by the creativity of inventors. SCReWbase© describes the following eclectic mixture as 'Unclassified'.

Instruments of torture? *Left:* The leather strap on this odd kitchen tool is adjustable to fit jar lids for twisting them open. It is marked 'Master Eze Opener R.E. Collier 957 Umgeni Road Durban Pat 53.22793 Others Pend.', and relates to a 1955 South African patent. *Centre:* This bar tool is an ice chopper and is spring loaded to enhance the action. The cap lifter and corkscrew tool fits into the end of handle. The top of the chopper is marked 'Chip Chop Pat. Pend.' but the patent has not been found. *Right:* The adjustable spanner is from Jean-Albert Soustre's French 1928 patent, which was sold as 'Le Kou-to-kle' (derived from *couteau clef* meaning 'knife spanner'). It is marked 'K.T.K Breveté S.G.D.G. Made in France'. It was also patented in the USA by Soustre in 1931.

Right: Smokers' tools. *Left:* This very well made pocket tool has a six-prong spring on the inside of the U-shaped handle to hold all of the tools in place. They are a pricker, button hook, tobacco tamper, knife, pipe bowl scraper and a corkscrew. On the back of the handle are match striker ridges. The tangs of the tools are marked with the maker's name, 'Richardson Edinburgh' and it is an example of Stephen Winckworth Silver and Walter Fletcher's 1892 British Patent No. 7,318. *Centre and bottom:* Neither of these early-twentieth-century cigar cutters is marked but the larger one is probably American as characterized by the cigar box pry and wire snag at one end. The smaller one with bone scales is more likely to be German or British. *Right:* The protrusion on the cigar box pry is a small hammer for tapping the box top back on after use. It is American with very decorative silver scales marked 'Sterling'.

Smokers' tools with vestas for matches. *Left:* This has a decorative but slightly worn vesta with a monogram on one side, 'Remember Dunedin' on the other, and a striker at one end. *Right:* The vesta has two openings and a long striker along the bottom edge. The other side of the tool has a bone scale and a small pricker inserted by the side of the cigar cutter.

Left: Wire cutters with a folding corkscrew on the side are not particularly rare but they often seem to have damaged worms – probably through enthusiastic misuse. This is marked with a retailer's name 'B.B. Wells'. *Centre:* The small screw on one of the handles engages with the opposite one to hold the tool together for storage. It has a hammer, hatchet and folding blade plus a screwdriver and tack remover on the ends of the arms. The hammer is stamped 'Warranted Forged Steel'. Some rare versions are marked 'D.R.G.M. 120388' for Bader's 1899 registration for the locking screw. *Below:* This is a smaller, more delicate version of the one above and has a very strong spring to hold the worm in position. It is unmarked. *Right:* For such a simple tool, this example is very uncommon. The two sides lock together in the closed position due to the overlapping slot on one side. This unmarked 'Improved Device for use in Removing Bottle Closures' is shown in Mason's 1945 New Zealand Patent (1946 British Patent).

Champagne tools. *Top:* This type of elegant tool was shown in trade catalogues of 1860–80 as a 'Champagne Wire Cutter and Corkscrew'. Many were made without corkscrews, and some have had one added (often rather crudely) to increase their value. *Bottom Left:* Ernest Norwill registered the design for this champagne knife in 1896. It has a very slender handle, a folding fluted helix and is stamped 'G.H. Mumm & Co' on both sides, and 'J. Norwill & Sons Sheffield R*d* 280085' on the blade. *Bottom right:* This simple but uncommon pocket tool has a small folding blade and is marked 'Gesetzl. Geschützt' and 'F.A. Koch & Co' on the sides.

Left: The serrated 'bell' on this straight pull is actually a wire cutter. The shank is stamped 'Mercer's Patent Cory's Waters' and is an example of the 1891 British Patent No. 21,594 from John Mercer. *Centre:* The ring-shaped handle with eight tapered grips was made to grip screw stoppers on bottles. There are traces of bronze paint, suggesting it is from the late nineteenth century. *Right:* The straight pull has a cone cork splitter on the

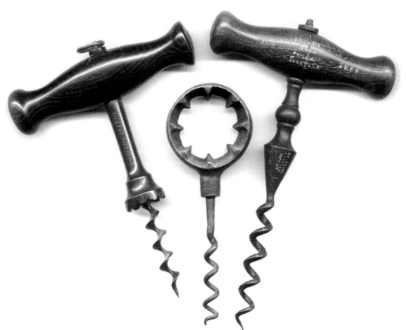

shank. The idea, from Walter James Holroyde's 1882 British Patent No. 1,406, is that you do not remove the cork from the worm after extraction; instead you just open another bottle and the second cork forces the first one up the cone and splits it in half, so it falls off. The wooden handle is very lightly stamped '1834 Patent Cone Cork Splitter 1355 T. Bradburn & Sons Sole Maker Birm.' The cone is marked 'By Royal Letters Patent'. The firm of Thomas Bradburn was established in Birmingham in 1834, which explains one number; the other is a serial number. Examples of this cone cork splitter were also made with a 'signet' finger hole.

Right: This is a rare, unmarked example of the 1887 British Patent No. 5,454 of John Stanley Garlick. It has a cone cork splitter, a Codd bottle opener, and a bronze handle at one end. This was claimed to allow the cork to be drawn more rapidly due to increased leverage.

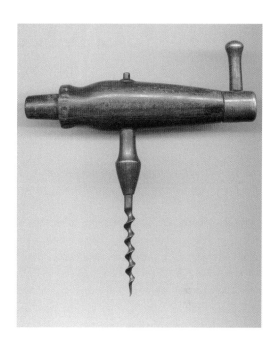

Below: Nutmeg graters. Most collectors dream of owning a silver nutmeg grater. These two examples, shown closed and open, come from travelling campaign sets with a knife, fork, spoon, condiments, beaker and corkscrew. The nutmeg was probably used for spicing up wine, but in the days before refrigeration, it could be used to disguise 'off' smells in food. It is often said that the shape of these lovely items is in the shape of a mace, a ceremonial club – a visual pun in that mace is the dried outer part of a nutmeg. The lid and grater of the smaller one screw on to the main body. As is fairly common on these old corkscrews, the head of the worm has a knop with a hole through it, so that a short steel pin could be put through it to create a pulling handle. The larger item has a hinged top with an integral grater and is well marked with hallmarks for 1803.

BAR CORKSCREWS

Wayne Meadows

Bar corkscrews, also called 'Barscrews', 'Automatic Corkscrews' or 'Mounted Corkscrews', occupy a fairly esoteric corner of the corkscrew-collecting world. These are cork-pulling devices that are designed to be fixed with clamps or screws to a counter or wall. Most are large and heavy, and are often in very poor condition when found, like the 'Sampson' shown below. If you have lots of display space, are mechanically inclined, have a reasonable workshop and love to take mechanisms apart to see what makes them tick or to renovate them, you will probably love them. If you don't have any of these things, you will probably not collect them. So, the good news is that not many collectors specialize in them; the bad news is that, compared to 'regular' corkscrews, very few were made.

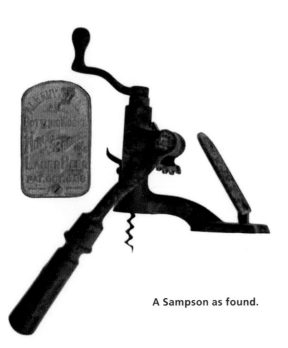

A Sampson as found.

Bar corkscrews are handled differently, in several aspects, from other corkscrews found in SCReWBase©. The SCReW© code follows the IDs shown in the Wayne Meadows' reference book *Compendium of Bar Corkscrews*. The collector can translate the SCReW© code into the book's code, and vice versa.

The first and simplest form of mounted corkscrew, introduced in the late 1800s in America, saw the worm and a mechanical advantage combined in one device. These corkscrews are commonly known as 'coffee grinders' or 'crank and pump' in the collector community. In most cases the worm was attached to a stem with a crank on it. In some examples the corkscrew is a copy of a patented mechanical corkscrew with a mounting bracket incorporated into the frame. These are not true bar corkscrews, as they were designed for home use – not necessarily for wine or beer, but for any product that came in a bottle. These do not have a complex automatic cork ejection mechanism, but as they are old and quite small, they tend to be prized by collectors.

With the advent of the mass production of beer in corked bottles and the proliferation of large hotel bars in America, the speed at which one could open hundreds of bottles in an evening became important. A low cost, faster mechanical system was required to insert the worm and eject the cork. A way was found to combine the two handles into one operating lever, pulling and ejecting the cork in a forward and rearward stroke of the handle. The very large number of mechanisms designed to do this were the subject of the bulk of the bar corkscrew patents aimed at the commercial market in the late 1800s and early 1900s.

American inventors produced by far the largest number of patents, not only in the USA, but also filing in many other countries.

Left: **Why you need a workshop – this is the same Sampson (patented in the USA in 1886 by John Hurley) after proper cleaning and polishing.** *Centre:* **The quintessential crank and pump patented by Edwin Walker in 1888.** *Right:* **The 'Simplex', patented by Henry Cliff in 1894.**

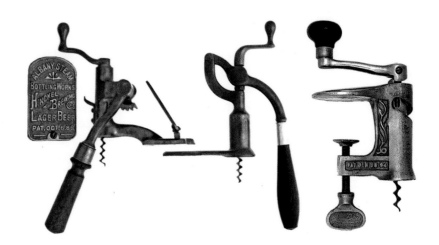

Gear mechanism.

Stem-nut mechanism.

At first glance, automatic corkscrew mechanisms appear to be extremely complex, but only the most impractical designs were very complicated. When one stops and thinks about it, there are very few operations required. First a worm is turned into the cork, and then the worm is pulled away from the bottle, removing the cork. In its simplest form, that's it. In an automatic corkscrew, one final operation is performed, when the worm is turned in the opposite direction, unscrewing or stripping the cork from the worm.

To make a corkscrew automatic, one must devise a method of turning the worm in both directions, while preventing it from turning during the cork extraction phase of the operation.

There are only three ways to cause the worm to turn in an automatic corkscrew. Two of these involve fastening a stem to the worm and causing the stem to turn. This can be accomplished either by attaching a gear to the stem or threading the stem and pushing it through a nut. The third uses the worm as screw.

In the gear mechanism, a gear (A) is attached to the stem (B) that is in turn attached to, or formed into, the worm (C). The usual method of turning the gear is to mesh it with a larger gear on a shaft, which is connected to a crank handle, which is turned to remove the cork. The gear mechanism was overly complicated, so was expensive to manufacture and thus very rarely used.

The stem-nut mechanism is mainly found in almost all British and a few Italian bar corkscrews. In the stem-nut mechanism a stem carrier (A) holds a threaded stem (C) which is free to revolve in its bearing. The worm (E) is screwed into the end of the threaded stem. The stem-nut (D) causes the stem to turn when the stem is pushed or pulled through it. In this example a bolt passes through the operating lever and through the hole (B) in the worm carrier. Pushing or pulling the operating lever causes the worm to turn clockwise or anticlockwise. This mechanism was moderately economic to produce and had a very long life expectancy.

The worm-nut mechanism is mainly found in almost all American and German bar corkscrews. As the worm (B) is already a form of screw, one can push or pull the worm through a worm-nut (C), causing it to rotate clockwise or anticlockwise. In the worm-nut mechanism a worm carrier (A) holds the worm which is free to revolve in its bearing (D). Apart from the worm, this mechanism was usually made entirely from cast iron, with a lead or babbitt alloy lining in the nut.

Little or no machining was required, thus it was very cheap to produce. The one drawback was that the lining of the nut wore out fairly quickly.

Britain produced the second highest number of bar corkscrews, primarily in cast brass rather than the cast iron that most of the rest of the world used.

Bar corkscrews were produced in many countries and many were copies or slightly modified versions of American corkscrew mechanisms.

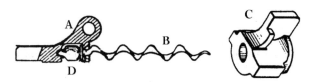

Worm-nut mechanism.

American examples. *Left:* Clamp-mounted 'Champion', patented by Michael Redlinger in 1896. This is the most commonly found American bar corkscrew; however, there are about ten different versions of it. *Centre:* The 'Quick and Easy', with clamp or top mount, was patented by Edwin Walker in 1896. *Right:* The 'Pullmee', patented by Albert Baumgarten in 1901. Other than the 'Yankee #1', American wall-mounted corkscrews are very rare.

British examples. *Left:* 'Original Safety', patented by American Raymond Gilchrist in 1894. This is the most commonly found British bar corkscrew. It was made in about fifteen different versions including cast brass and cast iron, with both clamp and top mount. *Centre:* The 'A1', patented by Samuel Mason in 1902, supplied with both top and clamp mount. *Right:* The 'Rotary Eclipse', patented by Frederick Marwood in 1885. This is a giant brass corkscrew that every corkscrew collector seems to want.

Above: European examples. *Left:* 'Hektor 1', a German adaptation of the Yankee #7 patented by G. Frings in 1925. This is the most commonly found German bar corkscrew. It was made in about nine different versions marked Hektor 1–3, with and without foil cutters on the side and different case decorations. *Centre:* The 'Milano', an Italian version of the US Champion. *Right:* 'L'Automatique', patented in France by Engelbert Renson d'Herculais in 1929.

Below: Further European examples. *Left:* 'Alfredo P.', a Spanish corkscrew manufactured by Perez-Quintanilla in Gijon. *Centre:* A Belgian fish-shaped version of the 'Titan', marked 'JV' with a rampant lion logo. *Right:* The earliest known patented bar corkscrew, patented in Sweden by P.F. Lindström in 1870.

NON-WORM EXTRACTORS

Reinhold Berndt and Joe Paradi

This class of 'corkscrews' is really not comprised of anything that screws into a cork. These should more appropriately be called 'cork removers'. But what difference does this make if, after all, the objective is to remove the cork so that we can enjoy the contents of the bottle? The answer is that it is just a matter of semantics that only a real corkscrew collector would be interested in.

There are five types of non-worm extractors, none of which has a worm or screw: prongs, hooks, gas injectors, retrievers, and spikes.

Prongs

These are the most common type of non-worm extractors and are usually equipped with a handle and

German examples. *Left to right:* An example with wire handle, marked 'Maro D.R.G.M.' (No. 1,483,417), registered in 1939 by Fritz Müchler. It is sold with wooden or tin sheaths. The next prong is a similar model also marked 'Maro D.R.G.M.' (No. 1,523,994), registered by Fritz Müchler in 1942. It is known with wooden and tin sheaths. A very popular cork puller *(second from right)* marked 'Maro D.R.P.' (1922 Patent No. 386,724 of G. Della Zuana), produced by Fritz Müchler in the 1930s. Finally, a cork extractor marked 'D.R.G.M.' (registration number not identified). Some similar pieces are marked 'RI-BI' for Richard Bickel, and the wooden sheath is available in different colours.

Further German examples. *Left to right:* The Korkenzieher 'Ideal' was produced in large numbers. The patent (No. 811,665) was registered in 1949 by Paul & Helmut Vitz, The next example, marked 'D.R.G.M. Ah-So – Garantie' is the 1932 registered design of Georg Hermann Usbeck (No. 1,242,981). The sheath is made of nickel-plated brass. The next example is a variant of the above, also by Usbeck, marked 'D.R.G.M. Ah-Ha –

Germany'. The final example has a plastic handle marked 'Monopol' and was manufactured by Monopol Usbeck & Soehne in around 1970.

British examples. *Left to right:* 'The 'Easi-Pull in its original box, made by Easi-Pull Co. in the 1960s. The next example, made in the 1930s by Arthur Balfour & Co., is marked 'W.U.F. Ideal Corkpuller'. A foil cutter is attached to the handle. The next is marked on the handle 'Wiggle 'n' Twist Cork Extractor and Corker'. It was sold by Heibo Products, London (Patent No. 1,525,678 from Heinrich Bordat's 1976 design) The final British corkpuller is marked on the leather case 'Ideal Cork Drawer, British Made, Reg-No. Reg-No. 708,714'. A cap lifter for crown corks is attached to the handle. The design was registered by Arthur Orol F. Brewster in 1924.

French pieces. *From left to right:* A cork puller with spare prongs in an aluminium sheath, marked 'Sanbri Bte. S.G.D.G.' It was patented in 1949 by Henri Albert Tabard. The next example is unmarked with a wooden handle and steel sheath, probably made by Laurent Kertzmann around 1930. The 'JTR' was sold by Société (Emile) Jetter between 1933 and 1955. Finally, an example with a Bakelite sheath, marked 'GOL' on the handle, made by Goldenberg, 1938–48.

two slender steel prongs, usually (but not always) fixed into the handle. The prongs are inserted on either side of the cork, but to lift the cork it has to be twisted clockwise or anticlockwise with a back and forth motion to release the cork from the bottle neck and, while still turning, pull it up. The interesting added benefit is that the cork remains intact, so the bottle can be re-corked by repeating the above process, but in reverse.

American examples. *Left to right:* An unmarked puller (1980s) with plastic sheath advertising a Californian winery, The Christian Brothers. The boxed cork puller is marked on the sheath 'Vaughan's Quick & Easy Cork Puller and Bottle Opener'. The Vaughan Novelty Manufacturing Co. applied for a US Patent in 1935 but it is not clear if the patent was ever granted. The next example *(second from right)* was a popular cork extractor, the 1899 US Patent No. 624,457 of Maschil D. Converse. It is marked on the sheath 'Patented May 9th, 99', and it was sold in large numbers and also exported to France. Lucian Mumford's US Patent No. 212,863 of 1879 *(right)* with nickel-plated prongs is marked 'Magic Cork Extractor, Pat: March 4 – 79, May 10 – 92'.

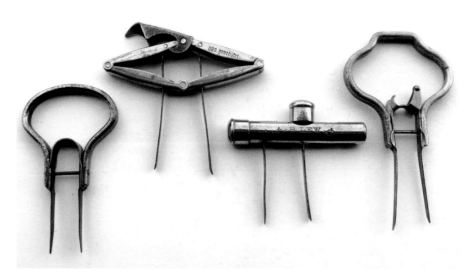

Folding or pocket pieces. *From left to right:* Unmarked cork extractor with folding mechanism, an example of Théodore Detroyes' 1929 French Patent No. 678,196. Next, an unusual folding extractor marked 'Ges. geschützt' for 1924 German Patent No. 476,777 of Otto Klemer. It is similar to the Hollweg folding corkscrew, and there is also a variant without a cap lifter. Benjamin Lew's famous adjustable two-prong pocket extractor *(second from right)* is one of the earliest German corkscrew patents (Patent No. 16 of 1877). Eugène Serre's 1934 French Patent No. 772,702 is a multi-tool with folding prongs, crown cap lifter and glass cutter.

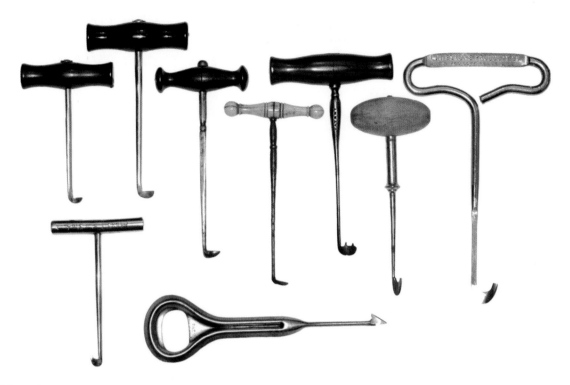

Hooks

Top, left to right: Two American examples made in large numbers by Benjamin Greely, US Patent No. 379,010 (1888). They have a groove to let the air back into the bottle. An unmarked hook, probably French. An unmarked example of the 1919 French Patent No. 499,727 of Paul Schnurr. The example with two teeth on the hook is marked 'Patent Sims and Law', and is the provisional 1868 British Patent No. 1,810 of James Law. An unmarked example of 1938 German registration DRGM 1,440,183 of Emil Rietz, and finally a hefty all-steel American hook marked 'Lakeshore Products Co. 783 Cork Puller'. *Bottom left:* Marked on the handle 'Le Parisien Bte', this is an example of Edouard Ygoumenc's 1924 French Patent No. 565,931 with flat-topped hook. *Bottom right:* Punched sheet metal piece with cap lifter, marked 'Pat. Jan 19 1926' for the US Patent No. 1,570,306 of William Johnson (also covered in 1930 Patent No. 1,779,170). It also claims to be useful for sewing up chickens.

Hooks

Cork extractors with hooks were made by all the major corkscrew manufacturing countries and there is a very good variety available for the collector. They typically have a T-handle with a slender shaft and the end is fashioned into a hook. The shaft is inserted alongside the cork, with the hook turned so that it slides past the cork. When it has completely passed the cork, the handle is turned through 90° so that the hook is right under the bottom surface of the cork, and the handle is then pulled up to remove the cork.

Gas injectors

These cork removers are equipped with a needle that penetrates through the cork and then air or gas is injected into the bottle, and the pressure of the gas will either ease out or pop out the cork – champagne of course does this on its own. They usually have a handle to push the needle through the cork and then either pump in air or release a compressed air or carbon dioxide (CO_2) capsule to increase the pressure until the cork comes out. These devices were banned in some countries as they can explode a structurally weak bottle if the pressure is too high.

Left to right: An unmarked air injector made in Germany by Emide, an example of the 1965 Swiss Patent No. 433,041 of Werner Streicher. The next air injector is an unusual piece with the needle at 90 degrees to the pump barrel, with a needle cover (the white plastic cone has been removed for the photo). It is marked 'Corky Made in Switzerland' and it has a Swiss cross and 'Patent' and 'Pat Pend.' on the end of the barrel. This refers to the 1965 Swiss Patent No. 403,526 of Franz Tschappu. The next example is also Swiss, with the pump handle shown in the open position. It is marked 'Corkex' and is labelled 'Made in Switzerland'. This was the 1965 Patent No. 390,072 of René Besançon. The final example contains a carbon dioxide cartridge in the handle. The needle is inserted into the cork and pressing the black button releases the gas to pop the cork. It is the1965 British Patent No. 994,203 of Brian Sidney Bennet.

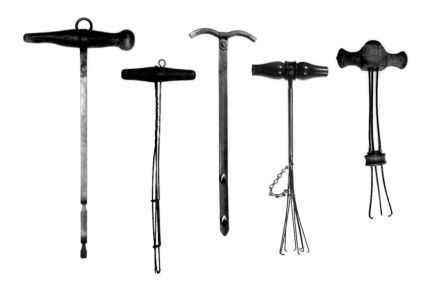

Retrievers

Left to right: A large cork retriever with a flat shaft marked 'Pat Nov 25 1890' for the US Patent No. 441,604 of Bernard Tormey. Note how the left of the handle is shaped such that it can push the cork down into the bottle. The next example has a turned wood handle with three prongs made out of stiff wire, twisted together and wrapped around the handle. Another wire is threaded through the handle (see the loop above the handle) and is formed into two loops that encircle the three prongs that are inside these rings. The loop at the top is used to slide the wire up and down to open and close the retrieving wires. The maker is unknown. The French retriever *(centre)* is Jean Deniard's 1932 Patent No. 742,331. One of the rarest and most prized of this type *(second from right)* is the 1890 British Patent No. 8,879 of Thomas Andrew McKee and Henry Spillar McIntosh. It has a beautiful turned wooden handle and a brass tube that is used to close and open the wires. Finally, a piece of unknown origin with a turned wooden handle and a wooden ring to close the retrieving wires.

Retrievers

One of the ways a cork can be removed is first to push it into the bottle and then, using one of these retrievers, to 'fish it out'. There is often a ring or sleeve that is used to compress the wires or prongs for insertion into the bottle. The ends of the wires or prongs are fashioned into hooks, which are used to grab the cork in an upright position before pulling it up through bottle neck.

Spikes

Perhaps the most unlikely technology used to remove corks from a bottle is the use of 'spikes'. These unusual devices are driven into the cork prior to the twisting/prying motion that is required to ease the cork out of the bottle. Many wine aficionados consider these to be the least effective method of removing today's larger and tighter corks, as they are not strong enough to tackle a tough cork, but for corkscrew collectors, these are great finds, nevertheless.

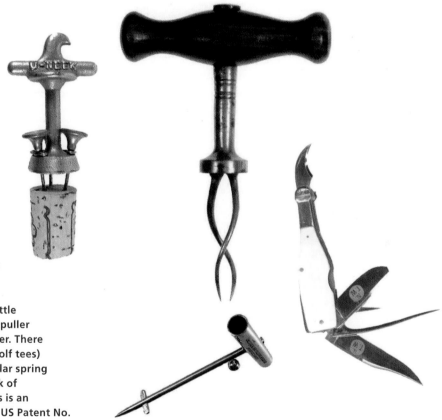

Top left: The '**U-Neek**' – indeed a unique item as there are no others like it. This is a cast steel combination milk bottle top opener and cork puller with a crown cap lifter. There are three pins (like golf tees) positioned by a circular spring ring that do the work of removing a cork. This is an example of the 1917 US Patent No. 1,213,452 of Wilson M. Brady. *Top:* Bradnock's 'Magic Twist' is an unusual piece, covered by the 1883 British Patent No. 3,221 of Richard William Bradnock. Most are marked 'Magic Twist' and they are hard to find. *Right:* A pocket knife with extractor, marked on several surfaces 'Korn's Patent', 'Henry Sears & Son 1865', and 'Registered'. US Patent Number 283,900 was granted in 1883 to George Korn, who also patented it in France and Germany. The twin spikes of uneven length between the two knife blades form the working device. *Bottom:* Unlike some of the other examples, this one can work well – the knob below the handle slides up and down opening the crossbar at the pointed end (as in the picture) or folding it into the shaft. When it is in the latter position, the spike is driven through the cork, the crossbar is turned out and the cork is pulled. It is marked 'Call's Ideal Cork Puller Pat. Applied For Springfield, Mass', and is an example of the 1909 US Patent No. 911,292 of Charles C. Call.

CHAMPAGNE AND SODA TAPS

Joe Paradi and Barbara Ellis

Champagne and soda taps, collectively called 'taps', are surprisingly rather unappreciated corkscrews, but there are collectors who specialize in them. Beginner collectors will easily find some of these very interesting devices, they are usually not very expensive, and they are worth collecting. There are several different types of champagne and soda tap, which will be described. Other champagne-related items are also included in this section.

The unique characteristic of champagne being under pressure really defined the need for these devices. Champagne was also considered by the medical profession to be a special medicine that would cure many ills. If this 'medicine' was to be taken without drinking the whole bottle, some method to meter the liquid was needed, and so the champagne tap was born. These devices have been around since the early nineteenth century. They were also used for soda and

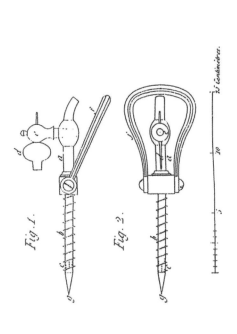

The first patent for a champagne tap was issued in France in 1828 to François Rever, Patent No. 3,571 – this was the first corkscrew patent granted in France. The patent drawing and an example are shown.

other 'aerated' liquids, and they are sometimes known as 'soda taps'.

Taps were designed to penetrate the cork without actually pulling it out, and then to draw off the liquid. They always have a valve with a handle, allowing liquid to be drawn off by opening the valve, and then stopping the flow of liquid and preserving the bubbles by closing the valve. They have an internal pipe with holes at the bottom for the liquid to move through. They have a pointed end to pierce the cork, which may be small short worm (tip worm) or just a spike. There may be a worm fixed on the shaft/pipe to penetrate the cork in the usual corkscrew way, but some have just a smooth shaft or pipe with no worm.

The design of the valve and handle is another distinguishing feature. There are six different operating mechanisms for combinations of the valve and handle, illustrated below. Some valves open and close by turning a valve handle through 90 degrees. This method is used by the side handle, top handle, double handle and spring valves. Starting or stopping the flow of liquid is achieved via a hole through the valve that aligns with the pipe carrying the liquid. In the other mechanism the valve plugs up or opens the end of a pipe or the base of the valve housing. This technique is found in taps with screw valves and lever valves.

VALVE AND HANDLE MECHANISMS

The most common taps have a single side valve handle. They open and close by a 90° turn and sometimes have a stop mechanism to limit the turning.

Screw valves open and close the fluid flow by moving a screw that threads itself in and out of the housing and thus opens or closes the tap. The screw can be located on the side or at the top.

The spring valve uses a spring to operate the valve. To open, the handle is pressed down and the fluid flows; once the handle is released the spring closes the valve. The handle can be on the side or on the top.

The top valve handle is located on the top of the piece, but it works in the same way as the single-handled valve shown above.

VALVE AND HANDLE MECHANISMS *(continued)*

In double-handled valves the handles are on both sides of the pipe, perpendicular to it. The on/off mechanism is the same as the single-handled taps and they can have a stop mechanism as well.

In the lever valve, the open-close cycle is accomplished by a lever that moves the tip of the tap up and down, using a wire that runs the length of the tube.

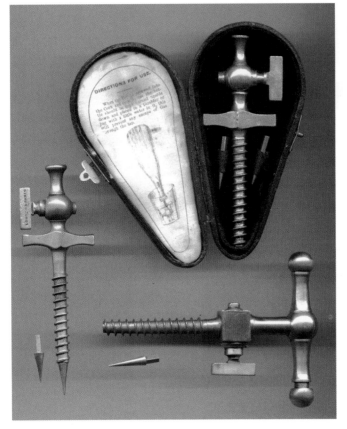

Drop points

Some taps come equipped with a detachable point or tip that fits into the end of the hollow shaft, which is used to drain the liquid. Once the tap is inserted through the cork, the point or tip falls into the bottle, and the valve handle is turned to dispense the liquid. When the bottle is empty, the point or tip is recovered and re-used. These taps usually came in a leather-covered, teardrop-shaped case, with small leather holders for the points.

Drop points. *Left:* A classic drop point marked 'Farrow and Jackson' for the British maker. One drop point is inserted and a spare is shown. *Top:* An unmarked example with two points in a case, with 'Directions for Use' printed on to the satin liner of the case. *Bottom:* An unmarked example with the spout underneath. The two ends of the handle unscrew to house the points – one end is shown slightly unscrewed.

Long and medium taps

Taps were often used for soda, cider and other carbonated beverages as well as champagne. These drinks came in containers of different sizes, from large (containing 8–12 litres) to small (containing 2–4 litres), so taps of different lengths were needed. Long taps are generally, and arbitrarily, defined as being longer than 20cm (8in), while medium taps are less than 20cm (8in). All of these taps have a short three- to four-turn screw fashioned at the end of the pipe, called the tip worm, which serves as the corkscrew. They also have holes in the pipe, just above the tip worm, to allow the liquid to enter the pipe. The flow of liquid is controlled by the valve handle.

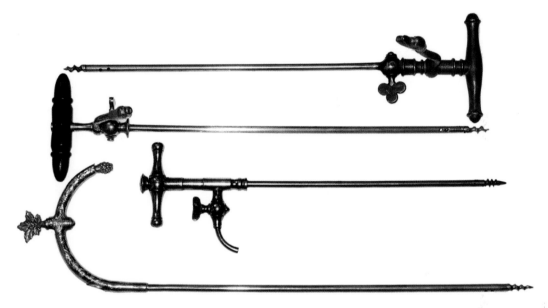

Above: Long taps are found with wooden or steel handles and the spout often ends in the shape of a dolphin's head. Soda bottles were not corked as tightly as champagne bottles and the idea was just to penetrate the cork and then force the long pipe down into the liquid.

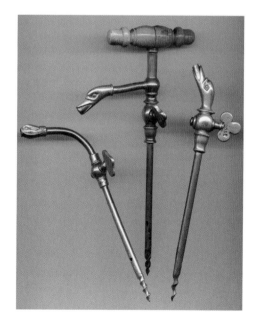

Right: Medium taps were used for champagne as well as soda and other carbonated drinks. Note the attractive dolphin head spouts. The two all-steel examples are marked 'Déposé' on one side of the valve handle, and 'LG' in a triangle on the other. This was the trademark for Louis Gilles who manufactured various taps up to 1920. The example with a wooden handle is marked 'Breveté J-P Paris' on the handle for Jacques Pérille. The patent has not been identified.

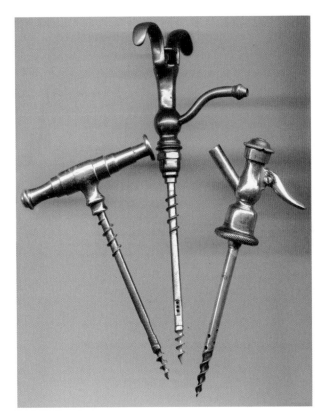

This wonderful tap with a fish handle is a medium tap as it has the short tip worm at the end. It also has another worm fixed on to the pipe. It is an example of the 1892 French Patent No. 216,953 and British Patent No. 3,436 of Charles Soulier.

Left and centre: These two French medium taps have a spring valve marked 'Bte S.D.G.D., J.D. Paris'. The patent has not been identified but the maker was J. Depagne who was active up to 1920. The spring valve is on the right side of the handle of the first example and at the top of the eyebrow example in the centre. Both have a partial worm fixed at the top end of the pipe. *Right:* This medium tap has a spring valve on the side. It is indistinctly marked 'Geraut Patented London' underneath the button at the top of the pipe. The patent has not been identified so far.

Pipes

Taps described as pipes are usually closed at the end, where the metal is formed into a sharp point to facilitate entry into the cork. They usually have a worm fixed on to the outside of the pipe, which runs up the whole length of the pipe. The worm allows easier cork penetration, as in traditional corkscrew use. The taps also have holes near the tip for the liquid to enter, and liquid flow is usually controlled by the valve handle, although there are some without such handles. There are a few examples that do not have a worm fixed onto the pipe, but just have a plain pipe with holes, which is forced into the cork. There are many variations in design of pipe taps and several patents, usually relating to the valve mechanism, so this makes an interesting group for the collector.

Left: A classic champagne tap is the 'Holborn Champagne Screw', which is the 1877 British Registered Design No. 307,655 of Edwin Wolverson. This bronze-washed example is marked with a registration diamond on one side and the name on the other. They can be variously marked or unmarked and also come in a nickel-plated finish. The worm is inserted into the cork, the bottle is inverted, and the tap is opened to release the champagne. This is why the tap is apparently upside down. Note that the worm has holes near the bottom for the liquid to enter. *Right:* Wolverson's second registered design for a champagne tap, granted in 1879, has a large finger loop handle and is marked with a registration diamond on the side handle. This is not a very common piece, unlike the very successful Holborn Screw.

Left to right: This unusual pipe tap has a plain pipe and no worm. It has a screw valve handle on the side and is marked 'The Gem Tap' on the top. The next example is a simple pipe tap marked 'Law & Co 1917', for the Birmingham manufacturers. Next, an unusual tap with an acorn top that unscrews to open the pipe. It is marked 'Indus' on one side and 'Pat 93543', and is a 1928 Spanish patent of Alfonso Oliveras Guerris, who also filed in the USA. An early tap *(second from right)*, marked 'Registered J.H.S. 11 Aug 1865' for the British Registered Design No. 4,735 of John Cheshire and Francis Heeley, trading as James Heeley and Sons. The top handle unscrews to open the valve. Lastly, an attractive British tap marked 'SM Maw & Son London' on the decorative fleur-de-lis double handles. Maw also made a similar drop point tap.

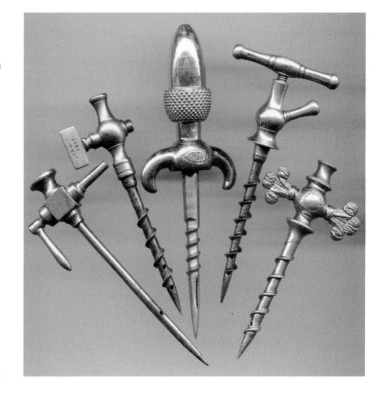

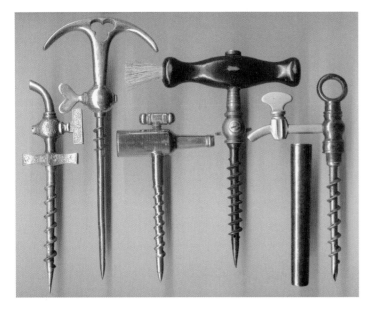

Left to right: A classic style tap with very decorative handles. Next, a stylish design with a spout at the back and just a small worm at the top of the pipe. An American Williamson's Tap, unmarked, but from a marked box, claiming 'Patent Applied For'. It has a characteristic bottle-shaped spout. The wooden-handled example is a simple tap with no spout, but with a hole at the top of the handle. Finally, an unusual old tap with a protective sheath that fits into the top hole to turn it into a picnic-type corkscrew.

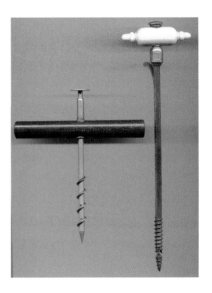

Right: These two taps do not have any valves and are thus 'tapless'. *Left:* This simple piece, marked 'Hoopers Patent Tapless' on the wooden handle, is the 1880 British Patent No. 980 of Frederic Edward Hooper and Arthur George Luke. It is also marked 'Perry & Co Limited Steel Pin Makers' on the other side. The top round disc is fixed to a hollow inner tube that can be moved up and down to open or close the holes in the outer pipe. *Right:* This quality French piece operates in a similar way. The bottom tip worm is fixed to the round brass handle at the top by an inner rod, which can be moved up and down to lock into the V-shaped opening at the bottom of the outer pipe. The spout can just be seen at the back. The ivory handle is the same as the Dordet patent below, so is probably from the same maker.

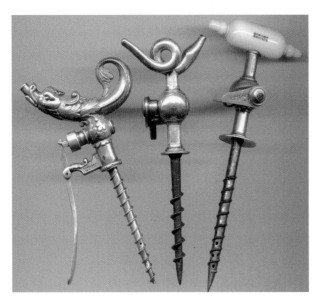

Left: French pipe taps. *Left:* This beautiful silver tap is crowned with a decorative dolphin with ornamental leaves, and has a long lever handle to operate the valve. It is marked 'Deleuze Breveté Paris' on one side of the arm to which the lever is fixed and 'Dutillet Breveté Paris' on the other. The patent was filed by Gustave Deleuze in 1830 (the other name may be the manufacturer). *Centre:* This elegant piece has a stylized curled dolphin spout and a handle with an external steel spring. The handle is marked 'Baudouin'. *Right:* An equally elegant example, with a carved ivory handle marked 'Dordet Breveté' and a spring handle, also with an external steel spring. The spring handle is marked 'Dordet Breveté Paris'. Jean Dordet was active between 1829 and 1861. The patent has not been identified.

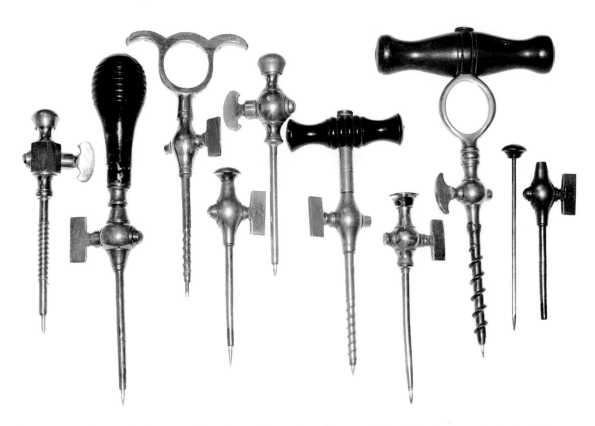

The trocar can be attached to a traditional wooden or three-finger pull handle (as in examples 3, 6 and 8) or to a screw handle as in the other examples. A removed trocar is seen on the far right. The trocar usually unscrews just above the valve.

Trocars

A 'trocar' is defined as a hollow pipe with a sharp point, but in the corkscrew world it refers to a long spike or wire that goes all the way from the top to the bottom of the tap inside the pipe. The end of the trocar spike can be seen at the bottom of the pipe and can be felt as being separate from the pipe. There are no holes drilled into the side of the pipe. This is an important difference from the taps described previously, where the pipe and pointed end are in one piece and have drilled holes for the liquid. Once the tap has been inserted into the cork, the trocar has to be unscrewed to remove it completely, and this then opens up the pipe for liquid to flow, controlled by the valve handle. The trocar is reinserted through the on/off valve when the valve is open and it passes through the hole in the valve. Care should be taken not to turn the valve handle while the trocar is in position inside the pipe, as this may cause damage. Trocar taps can either have a worm fixed on the outside of the pipe or just have a smooth pipe, as shown in the examples above. There are no spouts, just a hole for the liquid above the valve.

At a final extreme, a sabre or curved sword can be used to open a champagne bottle by dextrously sliding it down the bottle edge and forcing the cork out. This technique is called 'sabrage' and provides much amusement at parties.

Champagne tools

There are a number of useful champagne tools of interest to the collector. The tools are all designed to deal with the special conditions under which champagne is stored. Many such tools are marked with advertising for the champagne houses.

Knives

Champagne knives have short curved blades that help in cutting the retaining wires holding the champagne cork in the bottle. Many corkscrews and pocket knives have such blades as well, as discussed earlier.

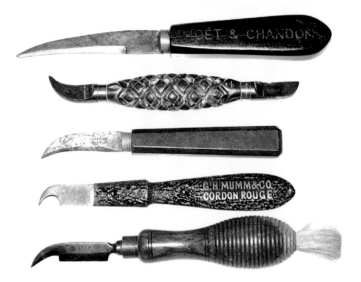

Left: **Examples of knives.**

Wire cutters

These tools resemble scissors or pliers, and they are used to clip the retaining wires from champagne corks.

Examples of wire cutters.

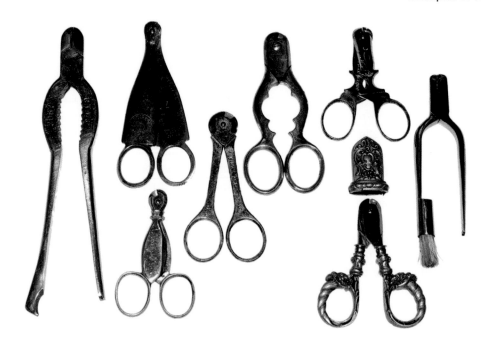

Examples of grippers.

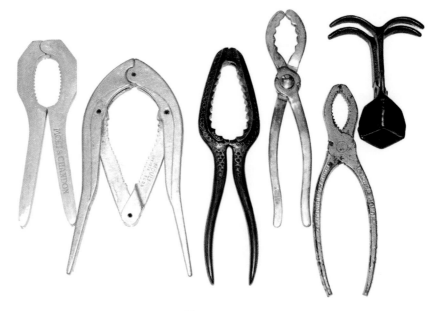

Grippers

Grippers typically look like a pair of pliers, but there are other shapes as well, as shown. These are used to grab the cork and twist or pull it out.

Easers

Easers are devices that ease the champagne cork out of the bottle, a gentle form of cork removal. The often spectacular popping of champagne corks can be dangerous and should be reserved for 'photo opportunities', according to Health and Safety fanatics. These easers will extract the cork in a safer but less exciting manner.

Examples of easers.

Cork stoppers and resealers

Cork stoppers and resealers are used to close the bottles of champagne after the cork is removed. They are designed to keep the gas pressure in the bottle, but not to dispense the liquid.

Examples of cork stoppers and resealers.

Cork replacers

Cork replacers are devices used to stopper the bottle after the cork is removed; they are equipped with a tap to allow the liquid to be dispensed into a glass.

Examples of cork replacers.

ACCESSORIES

Joe Paradi

Any corkscrew collector who is hunting for those elusive great pieces will come across common corkscrews he does not need or want, and sometimes cannot find anything he is interested in. But then, an item is seen that is not a corkscrew, but has a picture of a corkscrew or is in the shape of one. In fact, there are many such items around and collectors pick them up because they are interesting or educational – or because they can't resist them. Such items will often be bought for you by friends and relatives. There is a very wide range of such accessories, as listed below.

Art
Bottles and jugs
Cork tools
Dishes and tableware
Novelty
Paper and printed material
Screw tools
Videos and films
Wine accessories
Unclassified

Art covers paintings, photos, posters, sculptures, frames, music, rugs etc. It crosses over to another collectable world, as there are some very nice and valuable paintings and sculptures a corkscrew collector could acquire.

Painting by J. Durham.

A painting by Cartier.

A Seagram Museum poster.

Glengarry
whisky jug

Bottles and jugs include many collectable items
from Codd Bottles to whisky jugs.

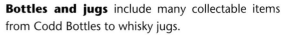

A Codd bottle
(left), and a
stoneware bottle
for ginger beer
(right).

Cork Tools are implements that are used to shape corks or insert them into the bottle. They include cork borers, cork cutters, cork presses, cork sizers, corking tools and corking machines.

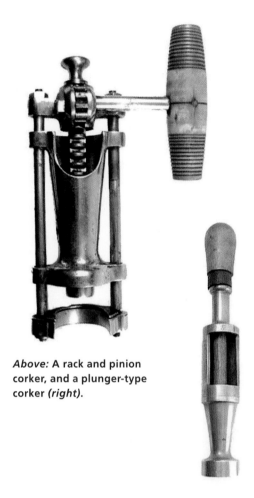

Above: A cast-iron cork press.

Above: **A rack and pinion corker, and a plunger-type corker** *(right).*

Dishes and Tableware are items that have corkscrew pictures on them. They include plates, decanters, glasses, and cups.

Below right: **A pottery wine cooler,**

Above: **a metal trivet, and** *(right)* **a commemorative plate.**

VINUM BIBENT HOMINES, ANIMALIA CETERA FONTES

MILANO ICCA AGM
1 9 0

Novelty includes a large assortment of objects from clothing such as neckties, aprons, shirts, socks and hats, to household items such as fridge magnets, ashtrays, chocolate moulds, cookie jars, coasters, and towels, through to tie pins, jewellery and even a match safe. Of course, all of them have an image of one or more corkscrews and they are very collectable!

Silk ties.

From left: An apron, tea towel and *(below)* serving tray.

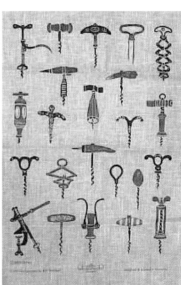

From left: Ceramic ash tray, chocolate mould, match safe, and *(below left)* CCCC club pin and tie pin *(right)*.

Right: The first corkscrew book by Watney & Babbidge.

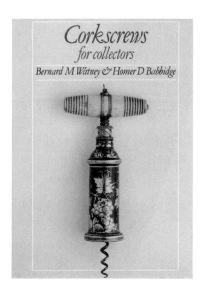

Paper and Printed Materials are probably the most useful accessories and without doubt, all collectors will have some of these – after all, if you are reading this piece, you have, or will have bought one of the books on corkscrews. Apart from books, there are a variety of items including catalogues, postcards, advertisements, wine labels, menus, paper napkins, bags and calendars.

The books are the most important items in this genre and for the beginner the six books shown below will provide an almost complete reference library. On the website www.corkscrewnet.com the reader can find a complete set of all corkscrew books published. The list has 75 different volumes, ranging from pocket books to beautiful, hardcover books.

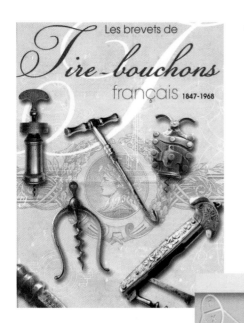

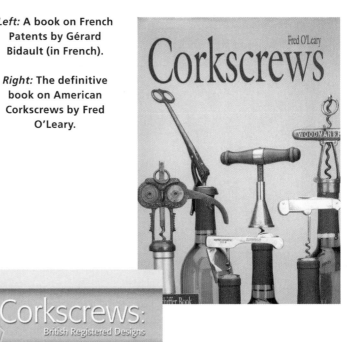

Left: A book on French Patents by Gérard Bidault (in French).

Right: The definitive book on American Corkscrews by Fred O'Leary.

*Right: A*n informative book on British Registered Designs by Frank and Barbara Ellis.

Below left: An authoritative book on British Patents by Fletcher Wallis; and (*below right):* the most complete book on Mechanical Corkscrews by Ferd Peters.

Postcards can be interesting and amusing items to collect.

A selection of corkscrew-related postcards.

Centre, Clockwise from left: Barrel bung puller, motor bearing packing tool, medical instrument (tumour screw), and *(below):* muzzle loading gun tool.

Screw Tools are articles that look like corkscrews but are not actually. These include barrel bung pullers, muzzle loading gun tools, motor bearing packing removers, medical instruments, tie downs and others.

Videos and Films include collectable segments of TV shows – many collectors have been invited to talk shows or antique and curiosity shows and these are the clips of these encounters. There are TV advertisements showing corkscrews, movie clips with corkscrews in action and interviews with expert corkscrew collectors. Obviously there are no examples shown here.

Wine Accessories include bottle locks, wine cradles, coasters, funnels, bottle labels, wine pourers, port tongs, bottle stoppers, and other related items.

Unclassified are those things which really cannot be easily assigned elsewhere. These include printer blocks, sugar devils, buttons, street signs, medals, tobacco tins and other items.

Above: Beer cap lifter with corkscrew logo, *(below, left):* ceramic bottle stopper, *(right):* pewter wine pourer.

Sugar devil.

Product tag.

Wine Expert Society Medal.

BRITISH REGISTERED DESIGN CODES

The class is denoted by Roman numerals as follows:

I	Metal
II	Wood
III	Glass
IV	Earthenware
V	Paper hangings
VI	Carpets
VII	Printed shawls

VIII	Other shawls
IX	Yarn
X	Printed fabrics
XI	Furnitures
XII	Other fabrics
XIII	Lace

Month letter codes

A	December
B	October
C	January
D	September
E	May
G	February

H	April
I	July
K	November
M	June
R	August
W	March

Years sorted by letter codes

1842 to 1867	
A	1845
B	1858
C	1844
D	1852
E	1855
F	1847
G	1863
H	1843
I	1846
J	1854
K	1857
L	1856
M	1859
N	1864
O	1862
P	1851
Q	1866
R	1861
S	1849
T	1867
U	1848
V	1850
W	1865
X	1842
Y	1853
Z	1860

1868 to 1883	
A	1871
C	1870
D	1878
E	1881
F	1873
H	1869
I	1872
J	1880
K	1883
L	1882
P	1877
S	1875
U	1874
V	1876
X	1868
Y	1879

Year letters sorted by years

1842 to 1867	
1842	X
1843	H
1844	C
1845	A
1846	I
1847	F
1848	U
1849	S
1850	V
1851	P
1852	D
1853	Y
1854	J
1855	E
1856	L
1857	K
1858	B
1859	M
1860	Z
1861	R
1862	O
1863	G
1864	N
1865	W
1866	Q
1867	T

1868 to 1883	
1868	X
1869	H
1870	C
1871	A
1872	I
1873	F
1874	U
1875	S
1876	V
1877	P
1878	D
1879	Y
1880	J
1881	E
1882	L
1883	K

Registration numbers

Corkscrews from 1884 onwards can be dated using registration numbers to determine the year. This table shows the approximate registration number used at the start of each year from 1884 to 1991.

1884	1	1920	673750	1956	879282
1885	19754	1921	680147	1957	882949
1886	40480	1922	687144	1958	887079
1887	64520	1923	694999	1959	891665
1888	90483	1924	702671	1960	895000
1889	116648	1925	710165	1961	899914
1890	141273	1926	718057	1962	904638
1891	163713	1927	726330	1963	909364
1892	185713	1928	734370	1964	913536
1893	205240	1929	742725	1965	919607
1894	224720	1930	751160	1966	924510
1895	246975	1931	760583	1967	929335
1896	268392	1932	769670	1968	934515
1897	291241	1933	779292	1969	939875
1898	311658	1934	789019	1970	944932
1899	331707	1935	799097	1971	950046
1900	351202	1936	808794	1972	955342
1901	368154	1937	817293	1973	960708
1902	385180	1938	825231	1974	965185
1903	403200	1939	832610	1975	969249
1904	424400	1940	837520	1976	973838
1905	447700	1941	838590	1977	978426
1906	471800	1942	839230	1978	982815
1907	493900	1943	839980	1979	987910
1908	518640	1944	841040	1980	993012
1909	535170	1945	842670	1981	998302
1910	552000	1946	845550	1982	1004456
1911	574817	1947	849730	1983	1010583
1912	594195	1948	853260	1984	1017131
1913	612431	1949	856999	1985	1024174
1914	630190	1950	860854	1986	1031358
1915	644935	1951	863970	1987	1039055
1916	653521	1952	866280	1988	1047478
1917	658988	1953	869300	1989	1056076
1918	662872	1954	872531	1990	2003698
1919	666128	1955	876067	1991	2012142

SCReWBase©

A collectors' guide for categorizing and coding corkscrews developed by Frank Ellis, Fred Kincaid, Fred O'Leary and Joe Paradi

SCReWBase©, the Standard Corkscrew Reference Work, is a database for cataloguing all significant corkscrews. A SCReW© code is applied to each item, whether it be a simple straight pull or an elaborate patent. This code allows rational ordering within the database and a means of searching.

The system developed for SCReW© is of use to all collectors, whether they use SCReWBase© or not. The basic Class, Type and Style code can be used in many ways. This Appendix shows how to derive these basic three letter codes, e.g. ABc.

Within SCReW©, all corkscrews and associated collectibles are organized into thirteen Classes, each designated by the initial letter of the Class (except Z). Ten of the Classes are specifically for corkscrews. The full SCReWcode© is in the form ABc123 representing the Class, Type and Style as letters, followed by a three-digit number assigned to keep similar things together in series. Types and styles mostly have easy to remember letters (in English!). The tables have been simplified for this book and not all styles are shown.

To use the system, you first need to use SCReW© Decision Tree to select the right Class.

Code	Class	Contents
A	Accessories	Collectibles that are not actually corkscrews
B	Bar screws	Mechanical corkscrews that are designed to be fixed to a wall or a bar
C	Combinations	Corkscrews with a tool or a design having one or more secondary functions
E	Easers	Corkscrews designed to ease the adhesion of the cork before pulling it out with a direct pull
F	Figurals	Corkscrews in which the whole item, or a significant part of it, represents a tangible object
K	Knives	Knives (folding or fixed blade) with a folding corkscrew
L	Levers	Corkscrews that have a mechanical action through the use of a simple lever and fulcrum
M	Mechanical	Corkscrews which have a mechanical feature using a thread, ratchet or rack and pinion action
N	Non-worm extractor	Cork removers that do not have helical worms
P	Pocket and Protected	Corkscrews in which the worm is covered or otherwise protected for safety or travel
S	Self pullers and partial pullers	Corkscrews based on the principle that continuous turning of the worm draws the cork up the helix
T	T-screws and other straight pulls	Corkscrew with no mechanical features and no other tools
Z	Champagne and soda tools	Tools for opening or tapping sparkling drinks bottles

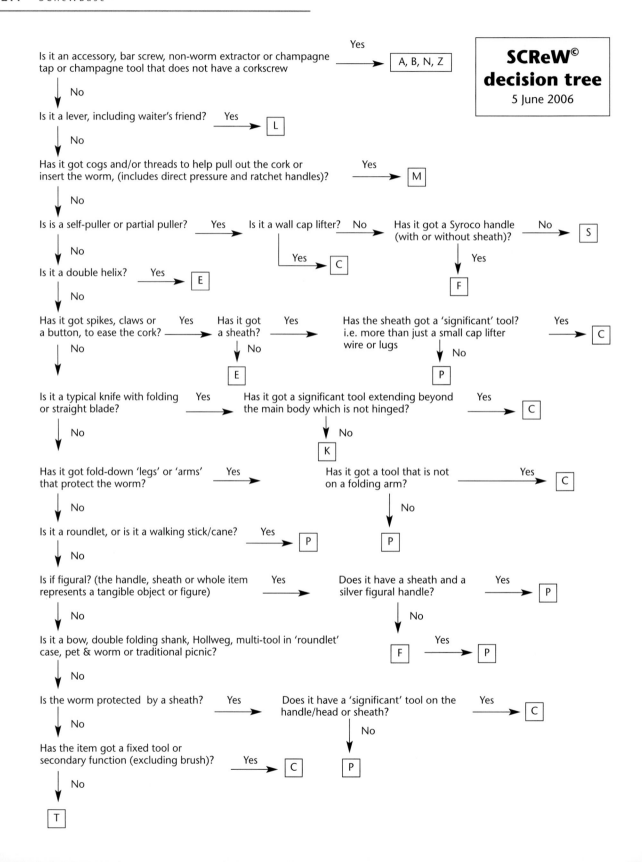

Is it an accessory, bar screw, non-worm extractor or champagne tap or champagne tool that does not have a corkscrew — **Yes** → A, B, N, Z

**SCReW©
decision tree**
5 June 2006

No ↓

Is it a lever, including waiter's friend? — **Yes** → L

No ↓

Has it got cogs and/or threads to help pull out the cork or insert the worm, (includes direct pressure and ratchet handles)? — **Yes** → M

No ↓

Is is a self-puller or partial puller? — **Yes** → Is it a wall cap lifter? — **No** → Has it got a Syroco handle (with or without sheath)? — **No** → S

No ↓   **Yes** ↓ C   **Yes** ↓ F

Is it a double helix? — **Yes** → E

No ↓

Has it got spikes, claws or a button, to ease the cork? — **Yes** → Has it got a sheath? — **Yes** → Has the sheath got a 'significant' tool? i.e. more than just a small cap lifter wire or lugs — **Yes** → C

No ↓   **No** ↓ E   **No** ↓ P

Is it a typical knife with folding or straight blade? — **Yes** → Has it got a significant tool extending beyond the main body which is not hinged? — **Yes** → C

No ↓   **No** ↓ K

Has it got fold-down 'legs' or 'arms' that protect the worm? — **Yes** → Has it got a tool that is not on a folding arm? — **Yes** → C

No ↓   **No** ↓ P

Is it a roundlet, or is it a walking stick/cane? — **Yes** → P

No ↓

Is if figural? (the handle, sheath or whole item represents a tangible object or figure) — **Yes** → Does it have a sheath and a silver figural handle? — **Yes** → P

No ↓   **No** ↓

Is it a bow, double folding shank, Hollweg, multi-tool in 'roundlet' case, pet & worm or traditional picnic?   F — **Yes** → P

No ↓

Is the worm protected by a sheath? — **Yes** → Does it have a 'significant' tool on the handle/head or sheath? — **Yes** → C

No ↓   **No** ↓ P

Has the item got a fixed tool or secondary function (excluding brush)? — **Yes** → C

No ↓

T

Next decide the Type and Style using the following guides.

Class A – Accessories

Type	Description	Examples
A	ART	Paintings, photos, posters, sculptures, music, video, rugs
B	BOTTLES & JUGS	Codd bottles, jugs, stone bottles
C	CORK TOOLS	Borers, cutters, presses, sizers, corking tools
D	DISHES & TABLEWARE	
N	NOVELTY	Hats, neckties, shirts, socks, towels, ashtrays, glass, mugs, plates, trays, charms, ear rings, pins, tie clasps, buttons, matchbooks, refrigerator magnets
P	PAPER & PRINTED MATERIAL	Advertisements, post cards. books, catalogues, letters, menus, napkins, photos (non-art)
S	SCREW TOOLS (not for corks)	Bung pullers, gun tools, packing tools, tie downs
U	UNCLASSIFIED	
V	VIDEOS & FILMS	
W	WINE ACCESSORIES	Bottle locks, cradles, coasters, funnels, labels, pourers, port tongs, stoppers, tastevins

Class B – Bar screws

There are no specific Types and Styles for bar screws. The codes in SCReWBase© are designed to be consistent with Wayne Meadows' book *Compendium of Bar Corkscrews* (Kitsilano Cellars, 2001) and you can translate the SCReWcode© into Wayne's book code.

Class C – Combinations

This is a very complex Class of corkscrews. The SCReWcode© depends upon the tools that are present. The Types are applied in alphabetical order (except that U is always considered *after* W).

There is a potential overlap of Combinations with Figurals, Knives, Pocket and Protected and T-straight pulls. Follow the SCReW© Decision Tree to identify the right Class.

Type	Description
B	Blade or spike on the end of a T handle
C	Can opener (includes blade and slotted sardine versions)
E	Eating implement – knife, fork or spoon from canteen or campaign sets (but not medicine or cocktail spoons)
F	Funnel (all wine funnels)
G	Glass cutter wheel
I	Ice pick/hammer/chopper
J	Jigger
K	Knife sharpener – 'wheels' and steels (including picnic type)
L	Cap Lifter
M	Marble pusher for Codd bottles
P	Can Piercer (triangular blade with lever action)
S	Spoon – medicine or cocktail (not an eating spoon from a canteen set)
U	Unclassified (none of the others)
W	Wall mounted cap lifter (Wall mounts (Brown type))
X	No other tool (styles only – it is not possible to have Type X)

Class E – Easers

These have a basic device to give the cork a twist once the worm is fully inserted.

Type	Description	Examples
B	Buttons	Henshall types, fat thick buttons
C	Claws	Claws or grippers at the base of shank; Gamble's Lever, Viarengo
D	Double helix	ALL double helix; Barnes, Williamson, Wilson, Magic Twist
S	Spikes	Maud (but not Jones I & II – *see* Mechanicals)
U	Unclassified	

Class F – Figurals

Type	Description	Examples	Style	
A	AQUATIC	Fish, alligator, seal, seahorse, serpent, sea shell, turtle, etc.	b	brass British flat back or hollow back (sometimes 2 sided)
B	BIRDS			
C	CATS		c	combination – separate parts fit together to form a whole figure
D	DOGS			
E	EXTREMITIES OF PEOPLE, EROTIC	Hands, feet and other body parts (excluding heads)	f	free standing (with a fixed worm)
F	FARM ANIMALS	Bull, cow, donkey, horse, mouse, pig, rabbit, squirrel		
G	GUNS AND WEAPONS		h	hinged worm (takes precedence over other styles)
H	HEADS OF PEOPLE	Head, or head and shoulders		
I	INSECTS AND PESTS	Insects and other household pests (spider, snail, etc.)	p	plain sheath with a figural insert
K	KEYS	Keys, letter openers		
L	LIFESTYLE	Banners, bottles, clothing, corks, drinking, flags, gambling, golf, hockey, medallions, music, smoking, sports	s	sheathed figural – the corkscrew is not part of the figure
O	OTHER WORDLY	Bacchus, cherub, devil, dragons, gnome, pixie, Popeye, satyr, sci-fi, skull, snowman	t	straight pull (T) – fixed worm, no sheath
P	PEOPLE – WHOLE		u	unclassified
R	REAL ESTATE	All buildings		
S	SYROCO	All Syroco pieces		
T	TRANSPORTATION	By land, sea and air; cars, motorcycles, horse & rider, ships, anchors etc.		
U	UNCLASSIFIED	Bells, numbers, letters		
V	VINE & VEGETABLE	Vegetable, vine, grapes, fruit, flowers		
W	WILD ANIMALS	Bear, boar, buck, elephant, fox, monkey, mountain goat, tortoise, zebra		

Class K – Knives
with corkscrews

Type	Description	Comments
A	ADVERTISING, SOUVENIR, POLITICAL	Includes some words, figures or symbols
B	BOTTLE	Bottle shaped scales
C	CAP LIFTER	Tool is integral with main body (*tools that extend well beyond the main body are in Class C*)
D	DECORATIVE	Knives with a generic design integral to the handle
E	END PIVOT	The corkscrew is hinged at the end of the knife
F	FIGURE SHAPED	Figure-shaped scales
G	GUN TOOL (CARTRIDGE EXTRACTOR)	Tool is integral with main body (*tools that extend well beyond the main body are in Class C*)
H	HORSEMAN'S	Hoof pick folding over the body
I	ILLUSTRATION	A speciality knife in which a picture or inscription appears under a clear protective celluloid surface
K	KNIFE BLADE FIXED	Daggers
L	LEGS, LAGUIOLE	
M	MINIATURE (UNDER 6CM)	The size criteria of 6 cm is pre-emptive except for CAPLIFTER (C) and END PIVOT (E)
P	POCKET CLASSIC	
R	RELEASE MECHANISM	The master blade is controlled by a locking mechanism
S	STRAIGHT BLADE	Fixed blade – dagger
T	TRAVEL SET	Folding knife with fork and/or spoon on same item – includes sets that slot together
U	UNCLASSIFIED	
W	WATTS' PATENT TYPE	Spring loaded arm that acts as a handle for nippers etc.
X	EXTENDED CORKSCREWS	A design that allows the worm to be longer than normal – Paffrath, Hammesfahr, Williams (Kastor), Steinfeld, Müller

Class L – Levers

Type	Description	Comments	Styles & examples	
C	COMPOUND	Several attached lever arms	e	eight arms – *Ideal, Perfect, Polichinelle, Rapid*
			s	six arms – *Armstrong, Debouchtout, Peerless, Perfect, Pullezi, Reliable,*
			z	ten arms – *Eclair, Kis-ply, Southplex, Tric Trac, Yprim, Zig Zag, double & normal Wier*
D	DOUBLE	Two lever arms	c	cam – *Baker*
			f	figural – *Anna G, Somellier, clown, girl, waiter*
			p	pivot – *A1, Empire, Goliath, Gropelli, Vogliotti*
			r	rack – *Chudzikowski, Campagnolo, Eterno, Magic Lever, Murray & Stalker*
L	LUND TYPE	Upper single lever arm and a static lower arm	j	joined – *Dordet, Hampton*
			t	two-piece – *BB, Coney, Lund and derivatives, Tangent*
S	SINGLE	One lever arm	c	cam – *Francois, Rasch, Royal Club, Russel*
			p	pivot – *Bechon Morel, Burgess & Fenton, L'Express, Le Presto, Noyes, Sperry, Subito, Tucker*
			r	rack – *Hipkins, Le Parfait, Puigpull, Rousseau, Traifor*
W	WAITER'S FRIEND	Sub-group of single levers, includes figurals		

Class M – Mechanical

Type	Description	Examples	Styles	
C	CRAB PIECE	Shaft joined to handle and threaded to crab piece or clutch; Brown, Fischer, Twigg & Bateman, The King, L'Extract	b	barrel
			c	collar, cone, bell
F	FREE FLY NUT	Shaft joined to handle and threaded to fly nut; Aero, Victor, Helice variants, etc.	f	frame (fixed)
			h	Hinged frame
I	INTERLOCKING SHAFTS & SNAIL FACE	Inner shaft rises after interlocking with outer shaft – includes snail faces: Diamant, Alvord and Brown, Twigg & Bateman, Kummer	o	open frame (no bottom ring
			s	spring barrel/frame
K	KINGS SCREW	Narrow rack, wide rack; Kummer	w	window barrel
L	LOCKING HANDLE	Shaft threaded to handle which has a locking device device; Bateman, Bodega, Ehrhardt, Gounevitch, Kampf, Shrapnel, Twigg, Voigt, Woodman, Wulfruna	x	not designated
P	PERPETUAL	Cotterill, many German frame and barrel versions, DICO		
R	RACK	London Rack, Perille, JB, Korkmaster, many German & Italian versions		
S	SWIVEL LOCK	Shaft is threaded to handle and has a swivel-over locking top; Bague, Challenge, Korkmaster Jr., Williamson Burgundy		
T	THOMASON	Thomason patent (I, II, IV, VI–XVI), French spring barrel, VULCAN		
V	VARIANTS	Thomason Variants (Patent III), Thomason Serpent (Patent V)		
D	DIRECT PRESSURE	Hull Presto, Van Gieson (& frame), Qvarnstrom (Sloor)		
G	GRINDER-COFFEE	Mostly Italian, Perille	x	not designated
N	NECK, THREADED	Threaded shank acts through a threaded neck: Left-hand thread – Williamson Power Screw Mabson, G. Karl; Right-hand thread – L'Excelsior, Coney, many English 2 pillars; Two-handled – Club, Valezina	l	left-hand threaded shank
			r	right-hand threaded shank
			t	two handles
			x	not designated
W	WING NUT – FIXED	Threaded shank, wing nut fixed to frame: Farrow & Jackson, Perille's Helice, many Italians		
U	UNCLASSIFIED	Phillips electric; Used fluid or gas to pump up the shaft & lift it, Artmer CO_2; Jacks; Fortunato Ratchets: Dixon, Newton; Telescopic, Walton's windlass; Unclassified – Dupuis, Kemper, Syme, Jones I & II	e	electric
			g	gas, hydraulic
			j	jack
			m	mechanical ratchet
			p	pulley, windlass
			u	unclassified
			x	not designated

Class N – Non-worm extractors

Type	Description	Examples
H	HOOKS	Inserted between cork and bottle, then hooks on to the cork before pulling
I	INJECTION	Inserts a needle through the cork and injects air or gas
P	PRONGS	Inserted between the cork and bottle and turned slightly to ease cork out
R	RETRIEVERS	Used to recover loose corks from the body of the bottle
S	SPIKE	Some partially pierce the cork and need a twist, others go all the way through
U	UNCLASSIFIED	

Class P – Pocket and Protected

Type	Description	Examples
B	BOWS & HARPS	Worm folds out for action from protective 'bow' through 180°
C	CANES & WALKING STICKS	
F	FOLDING	Protective 'arms' (plain, animal legs, shoes), clam shell/peapod, champagne wire cutter 'scissors', barrel with double folding worm
H	HOLLWEG TYPE	
L	LEGS & PEOPLE (FOLDING)	Lady's legs, Amor
O	'O' HOLE FINGER PULL & SHEATH	One or more finger holes in handle
P	PICNICS	The sheath fits snugly into the head to form a T handle
R	ROUNDLETS	Normal roundlets & cased multi-tool sets
T	'T' HANDLE & SHEATH	Includes many Dutch silver corkscrews (including figural handles)
W	PEG & WORM	
U	UNCLASSIFIED	

Class S – Self pullers and partial pullers

Type	Description	Comments & examples	Styles	
A	ALL SCREW	The frame remains stationary while the cork works up the worm until it is clear of the bottle; e.g. Screwpull	b	barrel
			c	cup/cone/bell (partial puller)
F	FREE – SLIDE & ROTATE	The frame or barrel is free to ride up and down the shaft and rotate at the same time; e.g. Chinnock	f	frame – joined at bottom
			h	hinged frame – sides or bottom pivot
L	LIMITED MOVEMENT; LOCK, RELEASE, STOP or LOCKING MECHANISM	The range of movement on the shaft is limited by the presence of a stop mechanism (e.g. Curley); or it has a locking mechanism for releasing the shank to remove the cork (e.g. many German frames)	o	open frame – not joined at bottom
			s	spring barrel
N	NO MOVING PARTS	No internal movement of any part of the corkscrew; e.g. Bennit, Plant's Magic	w	window barrel
			u	unclassified
R	ROTATE ONLY – NO UP/DOWN MOTION	Frames etc. that can turn but not rise or fall; some bells but excludes Walker & Williamson bells which are coded SW-	x	not designated
S	SPRING TENSION, FRAME ROTATES (Type L takes priority)	An internal spring or spring-over-shaft provides lift as it becomes compressed; e.g. Hercules		
U	UNCLASSIFIED			
W	WALKER & WILLIAMSON BELLS	A sub-section of SR-	a	Walker
			i	Williamson

Class T – T-Screws and other straight pulls

Type	Description	Comments & examples	Styles (handle material)	
D	DECORATIVE	Takes priority over all but Lever Hole	a	animal material (antler, bone, ivory, horn, tortoise-shell, tusk,
E	EYEBROW		b	brass, bronze
L	LEVER HOLE	Takes priority over *all* other types	c	composition (celluloid, catalin, plastic, bakelite, ceramic)
M	MEDICINE, PERFUME	Excludes vertical handles which are TV-	i	iron, steel (ferrous metals)
O	'O' HOLE, FINGER PULL HOLE	Note: excludes D-shaped cap lifter handles which are Class C	l	left-handed worm
			m	miniature (optional use)
S	SETS COTAINING T-SHAPE STRAIGHT PULLS	Includes only traditional Ts in sets: Bonsa type tool sets	o	other metal (pewter, aluminium, white metal)
			p	mother of pearl
T	T-SHAPED STRAIGHT PULLS	All standard plain straight pulls – may have advertising	s	silver, gold
			t	twisted wire shank
			u	unclassified (glass, agate)
U	UNCLASSIFIED			
V	VERTICAL HANDLE & NECESSAIRES	i.e. not T-shaped; Many perfume screws	w	wood
			x	not designated

Class Z – Champagne and soda taps and related tools

Type	Description	Comments
C	CORK REPLACER	A mechanical cork equipped with a valve to dispense the liquid
D	DROP POINT	The point is put into the end of the pipe to penetrate the cork. The point drops into the bottle and is recovered later
E	EASER	Mechanically eases the cork out of a champagne bottle
G	GRIPPER	Grips the cork and then twists and pulls it out
K	KNIVES	Champagne knife to cut the cork retaining wire
L	LONG TAP	Soda taps, length under 20cm or 8 inches
M	MEDIUM TAP	Soda taps, length under 20cm or shorter than 8 inches
P	PIPES	Tubes with a fixed point; with or without a worm on the shaft
S	STOPPER/RESEALER	Used to retain the gas in the bottle
T	TROCAR	Pointed wire down the inside of the pipe; with or without a worm
U	UNCLASSIFIED	
W	WIRE CLIPPER	Without corkscrews

Some examples

Accessories

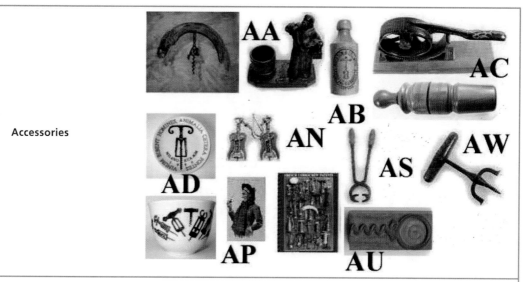

AA

AC

AB

AN

AW

AS

AD

AP

AU

Bar screws

Combinations CB-CK

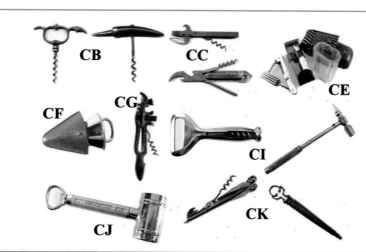

CB

CC

CE

CF

CG

CI

CJ

CK

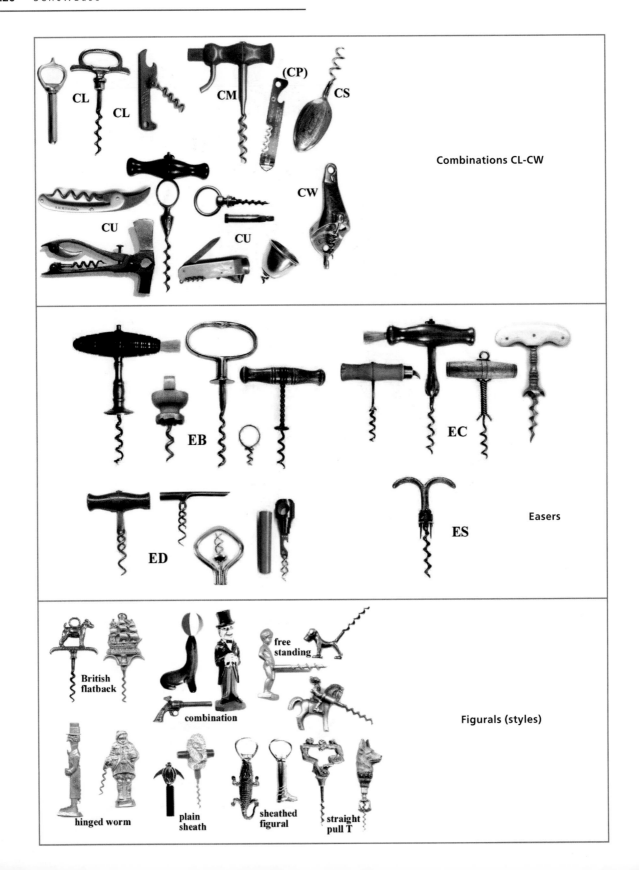

Combinations CL-CW

CL

CL

CM

(CP)

CS

CW

CU

CU

Easers

EB

EC

ED

ES

Figurals (styles)

British flatback

combination

free standing

hinged worm

plain sheath

sheathed figural

straight pull T

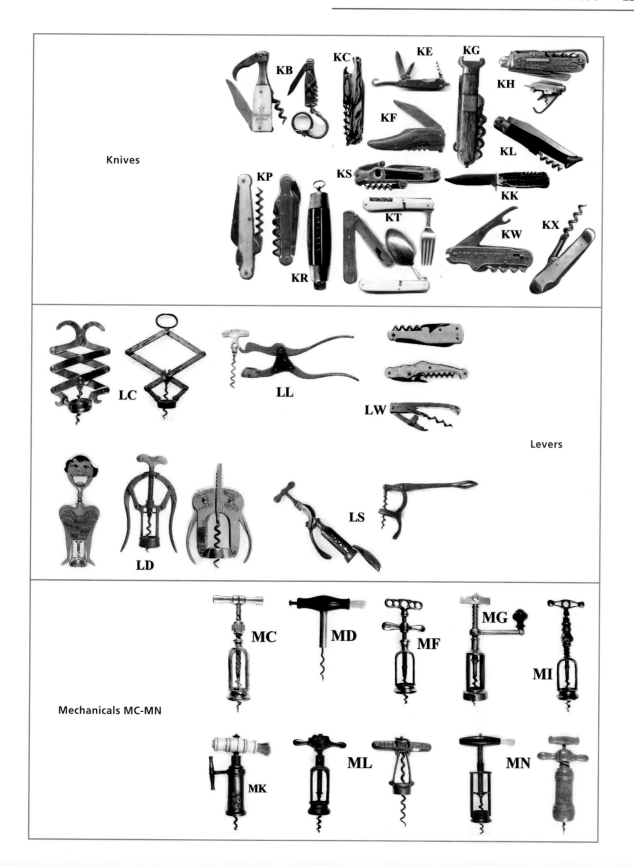

Knives

KB · KC · KE · KG · KH · KF · KL · KP · KS · KK · KT · KR · KW · KX

Levers

LC · LL · LW · LD · LS

Mechanicals MC-MN

MC · MD · MF · MG · MI · MK · ML · MN

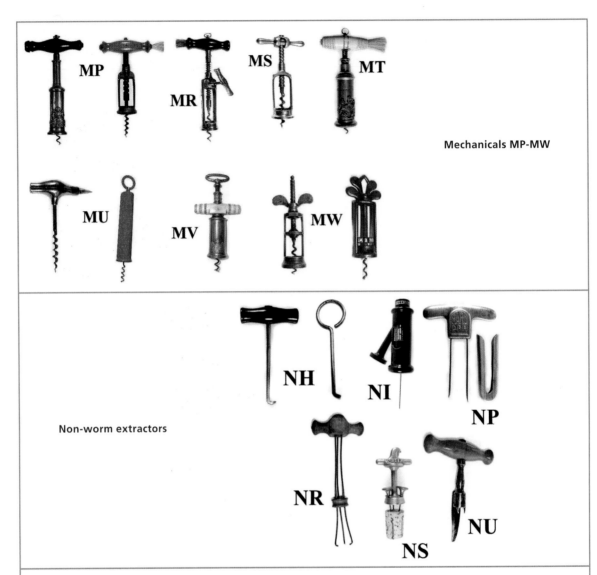

Mechanicals MP-MW

Non-worm extractors

Pocket and
Protected

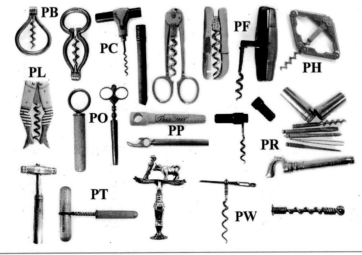

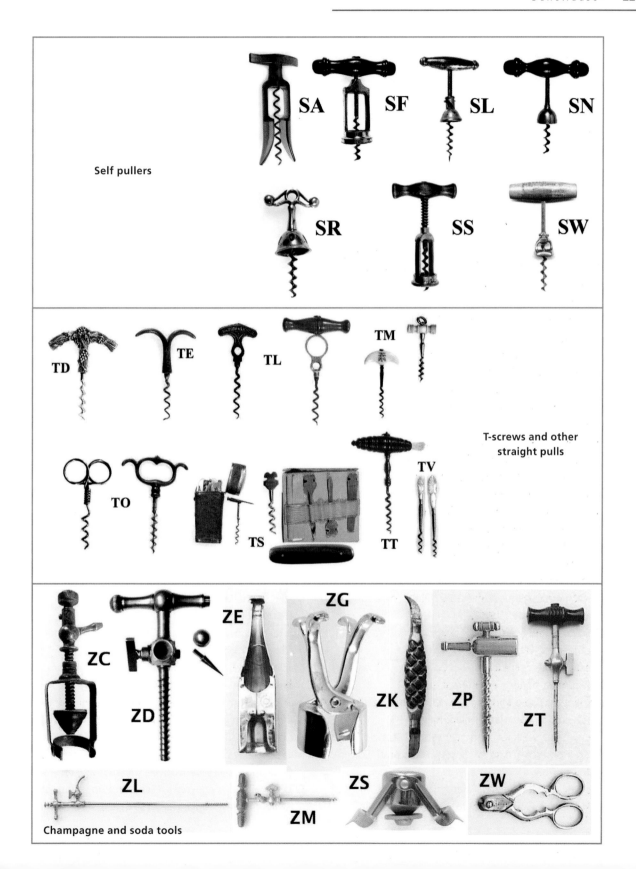

Self pullers

SA SF SL SN

SR SS SW

TD TE TL TM

T-screws and other straight pulls

TO TS TT TV

ZC ZD ZE ZG ZK ZP ZT

ZL ZM ZS ZW

Champagne and soda tools

BIBLIOGRAPHY

Berndt, Reinhold, *Federzungen* (Egelsbach, Germany, 2002)

Berntson, Bustor and Ekman, Per, *Scandinavian Corkscrews* (Tryckeriforlaget, Taby, Sweden, 1994)

Berazzo, Ottilia Munaretti, *The Art of Corkscrews* (Skira, Milan, Italy, 2005)

Bidault, Gerard, *Les Fabriques Françaises de Tire-bouchons, 1820–1970* (self-published, France, 2000)

Bidault, Gerard, *Les Brevets de Tire-bouchons Français 1847–1968* (self-published, France, 2007)

Bull, Donald A., *Bull's Pocket Guide to Corkscrews* (Schiffer Publishing Ltd, Atglen, Pennsylvania, USA, 1999)

Bull, Donald A., *The Ultimate Corkscrew Book* (Schiffer Publishing Ltd, Atglen, Pennsylvania, USA, 1999)

Bull, Donald A., *Corkscrew Patents of Japan* (Bullworks, Wirtz, Virginia, USA, 2004)

Bull, Donald A. and Stanley, John R., *Just for Openers: A Guide to Beer, Soda, & Other Openers* (Schiffer Publishing Ltd, Atglen, Pennsylvania, USA, 1999)

Butler, Robin and Walkling, Gillian, *The Book of Wine Antiques* (Antique Collectors' Club, Woodbridge, Suffolk, England, 1986)

Coldicott, Peter, *A Guide to Corkscrew Collecting* (self-published, UK, 1993)

Crestin-Billet, Frederique, *Collectible Corkscrews* (Flammarion Inc., Paris, France, 2001)

de Sanctis, Paolo and Fantoni, Maurizio, *Le Collezioni Cavatappi* (Bompiani, Milan, Italy, 1993)

de Sanctis, Paolo and Fantoni, Maurizio, *The Corkscrew: A Thing of Beauty* (Marzorati Editore, Milan, Italy, 1990)

Dippel, Horst, *Korkenzieher* (Ellert and Richter, Hamburg, Germany, 1988)

Dippel, Horst, *Korkenzieher* (Ellert and Richter, Hamburg, Germany, 1997)

Ekman, Per, Kohler, Anne-Lise and Solheim, Helgir Gees, *Scandinavian Corkscrew Patents, 1867–1973* (Helix Scandinavica, 2004)

Ellis, Frank and Ellis, Barbara, *Corkscrews: British Registered Designs* (Cod Beck Publishing, Bedfordshire, England, 2007)

Ellis, Phil, *Corkscrews & Wine Antiques: A Collector's Guide* (Miller's, UK, 2001)

Fantoni, Maurizio and de Sanctis, Paolo, *Corkscrews* (BE-MA Editrice, Milano, Italy, 1988)

Giulian, Bertrand B., *Corkscrews of the Eighteenth Century, Artistry in Iron and Steel* (WhiteSpace Publishing, USA, 1995)

Heckmann, Manfred, *Korkenzieher* (Fasanen Edition, Berlin, Germany, 1979)

Hoefer, Peter, *Osterreichische Korkenzieherpatente 1882–1980*

Hutchinson, Francis, *Patents for Invention, Abridgements of Specifications, Class 125 Stoppering and Bottling, 1855 to 1930* (self-published for the ICCA, UK, 1983)

Kohler, Anne-Lise, *French Corkscrew Patents Found in Denmark* (Esbjerg, Denmark, 2003)

Maclean, Ron, *The Common Corkscrew, II–IV* (Ontario, Canada, 1989–91)

Maclean, Ron, *The Williamson Story, C.T. Williamson Wire Novelty Co.* (Ontario, Canada, 1994)

Maclean, Ron and Nugent, Bob, *William Rockwell Clough, Inventor and Manufacturer of over a Billion Corkscrews* (Bullworks, Wirtz, Virginia, USA, 2004)

Meadows, Wayne, *Compendium of Bar Corkscrews* (Kitsilano Cellars, Vancouver, Canada, 2001)

O'Leary, Fred, *Corkscrews* (Schiffer Publishing Ltd, Atglen, Pennsylvania, USA, 1996)

Olive, Guy, *French Corkscrew Patents 1828–1974* (self-published, France, 1995)

Pascal, Dominique, *Collectible Pocket Knives* (Flammarion Inc., Paris, France, 2001)

Perry, Evan, *Corkscrews and Bottle Openers* (Shire Publications Ltd, Aylesbury, UK, 1980, Reprinted 1985 and 1989)

Peters, Ferd, *Mechanical Corkscrews: Their evolution, actions, and patents* (Beheermij Pintex B.V., Netherlands, 1999)

Peters, Ferd, *German Corkscrew Patents, D.R.P. 1877–2000* (Beheermaatschappy Pintex B.V., Netherlands, 2002)

Peters, Ferd, *German Corkscrew Registrations, D.R.G.M. 1891–2000* (Beheermaatschappy Pintex B.V., Netherlands, 2002)

Peters, Ferd and Giulian, Bert, *The History of Pocket Corkscrews and Pocketknives* (Beheermij Pintex B.V., Heel, Netherlands, 2006)

Pumpenmeier, Klaus, *Deutscher Gebrauchsmuster-schutz fur Korkenzieher 1891–1945* (self-published, Germany, 1997 (second edition))

Taylor, Leslie B., *A Brief History of the Westley Richards Firm, 1812–1913* (Shakespeare Head Press, Stratford-upon-Avon, UK, 1913)

Turler, Hans Joachim, *Swiss Corkscrew Patents* (2002)

Tweedale, Geoffrey, *The Sheffield Knife Book: A History and Collectors' Guide* (The Hallamshire Press, Sheffield, UK, 1996)

Wallis, Fletcher, *British Corkscrew Patents from 1795* (Vernier Press, Brighton, UK, 1997)

Watney, Bernard M. and Babbidge, Homer D., *Corkscrews for collectors* (Sotheby's Publications, London, UK, 1981, reprinted 1987)

INDEX

Index by subject and corkscrew type

Index of design registrants, patentees, manufacturers and trade names